We Were Next to Nothing

This book is dedicated to my parents with fond memories
and with gratefulness to all of my family,
who never gave up hope...
And with special love to my wife Fay
and our daughters, Carleen and Susan,
Carleen's husband Mike, and our grandchildren
Michele Tjader, Melissa Tjader, Mark Tjader, and Sarah Allan.

We Were Next to Nothing

AN AMERICAN POW'S ACCOUNT
OF JAPANESE PRISON CAMPS AND
DELIVERANCE IN WORLD WAR II

by Carl S. Nordin

McFarland & Company, Inc., Publishers
Jefferson, North Carolina, and London

The present work is a reprint of the library bound edition of
We Were Next to Nothing: An American POW's Account
of Japanese Prison Camps and Deliverance in World War
II, *first published in 1997 by McFarland.*

LIBRARY OF CONGRESS CATALOGUING-IN-PUBLICATION DATA

Nordin, Carl S., 1913–
    We were next to nothing : an American POW's account of
Japanese prison camps and deliverance in World War II / by
Carl S. Nordin.
        p.   cm
    Includes index.

    ISBN 0-7864-2162-2 (softcover : 50# alkaline paper) ∞

    1. Nordin, Carl S., 1913–   2. World War, 1939–1945—Prisoners
and prisons, Japanese.   3. World War, 1939–1945—Personal
narratives, American.   4. Prisoners of war—United States—
Biography.   5. Prisoners of war—Japan—Moji-shi—Biography.
6. Prisoners of war—Philippines—Mindanao Island—Biography.
7. World War, 1939–1945—Concentration camps—Japan—Moji-shi.
8. World War, 1939–1945—Concentration camps—Philippines—
Mindanao Island.   I. Title
D805.J3N66   2005   96-39692
940.54'7252'095222—dc21

British Library cataloguing data are available

On the cover: Japanese army photograph of Carl Nordin, October 1944. This
photograph was taken from an office of the Japanese army in August 1945.

Manufactured in the United States of America

McFarland & Company, Inc., Publishers
  Box 611, Jefferson, North Carolina 28640
    www.mcfarlandpub.com

Contents

Roster of Enlisted Personnel
of Det. 2nd Q.M. Supply (Avn)
(Lt. Carlyle Ricks, Commanding Officer)

1.	APPLEGARTH, FRED O.	Wenatchee WA	Died on Lasang detail hell ship
2.	BACA, ARTURO	Encino NM	
3.	BAILEY, GLEN L.	Thornton ID	
4.	BOWDEN, NICHOLAS	Salt Lake City UT	Died on Oryoku Maru hell ship
5.	CASTILLO, IGNACIO C.	Jerales NM	
6.	CHRISTENSEN, LEROY	Ogden UT	Died on Lasang detail hell ship
7.	CLUCAS, CLEVE G.	Arco ID	Died on Lasang detail hell ship
8.	CROMWELL, HARLEY, JR.	Waverly KS	Died on Lasang detail hell ship
9.	DAVIS, MACK K.	Provo UT	Died on Lasang detail hell ship
10.	DENNIS, ROBERT S.	Douglass KS	
11.	DIDIO, VINCENT J.	Detroit MI	
12.	EARL, MERVIN C.	McNary AZ	Died at Cabanatuan or on a hell ship
13.	EAST	?	Left at Ft. McKinley for surgery
14.	FADER, WALTER D.	Glenwood IA	Died on Lasang detail hell ship
15.	FOSTER, EDWARD D.	Newcomb NM	Died on Lasang detail hell ship
16.	GONZALES, PABLO V.	Claypool AZ	
17.	GOODLIFFE, CHARLES L.	Brigham City UT	
18.	GUERNSEY, GEORGE W.	Salem IA	Died on Lasang detail hell ship
19.	HICKS, OLIVER O.	Cahone CO	
20.	KOWIS, JACOB G.	Houston TX	Died on Lasang detail hell ship

21. LAMBERT, ARTHUR FRED	Seguache CO	Died on Lasang detail hell ship
22. LANCASTER, JOSEPH M.	St. Paul KS	Died on Lasang detail hell ship
23. LARSEN, KENNETH B.	Salt Lake City UT	
24. LeBEAU, BERNARD G.	Marshall MN	
25. LUCERO, FRANK D.	Old Laguna NM	Died on Lasang detail hell ship
26. McCABE, ANTHONY J.	Le Center MN	
27. McKAY, RODERICK	Hailey ID	
28. MELUCCI, ALBERT	Detroit MI	Died on Lasang detail hell ship
29. MINOTTI, MIKE J.	Duluth MN	Died at Cabanatuan or on a hell ship
30. NIELAND, ARTHUR B.	Wall Lake IA	Died on Lasang detail hell ship
31. NORDIN, CARL S.	Siren WI	
32. PARRY, EARNEST R.	Salt Lake City UT	Died on Lasang detail hell ship
33. PEERY, WILLIAM N.	Provo UT	
34. ROESKE, CLARENCE H.	Salt Lake City UT	
35. ROMERO, JUAN V.	Las Lunas NM	Died on Lasang detail hell ship
36. VALDES, SAMUEL O.	Pagosa Springs NM	Left in Hawaii with a broken leg
37. VANCE, DONALD L.	Fairview UT	
38. WEBB, JULIUS F.	Denham Springs LA	

Preface

It is almost a rite of passage for children and grandchildren to wish in later years that they had asked their elders more about things that happened in the past. I wish I had found out more about an ancestor who was a prisoner of war in Russia while serving in the Swedish army. He escaped and walked all the way back to Sweden, but that's all I know. The time may come when some of my descendants will hear that someone in the family had an unusual experience while serving in the military and may want to know more of the particulars. For such a possibility, I have set this account down in writing.

I guess I've always been one to make notes or keep track of things. I often develop some sort of record-keeping system, especially if I think it could be of value or importance, at least to me. So it was just part of the norm that when I entered the service I went to the post exchange and bought a little notebook. It became a book of many uses: a handy booklet for taking notes during basic training, an address book, and a record of important dates and happenings. I also started keeping a diary in prison camp. In writing this book I relied heavily on these notes and diary for an occasional reminder and also as a source of authentication. The rest is taken from memory, and those parts of the account are still as vivid as if they happened yesterday. The reader can be assured that I have provided a true account because even at this late date buddies of mine have come to me for reference and have gone so far as to tell officials of the Veterans Administration that if they want dates and happenings they should "contact Nordin."

I also want to state categorically that there undoubtedly were many who had it worse than I did, both during the fighting and in prison camp, and my hand and my heart go out to them. By the same token, I'm sure that there were those who had it better than I did. That, however, is of little consequence so far as this account is concerned because this is my story—this is what happened to me. The fear, the pain, the suffering, and the loneliness were mine alone.

Carl S. Nordin, Fall 1996

3

Diary made of cigarette packs in which Carl Nordin kept a daily record of his experiences as a prisoner of war.

Acknowledgments

When writing an account such as this, it is impossible to mention names without running the risk of being unfair. I would be remiss, however, if I did not mention the names of three people whose actions in difficult times were instrumental in saving my life. First there was Lt. Colonel Rogers, whose decision to send me back to the main camp when I was ill with dysentery spared me from being on the hellship *Shinyo Maru* when it was sunk. Closely associated with that incident was the action "Jug" Imlay took when he risked his life to convince an angry guard that I was too ill to continue work. The resulting scene brought my case to the attention of Lt. Colonel Rogers in a graphic manner. Unfortunately, both Lt. Colonel Rogers and Jug Imlay died on that ship. I am positive I would have also died if I had been on that ship because I would have been with Jug Imlay or with members of my outfit, all of whom perished because they were lying where the torpedo entered the ship. My life was later spared again by the bold and drastic action taken by Bob Dennis when I was desperately ill in Japan with dysentery. Without his demanding that I be given immediate medical attention, even after it had been denied me, I would very likely have succumbed. I almost died as it was.

In the last fifty years, I have been urged by a great number of people to write a book about my experiences. Among those encouraging me have been a number of pastors. Again, there are three in particular whom I believe deserve special mention. Two of them, the Reverend Robert "Chip" Salzgeber and the Reverend Keith Lueneburg, are former pastors of my home congregation. The third is the Reverend Michael Hellier, with whom I served on several synod committees of the church; he is now one of my best friends.

I am also deeply indebted to my family for the interest shown and the support given me in this undertaking. I owe special thanks to my brother Glenn for the extra effort he has put forth over the years in retracing my steps, locating the Abareces and Ikuta-San, and for the scores of pictures and other bits of information he has supplied to me over the years. I know that any other member of the family would have done the same, given the opportunity. My wife Fay also deserves special credit for her support, patience, and advice. It made the task significantly easier.

Finally, I am deeply grateful to Thomas Woznicki for critiquing the manuscript and putting it into final form for submission to publishers.

Part I
B.C. (Before Captivity)

The End of Peace
in Our Time

They made a wasteland and called it peace.
—Tacitus, Publius Cornelius, A.D. 55–120

Life in mid–America in the 1930s was relatively peaceful. The big war, hailed as bringing peace in our time, was over. People felt relieved and pacified that world statesmen were now working out the problems in a diplomatic way through the new world organization, the League of Nations. It suffered a severe handicap from the beginning, however, because of the refusal of the United States to join. The League's decay began with the Sino-Japanese War in 1931 and the withdrawal of Japan from the League. There were other instruments such as the Kellogg-Briand Pact, which was an agreement condemning war and proposing a peaceful settlement of international differences. But this pact turned out to be ineffective because it failed to provide for enforcement.

For a time in the decade following the First World War, it had seemed as if good days were here. But then things began to slowly and inexorably unravel. There was the stock market crash in 1929, an epidemic of bank failures, widespread unemployment, and then the longest and worst drought of the century.

Such were the conditions as I was entering manhood. Our dairy farm was of average size or above for that area and era. As the economy worsened, it became my lot to take the place of the hired help my father could no longer afford.

Then in 1933 I joined the Civilian Conservation Corps (CCC). This brought much-needed additional funds to the family because I received $5 a month for myself and $25 was sent to my father each month. In the early '30s, this seemed like a lot of money. Just as I was getting settled in doing forestry work in the CCC, a job opened up in the local post office, so on January 1, 1934, I began a career that was to be my life's work except for a five-and-one-half year stint in the armed forces.

Life became routine and quite pleasant in general. There were few radios and daily papers in our little town at that time, but there was an uneasy

Carl Nordin and Kenneth Carpenter, University of Utah stadium, October 1940 (soon after enlistment).

awareness of the fact that militarists on the other side of both oceans were rattling their sabres. A neighbor whom I had grown up with had purchased a truck and was buying scrap iron and hauling it to Duluth, Minnesota, for shipment to Japan, where there was a growing market for bomb-fragment material. There was general opposition to spending money on armaments. Many mothers were writing to their congressmen, saying, "We don't want our sons to die on foreign soil."

To me the possibility of war became more evident in 1937 when I was in Canada for a couple of days. In every town, small or large, young men were practicing military drill wherever there was a vacant lot available. Then in 1939 I was in Canada again for a Labor Day holiday, and as I stepped out of a movie theatre, newsboys were hawking daily papers with the headlines, "Mother Country Declares War on Germany."

By the summer of 1940, it was becoming quite obvious that our country would be involved eventually, so on September 18, 1940, I enlisted at Fort Snelling, Minnesota, with another young man from Siren, Kenneth Carpenter. In about ten days, we were shipped to Fort Douglas, Utah, a quiet, pretty post on the outskirts of Salt Lake City. We enjoyed it very much even though we had to live in tents until March of 1941.

Soldiering was easy and pleasant in what came to be known as the "peacetime army." Starting pay was only $21 a month, but we didn't need too much. Later on, I got myself an extra job—cleaning the six-chair barbershop every Saturday night. It got me out of the cold tent one night a week, I could listen to music on the radio, and the barbers paid me ten dollars a month.

The spring and summer of 1941 seemed to float by. I had gone from being a clerk in the Property Office to secretary/manager of the Post Carpenter Shop office, and later to manager of the Utilities Warehouse, which resembled a huge hardware store. Kenneth Carpenter had been transferred to Fort Warren, Wyoming, along with Al Siranian (of whom you will hear again). I had had visitors from back home, including my parents and sister Hazel (who had taken my place in the post office). I had also found a church home in a Lutheran church within walking distance of the Mormon Tabernacle, making it possible to attend my own church first, then take in the Sunday morning broadcast of the Mormon Tabernacle Choir. In late summer I was part of a group which went to Yellowstone Park for R. and R. (rest and recreation).

All in all, it had been a pleasant interlude, but there was a great void in my life. Something important—more important than anything else at the time—was missing, and I was determined to do something about it.

Furloughs were becoming hard to come by in late 1941, but I obtained one of fifteen-days duration, to commence the second week in October. With a three-day pass ahead of it, I could be home before my furlough actually began. I was going home to become engaged to my sweetheart, Fay Lewis, a teacher in the Siren school system. My sister Hazel and younger brother Glenn would meet me at the train depot in St. Paul early Sunday morning. On our way home, we would stop in Forest Lake to see my uncle Russell, who was dying of a brain tumor, and we would arrive at my folks' home for Sunday dinner on their thirtieth wedding anniversary. Fay and I would have our first date of this furlough on Monday night. It all sounded so good. After all, I had been gone thirteen months.

As it happened, my uncle died just before my sister, brother and I arrived home from the train station. My mother and I went to my grandfather's house to see what we could do. While we were there, a telegram arrived for me back at my parents' farm. My father delivered it to me at midnight. It read, "All furloughs cancelled—report back immediately. Commanding Officer, Fort Douglas, Utah."

Those six words marked a dividing point in my life. The world, as I had known it up until that moment, ended right then and there. That telegram would mark the beginning of four long years in which almost each day became worse than the one before, and often when it seemed things could get no worse, somehow they did.

There was a train out of St. Paul the next night shortly after 7:00 P.M., so only a day after bringing me home from the train station, my same sister was taking me back to St. Paul for my return to Fort Douglas. This time, however, we were accompanied by Fay. So what was to have been the first date of an engagement ended up being a farewell send-off into a complete unknown. We did make plans to marry the next year, however, if I was still in the U.S., and even if I was sent overseas someplace, we would marry after that. After all, overseas assignments were only of two-year duration, and if we had to, we could handle that.

As I sat by the window watching the southern Minnesota countryside rush by and listening to the train whistle cut the brisk October night, my thoughts were all of what might have been—days with family and friends and romantic nights with Fay. A rush of sadness came over me as I sat there recalling the tear-filled farewell at the station. And I became angered at the army for having done that to them, to me, to us. For the first time in my life, I was angry at the army and wished that it did not have this hold on my life. After all, I wanted to be able to control my own destiny. The dimensions had changed.

October 15, 1941—Arrived back in Salt Lake City. Naturally I was despondent at having been called back from furlough, but I was hardly prepared for what happened next. I had not only been transferred to a new outfit, but I had been assigned to a different barracks as well and we were kept locked in under strict quarantine awaiting sealed orders. We were told that our new address would be Plum, care of Postmaster, San Francisco, and that we could notify our friends and families of this change, so I sent this new address to Fay and my family immediately. Because of the ban on calling out, I had been unable to notify my friends, the Howard Hagglands, with whom I had spent so much time on picnics and outings, and also the Les Pedersens. Les and I had been in the same outfit for a year, and he had honored me by selecting me to be best man at his wedding that June. Quite naturally, these friends were interested in my forthcoming engagement to Fay. As it turned out, I had to leave Salt Lake City without saying good-bye to any of my friends. I did receive one piece of mail during this time of quarantine—a card from Kenneth Carpenter in Fort Warren, Wyoming, wherein he informed me that he was at Fort MacDowell awaiting overseas assignment—he thought to Trinidad.

October 23, 1941—Arrived in San Francisco and Fort MacDowell. Just as our convoy of trucks had taken a circuitous route from Fort Douglas to the Denver & Rio Grande train station (instead of the supposed Union Pacific), so too did we take a long and circuitous route to the coast. In both cases it was done ostensibly to foil any foul play by fifth columnists.

Our accommodations on the train were decent, but our food left something to be desired—cereal for breakfast and sandwiches (mostly peanut butter) for most of the other meals.

After being deposited at the pier in San Francisco, we were loaded in government ferries for transportation right past Alcatraz and on out to Fort MacDowell on Angel Island, where we began our final processing for overseas shipment. The view of San Francisco and Oakland from these high bluffs was spectacular, especially at night. We received passes to go into San Francisco several times, and on the weekend Mack Davis and I stayed with his cousins in Oakland. He and I had things somewhat in common because he had married his girlfriend of three years the weekend before we left Salt Lake City, and I had just experienced the sad farewell with Fay less than two weeks earlier. Mack was never to see America or his Jean again.

October 27, 1941—Embarked on USS Hugh L. Scott. The former liner *Franklin L. Pierce* had been converted to a troop ship and renamed the *General Hugh L. Scott.* Loading was done in a strictly military manner which moved men rapidly and efficiently. We were all lined up on the pier according to a previously prepared roster. An officer at the foot of the gangplank called out the man's last name, and he would respond with his first name and middle initial. Close by was the cargo ship USS *Meigs* loaded with supplies, plus trucks, ammunition, and other military materiel.

Before leaving the harbor, we were visited by a small government boat from which several bags of mail were hoisted aboard. To my great surprise and joy, I received two letters from Fay addressed to my new Plum address. These letters were of particular importance for two reasons—they contained two snapshots taken of her that year, and in one of the letters she said, "I'll wait for you even if it is two years" (the maximum tour of overseas duty at that time). I kept the snapshots protected in my little notebook which I carried in my field pack all through the war and prison camp. The letters were in my footlocker which I had to bury just before we were overrun by the Japanese, but by that time I had committed them to memory.

In the late afternoon, we weighed anchor and slowly sailed under the Golden Gate Bridge , heading into a huge unknown. The bright sunny afternoon had turned into a cold, damp evening with rain squalls in the distance. The deck was lined with men, their faces all turned eastward as we watched the Golden Gate fade from view. Then the lights of the city began coming on, but finally they too faded from view and we were filled with an indescribable emptiness. Every man aboard was leaving part of himself behind— family, parents, children, wife, a sweetheart, and our country. Our feelings were heightened because we knew not where we were going nor what the world of those unsettling times had in store for us. It seemed as if our particular world had taken a bad turn.

Quite a number of the men succumbed to seasickness brought on by the rough water just outside San Francisco Bay, made all the worse by a storm that had just blown in. I consider myself fortunate not to have ever suffered that unpleasant malady, even though I have crossed the Pacific twice and spent almost three months in the hold of a hell ship, including five days in a typhoon on the China Sea. After the weather cleared, we spent most of our time on deck, especially the enlisted men, because we were assigned to quarters below the water line. Our bunks were racks of tightly strung canvas hammocks about twelve inches apart, and stacked four or five feet high. For that reason many of the men spent their days as well as their nights on the steel decks. Daylight hours were spent playing cards, writing letters, watching the antics of the porpoises and flying fish, and of course engaging in the typical GI bull sessions. When we were about four days out, Colonel Ray T. Elsmore, squadron commander of the Fifth Air Base Group, opened the sealed order and informed us that our destination was the Philippine Islands (P.I.).

November 2, 1941—Arrived in Honolulu, T.H. Tied up to the pier as we docked was the luxury liner SS *Lurline* which, along with its sister ship, the SS *Mariposa*, plied the waters between Hawaii, America, Australia, and tropical ports of call along this route. Particularly noticeable also were the famed Aloha Tower, the huge Dole pineapple, and swarms of young native boys diving for coins. Compared to the touristy island we know in these late years of the twentieth century, Honolulu, as well as the entire island of Oahu, was quite unspoiled in 1941. There were only two hotels on Waikiki—the Royal Hawaiian and the Moana. The city of Honolulu was rather quaint, with narrow streets carrying little traffic and high sidewalks which were the cause of our first casualty. Samuel Valdez of our outfit had the misfortune of breaking a leg when he accidentally stepped off one of these sidewalks. This necessitated us leaving him behind in a local hospital. We never heard of him again.

We were informed ahead of time that there was an abundance of military personnel stationed in the area and that the streets were heavily patrolled by army military police (M.P.'s) and navy shore patrol (S.P.'s). Strict adherence to proper uniform and military manners was the order of the day. Men in uniform could not gather in groups of more than two, nor could they dawdle along engaging in window shopping. That did not stop us from enjoying our visit there, however, because we would get at least one swim a day in at Waikiki, and took strolls through the lovely Royal Palace and surrounding grounds. There was also a large two-story Army/Navy Y.M.C.A. with reading rooms, day rooms, snack bar, and a writing room of which I made use each day for writing letters to Fay and my family.

On a bus tour of the island, we saw Pearl Harbor and pineapple and sugar cane plantations where they ran small trains right out into the fields to haul the cane away just as I had seen pictured in the geography books I studied in school. Our tour also took us to Schofield Barracks and nearby Wheeler Field, both of which suffered heavy damage and loss of life in the surprise attack by the Japanese less than six weeks later. We also saw Haleiwa Beach, the first Mormon temple built outside the North American continent, the

Hawaii, 1941. *Left to right, back row:* Glen Bailey, Leroy Christensen, Edward Foster; *middle row:* Ben LeBeau, Joe Lancaster, Don Vance; *front row:* Charlie Goodliffe, Carl Nordin.

Blow-Hole, Coco Head, and Diamond Head, and we drove through dense jungle to Pali.

On our last day in Hawaii, a small group of us stopped by a place called the Black Cat, our favorite hangout for servicemen and a good place to pick up the latest news. We were easily recognized as newcomers because our sun-tan uniforms were packed away in our footlockers and stored in the hold of the ship. Noticing our wool O.D. uniforms, a couple of guys said, "You must have just come from the States—where you headed?" "The Philippines," we said. They exclaimed, "The Philippines—you poor devils! We just came from there and are mighty glad to be out of there. That's one hot spot. One of these days it's gonna blow, and when it does, we wouldn't want to be around that place." And that was the note on which our stay in Hawaii ended.

When we got back to the pier, the *Pierce*'s sister ship, the USS *Coolidge*, was tied up nearby, so we knew we would be leaving shortly because we had been waiting for this ship to join us.

November 6, 1941—Left Honolulu, USS Louisville convoying Scott and President Coolidge. When we boarded the ship that afternoon, we knew that our pleasant interlude in Hawaii was over and that we were indeed headed for foreign shores. We were also sobered by what had been said by the American servicemen at the Black Cat when they heard we were headed for the Philippines—"you poor devils."

The *Coolidge* was a beautiful ship, newer and larger than the *Pierce*. Her stop in Honolulu was for just a matter of hours, so the troops she was carrying had no opportunity to go ashore as we did, but such are the fortunes and misfortunes of life. In the next few years, we would find out that an agenda of difficulty, disappointment, and poor fortune would be pretty much the norm of our lives.

The heavy cruiser USS *Louisville* which joined us as we steamed past Pearl Harbor seemed to have plenty of armament, including two navy float planes which made daily patrols of a large area. Occasionally the cruiser itself would wheel out of the convoy and rush over to check on a ship that did not respond to its challenge. From now on we traveled "black-out," so there were no lights above deck, and smoking was not allowed on deck after the announcement over the ship's speaker system, "Now hear this—the smoking lamp is out." Strict radio silence was maintained (except for incoming news bulletins), so communication between ships was by signal light using code, as were challenges to other ships, such as "friend or foe." There could be no denying that these were the earmarks of war.

November 9, 1941—Crossed the International Date Line. Two humorous incidents occurred on this occasion. First, Walter Fader of our outfit had been hinting for several days that he expected special respect, possibly even a treat, on November 9 because it was his birthday. But he was pretty deflated the next day when he found out that it was already November 10; the ninth had occurred for just an instant at 2:00 A.M. when we crossed into another day. The other people who got fooled were a group of junior officers who gathered on deck for a supposed opportunity to do some deep-sea fishing the morning of November 9, only to be informed that this was now November 10. (This explains why Pearl Harbor Day was Sunday, December 7, in America, yet for us in the Orient it was Monday, December 8. Likewise, the cessation of hostilities in 1945 was August 15 where we were and August 14 in the other half of the world. The same holds true for the date of the signing of the surrender aboard the *Missouri*.)

It seems difficult to comprehend that as we were enjoying a beautiful sea voyage accompanied by fair weather and gentle breezes, only a few hundred miles north of us Admiral Nagumo's Kidu Butai striking force was heading the other direction—east toward where our fleet lay peacefully at anchor.

It was about this time that I had to forego the enjoyment of the gentle trade winds and put in a day of KP (kitchen police) duty, an occasion on which I got one of the biggest surprises of my life. It seemed that no matter what I did or where I went that day the KP pusher, a big husky sergeant, was looking me over. I finally volunteered to go into the steam room and do the pots and pans. But even then he came and looked in on me. Later at lunch break, I got as far away from him as I could, thinking he might not bother me. But sure enough, he brought his coffee over, and after seating himself across the table from me, he looked me square in the eye and said in a soft, pleasant voice, "Aren't you Carl Nordin from Siren, Wisconsin?" After a moment of shock, I said, "Well, yes, but who are you?" His reply, "I'm Howard Lang from Webster" (about six miles away). He had seen me in the post office a time or two and finally decided that the guy on KP duty was the same person. What a surprise meeting out there in the middle of the world's largest ocean, thousands of miles from home.

In the visit that followed, I learned that Howard was in the 192d Tank Battalion which had just come off maneuvers in the swamps and bayous of Louisiana and had arrived for overseas shipment with us. Howard (Bud) Lang and I were to have another surprise meeting, but under far different circumstances.

As our convoy steamed steadily westward, it was perhaps well that no one knew what the future held. The *Hugh L. Scott* would proceed from Manila to Shanghai to pick up returning American nationals and from there would take up duty in the Atlantic, where it was subsequently sunk by German torpedoes. The *Coolidge* continued doing convoy duty in the Pacific, and it too was sunk in the South Pacific during the war.

November 16, 1941—Stopped at Guam Island. Although we did not go ashore, we could tell we were really in the tropics. Many who served there, including Leonard Monson, a brother-in-law, and Harold Olson, a cousin, have told me it doesn't get much better than this.

November 20, 1941—Thanksgiving Day—Arrived at Manila, P.I. Wieners and sauerkraut at Fort McKinley. The announcement came over the ship's speaker system, "Now hear this—on the port side of the ship is the island of Leyte and on the starboard side is the island of Samar—welcome to the Philippine Islands." Later, steaming past the island fortress of Corregidor at the entrance to Manila Bay, we could easily see why it was affectionately known as "The Rock." Little did we know then, nor would we be able to comprehend the terrible fate that would befall it in the next few months. Sailing past Corregidor, I was amazed to see, sticking above the water, masts of what remained of the Spanish fleet that had been annihilated by Commodore Dewey some forty years earlier in the Spanish-American War.

Then another coincidence occurred. Looking down at the crowd on the pier, Sergeant Roeske exclaimed, "There's Pete Moskalik," and sure enough there stood Sergeant Moskalik, the man I had replaced earlier that year when I took over as manager of the Utilities Warehouse. This was almost as big a surprise as meeting Bud Lang in the middle of the Pacific Ocean. There would be more such occasions.

As our convoy rolled down Dewey Boulevard, it was easy to see why Manila was known in those days as the "Pearl of the Orient." Once outside the city though, our long convoy kicked up great clouds of dust as we sped along that windy day. I couldn't refrain from getting a little jibe in to Bob

Dennis, a native of Kansas, who had been complaining all the way across the Pacific about being "stuck in this tub." "I'll sure take the clean salt breezes ahead of this awful dust," I said. His mustache was covered with dust, and his teeth were gritty, but he defiantly replied, "I love it." He probably didn't have to eat his words, but he had to eat dust to say them.

We were bivouacked temporarily in tents at Fort McKinley awaiting our next assignment. The middle of that afternoon we received our Thanksgiving meal at a temporary kitchen—wieners and sauerkraut with canned peaches for dessert. Of course we felt abused because we knew that all the other troops were having turkey and all the trimmings. Little did we know how we would have welcomed such a meal a few weeks later.

With no work assignments, we spent our time exploring the area and learning what we could of this new land and its people. Strolling along the Pasig River one day, we came across a native plowing with a single-handled plow that had a five-inch share and was pulled by a carabao (native water buffalo). "How quaint and behind-the-times," we thought. Little did we realize that in less than a year we would be doing the same thing, and as slave labor at that.

A few of us took in a movie at the post theatre. Featured was the movie *Sergeant York*, depicting the story of a Kentucky hillbilly who became quite famous in World War I for, among other things, having single-handedly captured a large number of Germans. The accompanying newsreel also had coverage of the delicate talks going on between Japanese and American diplomats. Were these omens of things to come?

November 29, 1941—Left Manila aboard MS Legaspi; saw K. L. Carpenter. Looking down at the backs of two men who were adjusting the idling of the truck directly behind us, I was suddenly seized by the thought "That's Kenny Carpenter." When he raised up, I called to him a couple of times. Sure enough, there we were, half a world away from where we were the last time we had seen each other. Riding in his truck to the pier, I learned he was stationed at Nichols Field, and he learned of my aborted furlough and sad parting from Fay and my family. I told him that I had heard that he might be at Nichols Field, but not having been paid since September, I had had no funds with which to go over there. Our ship was to leave at 2:00 P.M., so we decided to have lunch together aboard ship, but first he had to park his truck. Before leaving, he handed me six pesos ($3.00 U.S.) so I wouldn't be completely broke while waiting for payday. I was never to see him again.

The *Legaspi*, a new and somewhat larger ship than most interisland ships, left promptly at 2:00 P.M. Despite the fact that it was carrying us farther from home and family, the voyage among the more than seven thousand islands that make up the Philippine archipelago was a pleasant one highlighted by a stop in Cebu, Cebu.

As we arrived in the beautiful harbor, we saw one of the traditional

Kenneth Carpenter at Nichols Field, 1941.

beautiful Philippine sunsets. On the pier a small string orchestra was on hand to serenade us. In that tranquil, peaceful setting so suggestive of tropical romance, it was only natural that my thoughts were of Fay, wishing she was there and that we were enjoying it together. As the orchestra played "Harbor Lights," I kept thinking that at that place and time, I would transpose the words to say, "but *I* was on the ship and *you* were on the shore." Breaking the reverie was the skipper's announcement that we would be given three hours of shore leave. With my six pesos, I had plenty of company as we strolled downtown for some treats. It was to be our last opportunity to exercise this freedom in almost four years.

As our ship continued southward in this almost idyllic setting while the

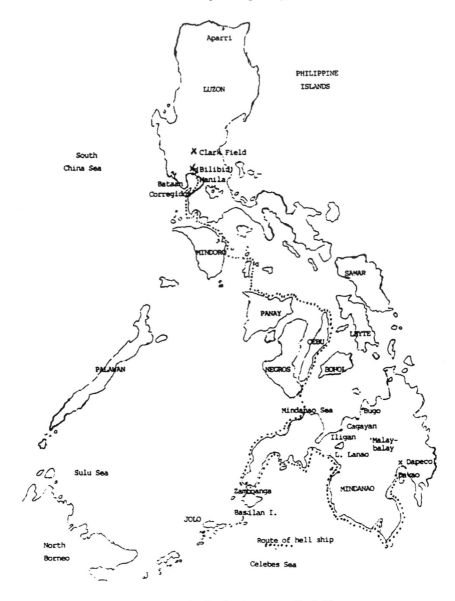

Philippine Islands, showing route of hell ship.

trade winds brushed us softly, it seemed that life couldn't get much better than this. And yet, gnawing at our subconscious was the anxious concern that seemed to be so evident in Manila and those words from Hawaii—"you poor devils."

December 1, 1941—Arrived at Bugo, Misamis, Oriental, Mindanao and Del Monte pineapple plantation. The island of Mindanao is the second largest in

Carl Nordin in front of his general supplies tent, Del Monte Field, Mindanao, December, 1941.

the Philippine group, with a land mass about that of the state of Indiana, although of a much more irregular configuration. It is rather primitive with a lot of jungle area, and sections of it are partly unexplored. Although the island is quite mountainous, there are large areas of fairly high plateaus affording a very pleasant climate.

Carl Nordin showing Filipino teachers pictures from the United States.

The island is about equidistant between Manila and the equator, both located roughly five hundred miles away. Most of the major cities are situated on the coast, as is Bugo, where a large Del Monte pineapple cannery was in full operation. A few miles inland and up on a very pleasant plateau was the Del Monte office and clubhouse enclave, surrounded by thousands of acres of pineapple fields. Not far distant was the huge cattle ranch owned by Mr. Elizalde, former high commissioner from the Philippines to the United States. This grazing land became the area where we developed the Del Monte Air Base.

In short order we had a small tent city set up, and we set about preparing revetments and gun emplacements and establishing field kitchens and all the necessary arrangements for sustaining a large group of men. I was put in charge of General Supplies, which operated out of a large circus-type tent. This operation was later moved to Tankulan, a nearby barrio. Personnel living in tent city had also been relocated by the time the area was attacked by Japanese planes. Since this was to be a major extension of the Pacific Rim defense, more support units were supposedly on the way. It all sounded so good. This then is where we found ourselves in early December 1941—on a primitive island in a strange land, halfway around the world. We only had a few planes, a few vehicles, a few guns, and a few bullets. This was *Plum.*

An early priority was the establishment of a supply line, so Sergeant Ben LeBeau, Charlie Goodliffe, and I were selected to go to Dansalan in the Lake Lanao area to establish contracts with the farmers in that area. Each of us was issued a Colt .45 pistol and a couple of cans of food as we set out in Lieutenant Ricks' staff car, a Buick sedan (right-hand drive). The other half of the negotiating team consisted of two Moros, ex-governor Heffington (of Lanao Province), and General Fort, who had served with John J. Pershing, then a captain, at nearby Camp Keithley with the main mission of trying to quell the head-hunting Moros around the turn of the century. (General Fort, a lieutenant at the time, had married a Filipino before going back to America at the end of his earlier overseas tour. But since she was not accepted in America, he had returned to the Philippines, where he joined the Philippine army and remained ever since.) Because of the respect Governor Heffington and General Fort had achieved among these people, we were able to establish a supply line that served us well in the months to come. We had one close call on the way down when guards of the datu (assistant to the sultan of Sulu) accosted us in Cagayan with the intention of settling a score another man had caused in a previous assignment. The other close call was when I took a picture of a young man and his mother walking along the road, with their betel-nut smiles and her traditional one-bare-breasted sarong.

Staying overnight at a hotel in Iligan, we met Lieutenant O'Brien from Madison, Wisconsin, who asked us to share in a seven-course birthday dinner. I still recall how good the chicken was. I will mention Lieutenant O'Brien again.

The success of the trip was matched by the pristine beauty of the coastal countryside, especially from Iligan to Cagayan. Again I found myself wishing Fay could have been there to share the beauty with me.

Back at Del Monte Field, there appeared to be the beginnings of normalcy. We had finally been paid, but there was no place to go and no way to get there. Bombers coming down from the north had brought some mail. I had received a letter from my sister Hazel as well as one from Kenneth Carpenter containing a snapshot of him at Nichols Field which, along with the two of Fay, I carried all through the war and prison camp. In turn I was waiting for mail service of some certainty to be established so I could write home and also send Kenneth Carpenter the six pesos he had loaned me. That time never came.

At War with Japan

December 8, 1941—Outbreak of war. The day dawned much as any other day.

We had been on the island of Mindanao for exactly a week and were getting somewhat organized at least enough that most of us knew what we had to do. One of our B-17s had taken off for Clark Field north of Manila to have some repair work done on a wing in the shops up there. All in all, it seemed like a business-as-usual type of day.

Sometime in the middle of the forenoon of that day, Monday, December 8, 1941, we were called together for an announcement. Col. Ray I. Elsmore, our commanding officer, mounted a truck bed and announced that Pearl Harbor and other military installations in Hawaii had been bombarded by the Japanese. It was not known exactly how much damage had been done, but early reports indicated that it had been massive. We were stunned. After an announcement and a plea for calm, he issued a directive that all hands would begin immediately to build revetments protecting our machine-gun emplacements around the field. We began work right away by filling Bemis bags with dirt, loading them on trucks, and hauling them to the various emplacements, where they were arranged to afford the greatest protection. Of all the hard work I have done in my life, that was close to the hardest. A Bemis bag filled with sand weighs over 125 pounds. That in itself is a significant amount of weight, but lifting them up to the bed of a GI truck is really hard work.

Our thoughts ranged far and wide as we worked. There were so many unanswered questions; had the Japanese proceeded further east with the attack? And if not, why not? Would the West Coast be able to defend itself? How about the Panama Canal? Would there be sabotage there? That would surely strain our commerce and our military movements. And why Hawaii? Why not the Philippines? These were the thoughts and questions that went through our minds that day. We knew we must be at war, but to us it was still thousands of miles removed.

Shortly after noon, we were called together again for the announcement that Clark Field had been bombed by the Japanese. Now we knew that war had indeed arrived. That was only a few hundred miles away. The war had definitely come to the Philippines.

This second great shock of the day was heightened by the realization that one of our own planes had gone to Clark Field for wing repair. What had happened to it, we wondered? Did its crew escape the carnage? Had they been forewarned, or did they get caught? Finally a radio message came in telling us they were on their way back but that they were pretty badly shot up. They requested that there be medics at the scene when they arrived, as there was a wounded crew member, and they were also not sure they could make a safe landing, because their plane was damaged. The plane was fortunately able to land safely later that afternoon. I was one of the witnesses as they brought the wounded man off the plane. He had been shot in the chest. We also got to see our first battle-scarred plane. So the war that had started a few hours earlier in Hawaii had also made itself felt way down in Mindanao.

Following is the Air Force Department of History account of the above mentioned incident:

> A B-17 coming up from Mindanao to have a wing repaired arrived over Clark Air Field at the exact moment of the Japanese high-level attack. Because of a report, relayed from Del Monte, that the field had been under attack, the crew approached cautiously, keeping within the cloud bank over Mt. Arayat and searching with field glasses through the overcast. But at 12:30 Clark Field lay peacefully in the plain, the unpainted B-17's and P-40's shining in the sunlight. They let down through the overcast, broke clear of it, and then, crossing the field at 500 feet, let down their wheels. At that instant the first bombs struck the rows of quarters, and the incredulous men at the windows of the big plane watched the string of explosives across the field. Tash took the B-17 down at full power to the treetops; and as they leveled the fighter planes closed in. They peeled out of their original formation and came in singly from the rear and banked away to the left as they finished their run. Sgt. M. Bibin, the bombardier, who had volunteered to handle one of the waist guns, was struck in the chest by the opening burst from the Japanese planes. He was knocked to the floor but did not lose consciousness. The Jap pilot came in so close on the B-17's tail that the tracers from his guns were converging out in front of Tash and his co-pilot, Lt. R. H. Kellar. The aileron cables were half cut through and so were the flap cables; one of the propellers was hit. After that Tash had to fly the ship dead level for fear of spinning it in.

Sgt. Bibin's medical treatment and surgery required some skin grafting. This was only partially completed at the time of our capture, so he went to prison camp with a roll of skin about the size of a large finger on the exterior of his upper body, as part of the process of moving new skin to where it was needed for replacement. Mike and I were in the same prison camps and traveled on the same hell ships, so I can personally attest to the fact that he wore that roll of skin on the surface of his upper body for over three-and-one-half years before the graft could be completed.

The military devastation caused by the Japanese coup in just one day almost defied comprehension. A major part of the U.S. Pacific Fleet had been sunk as it lay at anchor. There had been tremendous loss of life in Hawaii and fearsome destruction of military bases besides. In just 45 minutes, Clark Field as a tactical base was virtually destroyed. The casualties were very high—250 wounded, besides civilians, and 100 dead. There had also been much damage to other installations on Luzon, more casualties, and loss of life. According to the air force history: "Numerically the strike force of B-17's had been cut in half. But in efficiency their loss was infinitely greater, for now all B-17's would have to be based in Mindanao and would have to use Clark Field merely as a staging area. The wear and tear on engines and air crews alike would be far more than doubled, and so would the time spent in reaching targets."

Taking everything into consideration, what had been a rather bleak outlook for us militarily suddenly became even bleaker. The military significance of Mindanao was at once evident, and we had had only one week to prepare and become operational. More than ever we needed the bomb squadrons, tactical units, and support groups that were supposedly on the way. We needed them desperately. Would they come in time?

Shortly after the debacle at Clark Field, various air corps units were sent down to Mindanao. One such unit was the 30th Bomb Squadron, which was bivouacked in a canyon just outside of Bugo. Another unit was sent to Malabang. Some ended up in the Butuan and Surigao area. Other personnel remained on Luzon and fought with infantry and artillery units. Japanese bombers made the 400-plus-mile voyage hazardous by attacking the interisland ships that were carrying them. One ship attacked was the M.S. *Mayan*, which was carrying the 30th Bomb Squadron. Some of the men jumped overboard, thinking they would be safer. The ship received no direct hits, but at least one man was killed from the concussion of a near hit. A few other men came down to Mindanao on planes. One such person was Al Siranian, who had been stationed at Nichols Field. He and Kenny Carpenter had left our unit at Fort Douglas in early 1941, when they were transferred to Fort Warren, Wyoming, and they were subsequently sent to Nichols Field. Al informed me that there had been a sign-up sheet at Nichols Field for a ride to Mindanao. Al was second on the list, and Kenny was third. There was only room for two. Unfortunately, Al didn't survive either.

It was at about this time that our unit moved off the field and into a little barrio named Tankulan (its name was later changed to Manolo Fortich), about four or five kilometers east of Del Monte Field. The barrio's normal population was only about 125, but by this time most of its residents had evacuated to the hills for safety. There were two or three stores, a telephone office, a small Catholic church, and a village pump at the center of town; there was neither running water nor a sewer. There was also a school, which was the nicest building in the barrio. This building served as a sort of headquarters for our detachment. My General Supplies tent was situated under some mango trees near the little church. We also utilized the domestic science building for overflow storage space of General Supplies. Pyramidal tents were set up under mango trees on the back part of the school grounds for commissary storage and for quarters.

Another unit, the 89th Quartermaster (Maintenance), was also stationed in Tankulan, about a block and a half from my supply tent. Al Siranian, who had been in my outfit in Fort Douglas, had signed on with this unit after arriving in Mindanao from Nichols Field.

It was in Tankulan that I met Salvador Albarece, a Filipino who turned out to be a lifelong friend. He was the principal at the Tankulan school, which had been disbanded, and he had been most cooperative and helpful to us in getting set up in Tankulan. His wife, Marcelina, was a teacher in the school. Salvador was a very knowledgeable man and was very conversant on a broad range of subjects. He spoke Illacano, his native tongue, Visayan (the dialect of Mindanao), Tagalog (the official Philippine dialect), Spanish, and English, all fluently, and he could switch from one to another without a hitch. By this time, he and his family had evacuated to the hills. He did have access to a radio, so between that source and what came through Del Monte headquarters, we knew pretty much what was going on in our part of the world and it was not good.

On December 10, 1941, just two days after the twin debacles of Pearl Harbor and Clark Field, the Japanese sank the supposedly near-impregnable British warships HMS *Repulse* and *Prince of Wales* in the Indian Ocean, not far from Mindanao. On that same day, Japanese forces invaded the northern Philippines at Appari and Vigan on the island of Luzon. On December 13, another invasion force struck at Legaspi on the southeast coast of Luzon.

Then on December 19, the war came directly to Mindanao when eight Japanese planes carried out a fairly extensive strafing raid of Del Monte Field. It was fortunate that the field had been cleared as a bivouac area because they really worked over the places where our tents had been. There were, however, various personnel working on the field, so there were casualties. One of our own men, "Chief" Foster, came very close to getting hit as he lay flat on the ground, with bullets hitting the dirt on both sides of him and splashing dirt in his face besides. We also were treated to a couple of the aerial dog fights as some of our P-40 pilots rose up to challenge the invaders. The very next day, December 20, invasion forces landed on southeastern Mindanao at Davao. One day later, December 21, Del Monte Field suffered its first bombing raid by a fleet of thirty-three planes. On the twenty-second, the invaders made another landing at San Fernando in the province of La Union on the northwest coast of Luzon; on the twenty-fourth, another landing was made on the southeast coast of Luzon.

Christmas, 1941. I was raised in a family where Christmas was important, and for the right reasons. To be sure, there were gifts, but they were few and modest. Mostly they symbolized our love for each other, but they were not

Salvador Albarece family at their home in Tankulan, 1955. Photo by Glenn Nordin.

at all excessive. Our parents, to their everlasting credit, sought to imbue us with the true meaning and spirit of Christmas: a revelation of God's great love for us. The observance would begin with a very simple, humble meal, symbolic of the humble circumstances surrounding the birth of Christ. But before the meal, our father would always read us the Christmas story from the Bible, as recorded in the second chapter of Luke. Later on that night or sometimes early Christmas morning, the entire family would attend church. This tradition had become very meaningful to me. But on Christmas of 1941, there would be no sitting down to a family meal preceded by hearing the Christmas story. Fortunately though, there was a midnight mass at the little Catholic church behind my supply tent. Being a Lutheran raised in an era when there was much misunderstanding and divisiveness between Catholics and Protestants, I had never set foot in a Catholic church before. But the importance and solemnity of the occasion overrode my bias, and for the first time in my life I attended a Catholic mass. Although the service was interrupted when one young lieutenant who was overcome by fear, homesickness, and emotion disrupted the proceedings, I found that my need really had been fully met, even though I was in a different church in a foreign land, surrounded by people whom I didn't know, in the middle of a very black night.

Christmas Day dawned bright and beautiful. Our company commander had arranged for turkey and all the trimmings to be brought in, so everyone broke out in clean suntan uniforms and spent the forenoon in eager anticipation of a back-home meal. It turned out to be an unlucky day for me, however.

Catholic church in Tankulan, where author attended mass on Christmas Eve, 1941. Later his supply tent was right behind the church. Photo by Glenn Nordin.

A few days earlier, our lieutenant had procured a case of beer and had secretly brought it to my tent to be kept a surprise for the troops at Christmas. So I hid it back among my supplies for that day. But when the lieutenant came to get it before our meal, to my utter consternation it was gone, I couldn't believe my eyes, and of course he had a hard time believing my protestations of innocence. I later asked Lucero, my helper, about it, but he claimed not to know anything about it. It not only ruined my day, but it became a negative factor when I was up for promotion. It wasn't until about forty years later when a guy from our outfit was laughing about the Christmas beer they had stolen from the supply tent that I found out that Lucero had moved it to the end of the tent opposite where I slept, thereby making it possible to slip it out by lifting the bottom edge of the tent. It was a costly prank for me in terms of my foregone promotion, but I do have the satisfaction of a clear conscience.

We were brought back to the real world in short order, however. Word reached us that Hong Kong had fallen to the Japanese on Christmas Day. We were also getting reports that there was heavy fighting on Luzon and at Davao. There began to be more and more calls for supplies, and each time that I was visited by someone from another sector, I began to hear more details of the fighting. It was not long before the Japanese made a landing at Cotabato, on the south side of Mindanao. Our troops were developing a Davao-Cotabato front, and the various air corps units were developing alternate airfields in different parts of the island, some quite secret and well camouflaged. All this time we lived in hope of the relief we would receive when the fifty-ship convoy arrived. We were going to be ready.

December 29, 1941—Received cablegram from Fay; afflicted with dysentery at the time. There is a certain amount of poignancy in the above notation. Probably nothing in the world could have made me happier or lifted my spirits more than a cablegram from Fay, affirming her love for me, assuring me of her prayers for my safety and well-being. I needed to hear both, as the situation in our part of the world was becoming more ominous each week. What took the edge off my joy though was my physical condition. I had been plagued by diarrhea for some time, so I finally sought help from the Medical Corps. In order to make my case, I kept count of my trips to the latrine. During an eight-hour period, I had nineteen bowel movements; it was dehydrating me and really sapping my strength. It was at this low point that I received the cablegram; it lifted my spirits, but I really had a medical problem.

During these early days of the war, there was a detail going around foraging and confiscating various supplies, especially from Chinese stores. These items would be brought to General Supplies, so I had quite a conglomeration of supplies in my tent . On one occasion they had brought ten or fifteen small bottles (about a pint each) of Chinese wine, which I dutifully stored. As the lieutenant and I were reading the labels, we couldn't help but chuckle about the uses for which the wine was supposedly manufactured. The list included such things as cooking aid, headaches, morning sickness, postpregnancy discomforts, dyspepsia, and diarrhea. Knowing of my problem, the lieutenant suggested that I should try some, which I did. It helped some, but it didn't cure my condition. At any rate, when my buddy Bob Dennis over in the commissary tent heard that I had some wine, he wanted to sample it too, only he did a little more than sample. This little episode may have been a contributing factor in the lieutenant's disbelief of me about the disappearance of the beer. It was a case of the danger and damage of circumstantial evidence.

As the year 1941 slipped into history, there was no denying the fact that a period of nervous peace had ended, and in its place was practically a whole world at war, a war that would be unsurpassed in size, horror, and ugliness. But it held one more macabre twist for me. New Year's Eve was about as dreary as any night could be. It had begun raining hard in the afternoon and had continued all through the night. I was alone in my big supply tent, and since I had nothing to read and only one candle as a source of light, I had retired by about 8:00 P.M. By bedding down in my cot, I could get off the dirt floor that was wet from rainwater seeping in around the bottom edges of the tent.

It was close to midnight when I was awakened by someone batting at the entrance flaps of the tent and calling my name. In response to my "Who's there?" inquiry, he said, "It's Mack Davis, and I've got a stiff in the back of my van; I need some help in finding his C.O." It seemed that a B-17 had landed at Cagayan late in the afternoon after a bombing raid up north. There had been several casualties, including one dead. Mack had been ordered to meet the plane because he was in charge of the burial detail for our part of the island. Before burying anyone, however, he would always contact the C.O. to report the death and leave valuables of the deceased. If items of clothing, canteens, or mess kits were needed by the unit, he would leave those of the dead soldier. Otherwise, they would be turned over to General Supply for reissue.

So I got dressed and went with him. I could understand why he might want company as we slipped and sloshed around on muddy roads and trails, with that corpse rolling around and hitting the sides of the van with every slip of the vehicle. Adding to the eeriness was the difficulty of seeing the road in the pouring rain when we had only black-out lights by which to see.

As we drove and searched in vain that miserable night, our conversation drifted to the girls we left behind: his Jean, with whom he had gone out for three years and whom he had married just days before going overseas, and my Fay, whom I was forced to leave so suddenly. Although events of the last few weeks had kept our minds and time occupied with things of gigantic importance, matters of the heart were never far removed from our consciousness. It was good therapy to air our feelings with a kindred heart.

After several hours and a number of dead ends, Mack accepted the futility of our search and decided to wait until daylight. Then he could alert the grave-digging crew to prepare another addition to the graveyard that we had already started. So ended 1941.

The War Continues
and Expands

January 4, 1942—First full pay of the war. The circumstances were much the same as they were when we got paid in early December—"no place to go, and no way to get there." The one big difference was that the men were more dispersed and more occupied, so there was very little poker being played. The men were also more inclined to hang on to their money because of the uncertainty the future held at this point. About the only way to spend money was when the natives would come in from the hills to pick up and deliver laundry, and they only charged a pittance.

News coming from the north revealed to us that the troops there were preparing for the long haul. Manila had been declared an open city, but the Japanese had violated the international code of honor attached to such a declaration, causing the slaughter of hundreds of innocent civilians as they bombed it relentlessly. And news from the south indicated heavy fighting in the Dutch East Indies, Malaya, Celebese, and other areas. In a word, we were being encircled by the enemy.

As the Japanese became more operational after establishing their beachhead at Davao, we noticed a distinct increase in air raids on our part of the island. At first, some of the raids would be made by the slower sea planes, but after our pursuit planes entered the picture, the raids were mostly carried out by high-level bombers.

One indication of the inadequacy of our capabilities was our so-called "early warning system." When the planes passed over Malaybalay, the operator in the telephone office at Malaybalay, would call the operator in Tankuklan, who would go outside and sound the alarm by using an iron pipe to strike the sides of a warning triangle hanging from the roof of the porch. It was crude, but it gave us a few moments to get to our foxholes.

Speaking of foxholes, I learned about them by experience. My first foxhole was under a poinsettia bush, which was about ten feet high with overhanging branches. In my naiveté, I thought that I would be safer if I could see the plane—but what if the pilot (or bombardier) could not see me? The one thing wrong was that my foxhole was across the street from my tent. Some men had already been killed while running for cover. I wanted my foxhole close, and I wanted it big enough to accommodate both me and my field pack, a mistake, as I later learned. So I dug myself another foxhole on my side of the street that was considerably larger. All was well and good until the next air raid. As I sat crouched down in that immense foxhole, I began to realize how much bigger and deeper it looked from that perspective, as compared to when I was digging it. And then I began to think that if a bomb landed close enough to cave that sucker in, I'd really be in the soup.

A few days later there was another air raid. Bob Dennis had come over for a little visit, so as the alarm sounded, I headed for my foxhole. Concerned for Bob's safety, I said, "Don't run Bob; lie down flat." His reply was, "Lie down, hell; I'm getting in there with you." So I made room and he squeezed in. We had just gotten settled and were looking up at the sky, trying to see the planes, when lo and behold, all we saw was arms and legs and a big blob as K. B. Larsen, the biggest man in our outfit, settled down on us. He had been walking down the street when the alarm sounded, and instinct sent him to the nearest foxhole in the vicinity. After that episode, I decided that it's nice to be hospitable and all, but there's no need to dig a foxhole for half the company.

On a serious note, it doesn't take a soldier long to learn that a foxhole doesn't have to be big or deep—just enough for protection from flying shrapnel. One other thing we learned to do instinctively as the war progressed, and we were on the move—the very first thing one does is dig a foxhole or find a low indentation or at least lie flat if an attack begins.

On January 2, 1942, the Japanese landed a force on Jolo, an island south of Zambaonga in southwestern Mindanao, and by the middle of the month they had made more landings on Luzon. Both sides were consolidating their forces on the Bataan peninsula. Withdrawal of our Luzon forces into Bataan was in accordance with prearranged military plans should the engagement of the two forces develop into a fight to the finish.

Meanwhile, B-17s operating out of Del Monte Field were carrying out missions over Luzon and other strategic targets. The fighting in the Davao area had stalemated for a while but was becoming aggressive again. On two different occasions, I was visited by a member of the "Moro battalion," so-called because they were a contingent of Moros only, who used stealth and knives as their weapons. According to my informant's report on the last visit, they had sneaked into a Japanese bivouac at night and cut the heads off quite a large number of Japanese. He brought along a pair of ears to make his point. Their requests for supplies were few, which was a good thing because there were getting to be fewer supplies from which to draw.

Food was a problem, so sometime in January we were cut to two meals a day—10:00 A.M. and about 3:00 P.M. Noticeable also was the deterioration of variety and quality of our meals. The situation was anything but a morale builder, and yet morale remained surprisingly high, though the future was anything but promising. It must be remembered that in those days there were no such things as helicopters to whisk us away from a dangerous place. In addition, we were on an island, an isolated one at that, and even if we left Mindanao, there was no place to go because the navy had been sunk at Pearl Harbor, leaving the Japanese in control of the surrounding seas. Consequently, in our more thoughtful moments, we began to realize that our much-needed support of men and war materiel would never arrive. We would thus be left seriously out-gunned and out-manned, and our ultimate fate would be that we would either be killed or captured before this scenario was played to its finish.

February 16, 1942—Transferred to duty at Bugo as convoy commander under Captain Gray. This assignment was not nearly as glamorous as it may sound, but it was not without its challenges. As foodstuffs (mainly rice, some sugar) and other miscellaneous items were shipped to Mindanao, it was our duty to transport them to various supply bases and other storage sites inland. There were not enough GI trucks to go around, so we had to scrounge up whatever we could find. Fortunately for us, the Western Development Company and a gold-mining outfit had ceased operations at the outbreak of the war and had put their trucks in a motor pool for the military use. There were many makes, models, and sizes, but all had been made for the Far East, so they were all right-hand drive. The drivers were all Filipino—some civilians and some members of the newly called-up Philippine army.

Another man from our outfit, Roderick McKay, had been on detached service to Bugo since shortly after the beginning of the war. He and I had our cots and gear in a little ten-by-twelve foot enclosure of wire netting with a galvanized metal roof between the water's edge and the bay side of the Del Monte cannery. We were attached for rations to the 30th Bomb Squadron of the 19th Group, which was bivouacked at the mouth of a canyon about five hundred yards away. McKay had been there long enough to become acquainted with the skippers of the various interisland ships that docked there and would always be invited to dine with the captain at his private mess, so he had a good deal. Dinner would usually be a seven-course meal, lunch a five-course meal, and breakfast would be three or four courses, complete with waiters, the captain's valet, and whatever it took to make the captain happy. I was fortunate enough to be invited for a couple of meals, and I was amazed at the food and the service. As for me, however, I would experience a vast difference in food in my new assignment.

The average size of a convoy would be five or six trucks, sometimes fewer but seldom more. The Filipino drivers were usually in their middle twenties and were good drivers. Most of them spoke little English, so there was a communication problem. This was alleviated to a certain extent, however, by the aid of one of the drivers, whose name was John. He too was a good driver, and he was a really fine person. I grew to depend on him. He was especially helpful in seeing that we were loaded and ready to move out on time. I delegated to him the authority of seeing that the drivers were also there on time, because he could communicate with them much more easily. In addition to overseeing the operation in general, I was also the person designated to ride shotgun. This entailed riding outside of the cab to keep a lookout for airplanes. Whenever I spotted some, I would bang on the roof of the cab and signal the other drivers to stop immediately so we could take cover. For this duty, my Colt .45 was replaced with an Enfield 30.06 rifle of Spanish-American and World War I vintage. I hated to give up my Colt .45, but the pistols weren't of much use against planes; neither were rifles. Normally, I would ride in the back of the lead truck, but that could change according to the circumstances.

Depending upon how heavily we were loaded and the road conditions, the round trip between Bugo and Maramag would take about twenty-four hours. We would try to be on the road between 7:00 and 8:00 A.M. The first forty or fifty miles were quite mountainous, with narrow, winding roads in some places that required us to travel at reduced speeds for many miles. After leaving Malaybalay, the road and terrain got better, but soon after leaving Valencia, we would encounter darkness. This slowed us considerably, as we had to travel blackout at night. Newer trucks came equipped with blackout lights, which were small, narrow horizontal lights. The blackout lights we used had been jerry-built by painting the top and bottom portions of the lens with black paint, leaving a horizontal rectangle of clear glass about one-inch wide a little below the middle of the glass. The purpose of blackout lights, of course, was to make it possible to travel at night with much less chance of detection from the air. They obviously made for slow going, especially over roads that were treacherous enough in daylight. This schedule would bring us to Maramag between 10:00 P.M. and midnight. Unloading time depended upon the kind of cargo we carried and the amount of help we could rustle up in the middle of the night, but we usually tried to begin our return trip by 2:00 A.M. That would put us back in civilization in time to catch the early mess from whatever outfit's breakfast we could scrounge a meal. This became an important objective for me because whenever we went out on a run, Captain Gray would give me my choice: I could have either a can of fish or a can of pork and beans as my ration for the trip, which often was twenty-four hours in duration. There was no opportunity to get rice or anything else that early. The Filipino drivers had their rice and viands, and sometimes they would share some of their rice with me, but they didn't have any too much either, so I wouldn't take unfair advantage of their generosity. We would normally stop at a little turnout place at Absalom Falls between Impasugo-ong and Malaybalay for a break and to give the trucks a chance to cool off. There was also a water fountain there, so we could replenish radiators and canteens, if necessary. We would normally get to Valencia in midafternoon, where we could gas up if need be, and we could also buy homemade candy made of coconut and brown sugar from roadside vendors. This was my only supplement in twenty-four hours, as they would not yet be open on our return in the morning. Some of our trips were to a place called Kitaotao, which was beyond Maramag. Not only was this a longer trip, but it was quite eerie to be roving along in a deep forest in the middle of the night. Sometimes this uneasiness was heightened by events on the way down there during the day, such as strafing raids by planes.

One of our worst air attacks occurred just east of Tankulan as we were starting down into a canyon. I was riding shotgun but didn't see the planes until they were almost on us because we were just below the rim of the canyon. I pounded on the cab of the lead truck, signaled the others, and we all dismounted and took cover. It was not to be the only time that I was caught in that particular spot. On another occasion, planes attacked in an open territory between Malaybalay and Valencia as we were headed south. The next day they attacked us in the very same spot on our return trip. This was almost too much for some of the drivers, who didn't want to come back to their trucks from their hiding places. Instead, about half of them to take off and join their families, who had evacuated to the hills. I used persuasion first, then gave them an order to return to their trucks. When they defied that, I reinforced my order by drawing a bead on them with my rifle explaining that the man with the gun was the boss. It was a desperate threat, but it was one they understood clearly and I had made my point. To be doubly sure, however, I finished that trip by riding shotgun from the truck in the middle of the convoy. It was the last and only time I had trouble with them for that or any reason. In fact, from then on, our sense of understanding and unity was without question. Fortunately, despite all the times we were shot at, there were no personal injuries except for sprains or scratches caused by jumping from trucks and not enough serious damage to our trucks to deter us. Once I was able to convince the drivers that there was no advantage to be gained by panic, things went much more smoothly, and a sense of self-assurance developed that made things easier for all. We encountered most of our air attacks south and east of Bugo, because that was the main flight corridor that Japanese planes used to attack Del Monte Field from their base in Davao. Thus our trips from Bugo to Kitaotao and points between were our most hazardous. Some of our trips involved handling supplies, primarily rice, to be warehoused in various schoolhouses in the area between Maluko and Valencia. These supplies would be used to feed our troops after the invasion of northern Mindanao and after the fighting progressed inland in that area. Mr. Albarece, the superintendent of the school in Tankulan, provided me with some valuable information in this regard because he was particularly well acquainted with the schools and the people in Bukidnon Province. A case in point was a barrio called Malitbog which, according to my map, was not far north and east of Tankulan. When I asked Salvador about the roads and if there was a schoolhouse there, he told me that there was a schoolhouse there that was used some. He recommended, however, that I not go there. He didn't elaborate much except to say in a very polite and generous manner that I might not find friendship there. When I went back there thirty-five years later, I asked Salvador about Malitbog, and he told me that, even after all that time, it was very primitive and still was not a safe place to go. As superintendent of schools for Bukidnon Province, he had tried to get the educational system started there. Teaching there was still considered hazardous duty, worthy of extra pay and shorter terms.

February 28, 1942—Shelling of Bugo. This had been a particularly long and taxing day. Our trip to Kitaotao had been interrupted several times by air raids. Night driving had slowed us more than usual, and we didn't get unloaded until toward morning. There were more air attacks on our return trip, so we didn't get back to Bugo until midafternoon. Consequently, after more than thirty hours of difficult travel, we were very hungry and dog-tired. McKay had had an exhausting day also. There had been two air raids at the pier, and one ship had been sunk as it was being unloaded. This, of course, had created quite a mess around there, so except for stopping to eat, we both worked until darkness overtook us and then we climbed into our cots which were set up in the small net wire shed between the factory and the beach for a much needed night's rest. At about 9:00 P.M., however, we were jarred to consciousness by tremendously loud shots or explosions, followed by sounds of tearing steel. McKay was the first to speak, "Oh my God, they're bombing the pier again!" "No," I said, "they're shelling us from the sea. They've got a searchlight on us. Hit the deck—now!" We lay there on the cement floor, pulling on our clothes as the shells flew over us, tearing into the galvanized steel sides of the Del Monte pineapple cannery. No sooner had we collected our thoughts than McKay said, "We've got to get out of here; I've got a key." "Yeah," I said, "they're probably softening up the beach, getting ready for an invasion." The next couple of minutes seemed like an eternity as we stood in the glare of the searchlight while McKay struggled with the key as he tried to unlock the padlocked door to the factory. Once inside, we groped in the dark, with only a little light coming in through the shell holes. A number of shells tore through the superstructure of the building as we made our way through, with shrapnel and steel falling around us. The minute we stepped out on the other side, a shell took off the top of a palm tree just ahead of us. Once we crossed the street and got past a row of nipa huts and into a rice paddy, we got a look at the source of the shelling because we learned really fast that if we watched for the flash of the guns, we had time to fall flat before the shell passed over us. It was then that we could see that it was a destroyer that had pulled in close to shore and was having a field day. It obviously made for a wild night for us. Because the beach was undefended at that time and, McKay and I thought that an invasion might follow, we walked all the way to Tankulan, a distance of twenty-six kilometers or approximately fifteen miles, arriving there about 2:30 or 3:00 A.M. Fortunately, the moon came out later, so it was a pleasant night, but our thoughts were mostly about what had just happened and what might happen next.

When we returned the next forenoon, General Sharp, commander of the Visayan-Mindanao forces, and his aides were already on the site, inspecting the damage. There were 27 five-inch holes on the bay side where the shells had entered the building. The interior of the building was a jumbled mass of beams and catwalks, all askew, with shrapnel and pieces of steel from damaged machines strewn everywhere except in the path or area where we had picked our way through the building on our way to safety. When we inspected the little shed where we had been sleeping, we saw something even more amazing. My canvas cot had a big five-inch hole right where my chest had been, and lying on the concrete floor directly beneath it was the four-and-a-half inch piece of jagged shrapnel that had caused the tear. If I had not rolled out when I did, that shrapnel would have gone right through my body. Surely I was being watched over that time.

Our trips to Malabang on Illiana Bay of the Moro Gulf were more interesting and pleasant for several reasons. The drive along the seacoast from Bugo to Iligan through miles and miles of stately coconut palm trees along pristine sand beaches is one of the most beautiful drives one can imagine. By going west and south from Bugo and Cagayan, we were also going away from the general flight path of Japanese airplanes, so air attacks against us were greatly reduced. Furthermore, the trip involved less night driving, although we did arrive at the jungle headquarters of an air corps unit (another eerie place) as late as midnight. Depending on our schedule, we could sometimes get a meal, usually breakfast at a mission house in Dansalan on the north end of Lake Lanao. In fact, I was even put up there for part of the night on occasion. It was an interesting place because missionaries from various parts of the southwest Pacific were seeking safe haven there as the islands where they had been stationed were being taken over by the Japanese. They had used Mindanao as a stepping stone to Manila, a main terminal for transpacific ocean travel. Unfortunately for them, that was no longer a possibility, so they ended up being captured eventually anyway.

The interisland ships were bringing cargo from the islands of Negros and Panay into the port of Iligan as well as to Bugo. For the drivers, this presented an uncomfortable obstacle: the pier at Iligan was long and narrow, so they had to back a long way, with little leeway, in order to load their trucks. It definitely was a hazard, but not insurmountable. There were no mishaps.

During my service with the convoy I met some men I will always remember. One of them was George Plowman, a true man of courage. Even though events would shorten the time of our association, we became very good friends. A Texan, he had made and lost two fortunes in the 1930s, one in cattle and one in oil. He salvaged a few thousand dollars from his last venture,

Left to right, Carl Nordin, ex-governor Heffington, a missionary, Mrs. George Plowman, and Clive Clucas in front of Mission House, Dansalan, 1942.

and he decided to take a trip around the world because he was young and footloose. As I recall him telling the story, however, an event at the American Embassy in Japan sort of changed his plans. While on a routine visit to the embassy, he had met a young lady whom he could not quite forget. He did take a little trip over to China, but rather than continuing on around the world, he came back to Japan. At this time it was no longer advisable nor desirable for American nationals to remain in Japan, so George came on down to the Philippines, the closest soil friendly to the United States. He told me that when he arrived in Cebu, he had fifty cents. He went to work in the logging industry, and in a short time had accumulated enough money to send for the girl he had met in Tokyo, whereupon they were married and began their lives together in the Philippines. His dream was to go into the logging business on a big scale. In fact, he wanted me to join him after the war to sort of take care of the clerical and office end of the business and to someday start a dairy. He even had the island picked out that he planned to buy and build his new fortune on. He was an enterprising and engaging young man, but he was more than that—he was courageous and fearless. Among the items he had accumulated was a rather large banca, which is a canoelike vessel with a sail and an outrigger to make it seaworthy. This was large enough to haul freight from island to island. So after the war started and the Japanese were making it difficult for the interisland ships, George began running the Japanese blockade with his banca. It was a ploy that worked very well because bancas were a very common mode of travel and transportation among the islands by the Filipino people in those days and thus caused little or no suspicion among the Japanese fleet. George was deeply tanned, dressed like a Filipino, and kept a low profile. He kept going from island to island, picking up cargo and bringing it to Mindanao, primarily to Bugo and Iligan. It was a fascinating and productive way to beat the Japanese at their own game, and we enjoyed many a chuckle over it. In fact, it was so productive that he was offered a commission in the army, but he refused it. He thought he could do more for the war effort doing what he knew best, and rightly so. Nobody could have done it better. No orders from higher up could have improved his method. Few, if any, would have been more courageous. I take my hat off to him because I saw firsthand what he did. I lost track of George Plowman at the time I became a prisoner, but have heard recently that he lived through captivity and returned to the U.S. He died in a plane crash almost fifty years after the outbreak of the war, however.

Another memorable man was called simply "John the Arab." At one time I may have known what his surname was, but it has faded from memory after all these years. But I do recall that his given name was John, or at least the Anglicized version was John. I first met him when I stopped at his place for water. He had a place by the side of the road that was distinctive because instead of being the normal nipa hut, it was a frame building, a little larger than the traditional hut, was rectangular, and had glass windows. It was set among tall, beautiful hardwood trees instead of palm trees, and it was close to the top of a long rise. He showed me the area back of his house, where quite close by was a fast-rushing, small river with quite a high waterfall. It was a place one had to love. It seemed so serene, so quiet and safe, yet close to the comings and goings of mankind. John the Arab had fought with Lawrence of Arabia in World War I, helping King Feisal I defeat the Turks. Having made the military his career, he lived in retirement, sustained by a military pension from Great Britain. He was a very knowledgeable person and a most interesting conversationalist. Added to that, he was a genial host and always seemed to have a bottle of Coca-Cola—almost unheard of in those days—or a bottle of sarsaparilla. And no matter what time of day it was, he would always insist on serving up something to eat. For one thing, he always had a big pot of baked beans ready to warm up. Obviously, when Captain Gray gave me a choice of beans or fish for trips where we would be going by John the Arab's place, I took fish.

There was very little furniture in John's house. My drivers would either sit on the floor or squat on their haunches along a wall, some distance from where John and I might be, in an attempt to be the least obtrusive. When it was time to eat, they started opening their food containers right where they were, but I told them to join us at the table. "Oh, no, seer (their way of say-ing 'sir,' which would rhyme with beer), we do not feel we should sit at the same table as you." I said, "Why not?" "But seer," John the driver said, "We are inferior to you—you are American." "Nonsense," I said. "No one is infe-rior to anyone here. We are all the same, trying to do the same thing. Now come and join us at the table." John the Arab gave me an approving nod, so I said, "Come now," and they came, almost sheepishly. It was either on that or a subsequent trip that Cleve Clucas had come down from Tankulan to join me for a trip to Malabang, just to get away. When he saw that I insisted on the Filipinos joining us at the table, he made it a point to tell me later how impressed he was with that gesture and said, "Now that's the way we should all treat people of other races." "Well, " I said, "they are people just like we are." (Sadly, Clucas was not to return home.)

Another point of interest on the way to Malabang was the home of the datu on the southwest part of Lake Lanao. A datu is sort of a holy man in the Moslem religion. Perhaps more correctly, he is a sort of regional repre-sentative of the sultan—in this case the sultan of Sulu, whose residence was on the island of Jolo in the Sulu Archipelago south of Zamboanga, Mindanao. The datu's compound was comprised of at least ten acres, with a large, rather rambling house set back from the road. There was a fence around it with Moro guards at the gate. It was tastefully landscaped and complemented with lush tropical vegetation.

My roster of memorable characters on convoy duty would not be com-plete without mentioning again my favorite driver, John. I never knew his last name, but he was proud of the fact that his name had been anglicized from Juan. He would have liked to have been an American, and he tried so hard to excel at everything. He spoke the best English of any of the drivers, was the best driver of the group, and took the best care of his truck. He was the most reliable in every way until one day when we were going to Talakag to pick up some vegetables. We were only going to take three trucks, but I wanted John to be one of the drivers. It was the shortest of any run we made, but the roads were by far the most treacherous. In fact, in some places to call the route a road was definitely an exaggeration. In places, it was little more than a trail carved out of the side of a mountain, with some difficult to nego-tiate curves. This route eventually led down to a mountain stream that had to be crossed by a ferry that had been built for passengers and carts, not for trucks.

On this day of all days, John did not show up, and none of the other dri-vers could explain his absence. So we took off and made it to Talakag, a lit-tle barrio on the northern edge of the Moro farming country. In fact, it was part of the crop-producing regions that entered into my negotiations with the Moros, General Fort, ex-governor Heffington, and Goodliffe LeBeau in early December. They had granaries full of camotes (similar to sweet potatoes), corn, beans, squash, and other vegetables. We took one truck out in the fields and loaded sacks of camotes, while the other two trucks loaded items from the granaries. Returning with the trucks loaded was slow going and fraught with danger, but we made it without serious incident.

The mystery of John the driver's disappearance was solved about ten days later when he showed up one morning ready for a trip to Kitaotao. He was carrying a poorly wrapped package which he bashfully, yet proudly, handed to me, saying simply, "For you." Inside was a beautifully crafted bolo encased in a handmade scabbard of Philippine mahogany, with silver inlay. It was the most beautiful bolo and scabbard I have ever seen. When I recovered from my initial surprise and protested that it was too much of a gift, he said, "But sir, you have been so kind to us. You have made me feel worthwhile, so I want to give you something of worth to show my gratitude. " Seldom have I been as touched by another person's action toward me as I was when John gave me that bolo and told me why he did it. He had noticed that almost everyone except me had a bolo of sorts by this time, so he went cross-country on foot down into the Moro country and had purchased it from one of the artisans with his hard-earned money. What a selfless act and demonstration of appreciation!

Farewell to Freedom

March 2, 1942—Put on Demolition Duty at Bugo. Sensing that there was not a great amount of defense capability on our part, the Japanese navy was getting pretty cheeky around northern Mindanao. They had bombed the pier at Bugo several times and had pulled in close and shelled the Del Monte cannery building. On one occasion they had even pulled into Tagoloan (the next barrio east of Bugo), tied a line to an interisland ship at the pier, and attempted to pull it free of the pier, all in broad daylight. Word of the hijacking attempt was relayed up to Del Monte Field. In just a short time, a couple of P-40s were dodging antiaircraft fire from the Japanese ship as the planes tried to drive the ship away by strafing it. Then one of the planes returned to the field, where they tied a bomb onto it. Since Tagoloan was only a few kilometers away from Bugo and separated only by a long, narrow, wooded point of land, McKay and I could see the whole aerial operation and hear all the firing. When the second P-40 returned with the bombs, we saw it go into its dive and could even see the bomb release. That did the trick. The Japanese pulled away without any booty that time. It was a great show while it lasted, but that and other events gave clear indication that time was drawing short for us.

We really had no defenses, but plans were being put into place to try and deter whatever aggressive action the enemy might take. Part of that plan was to install demolition sites at various places along the beach. McKay and I were given instructions how and when to set off the charges. In my case, the instructions applied only if I was not inland someplace with a convoy. Because McKay and I were in a supply unit and had no infantry training, Colonel Woodbridge, a West Point man, also gave us instructions and drilled us when we had some time to spare. What a way to have to fight a war. Some of this training came in handy later on, though.

March 13, 1942—PT Boats bring MacArthur to Mindanao. I had returned from another long and tiring trip, and I spent the rest of the afternoon getting things squared away so we would be ready to go where and when Capt. Gray told us. As can be expected, I was looking forward to a good night's rest, but that was not to be. Just before dark, a lieutenant whom I had never seen before contacted McKay and me and informed us that something special was going to happen some time in the night. He told us he could not say any more at the time except that some time in the night we would hear a mighty roar. He said it would sound like planes but would not be planes. Then he told us our mission. We were to guard the pier and allow nobody in the area—*nobody*—until he gave a certain signal that whatever it was that we were waiting for was about to happen. It was a long night, but about daybreak we heard the loudest roar you can imagine. He was right; it wasn't planes. It was PT (motor torpedo) boats bringing MacArthur and his entourage out from Corregidor. General Sharp and his party escorted them up to his headquarters at Del Monte. From there they were flown out to Australia.

The waterfront at Bugo got a little more interesting after the PT boats came in. For one thing, the sailors who manned them had been going out on missions around Luzon, so we heard a lot about their exploits up there. We also heard firsthand about the disastrous situation on Bataan and Corregidor. After the shelling, McKay and I had moved into one of the larger and better houses in Bugo, and the sailors moved right in with us, with the overflow moving into a couple of other houses. In the ten weeks we lived with them, we got to know them well. Especially interesting was being privy to the missions they conducted from Bugo. There was always tension and a certain sense of excitement among them before they went out on a mission. Their return, however, might be marked by feelings of elation over success or sadness over loss. Sometimes there would be a combination of the two. Their exploits make a story of their own and have been described by other authors. Suffice it to say that their operations out of Bugo were very damaging to the Japanese, whose greatest loss to the PT boats was a heavy cruiser. By the time their campaign out of Bugo was all over, the men of PT Squadron 3 had made an indelible mark in their type of warfare, but it had cost them two boats and the lives of several gallant men.

April 18, 1942—Doolittle raid on Tokyo. News of the Doolittle raid on Tokyo buoyed our spirits and caused our adrenaline to flow a little faster, at least for a moment. It was good to know that America, too, was capable of mounting an element of surprise, but of course we realized our country was not yet prepared to carry on a sustained attack against the Japanese homeland. The best we could do was inflict some damage on Bataan and Corregidor by utilizing what bombers we had left and an occasional flight of planes from Australia. In these cases the planes would land at Del Monte Field to refuel and take on bombs. Some of our P-40s were converted to bombers for attacks on Subic Bay.

But by the middle of April, reality was beginning to present a pretty grim picture. The fact that MacArthur was being sent to Australia for the purpose of retaking the Philippines gave a strong indication that eventually they would be lost. Ten days before he arrived on Mindanao, the Japanese had made another landing on our island, this time at Zamboanga. Bataan had fallen on April 8. Interisland ships were having more problems all the time. George

Plowman was still getting through the blockade with his banca, but it was becoming more iffy as time went on. And besides that, there were fewer supplies available to transport. Japanese incursions were becoming more frequent. Fewer flights from Australia meant less medicine and ammunition coming in. Food was becoming more scarce as time went on, and all supplies generally dwindled. And there was no relief in sight. It wasn't a pretty picture.

April 23, 1942—Relieved from Bugo. By this time the Japanese had sunk two ships at Bugo—one on either side of the pier—thus making in next to impossible for other ships to get in and unload cargo. The ships were also having more and more difficulty getting through the blockade. Much to the credit of the various interisland ship captains, they had been a willing and loyal group of people. They and George Plowman had done a magnificent and heroic job for almost five months. We had done the very best we could under daunting circumstances. It had been an interesting, though sometimes taxing interlude. But now we were moving into a new and final phase of our little part of the war. (Sadly, I was never to see George Plowman again.)

McKay was sent down to Maramag, where part of our outfit had been sent to handle the supply part of a sub–air base that had been built by the Fifth Air Base Group. I was sent back to Tankulan, from whence I had come before taking over convoy duty. Life for us now was just a matter of waiting and wondering. On April 29, the Japanese made a landing at Parang, which was only about twenty miles from Malabang. Thus they had made landings at Davao, Cotabato, Jamboanga, and Parang, all on the southern flank of Mindanao.

May 1, 1942—Japanese troops in the Parang area advance southward into Cotabato and northward in the direction of Dansalan. On May 3, we heard that one last plane was coming into Del Monte Field from Australia with ammunition and medical supplies. We were also told that it would take out mail, so I sat down under a mango tree and wrote a short note to my folks. Knowing that I would soon be killed or captured, I wanted desperately to get some word to them, yet not alarm them too much. It was not an easy letter to write. It went something like this:

> Tankulan, Mindanao
> May 3, 1942
> Dear Folks:
> It will soon be Mother's Day, so I'll be thinking especially of you that day, Mother, but I'll be thinking of all the rest of you also. There isn't a whole lot I can write about, but I have learned a lot in the last two or three months. I think this country would be beautiful in peacetime.
> You probably won't be hearing from me for a while, but don't worry about me—I'll take care of myself.
> Please greet my relatives and friends back there, and be sure to give my love to Fay. How I miss her, and long to be with her and all of you again!
> Love to all,
> Carl

It was a noble effort, but to my disappointment, it was all in vain, because I was not able to get the letter to the field before the plane took off.

Years later I read an account of the last trip of this plane. As they came in for a landing at Del Monte Field, they saw the Japanese transports arriving in the bay at Bugo, preparatory to the invasion. The plane crew was pretty nervous and anxious to take off. Their final words to the ground crew at Del Monte were the same as we had heard in Honolulu—"You poor devils." In the written account, they also said that we reminded them of trapped rats.

May 3, 1942—Invasion of Bugo. Ever since December our company truck had made daily trips to Cagayan, but when our driver Odell Hicks saw the transport out in Bugo Bay, he knew that was his last trip.

Specific details of events of the next week or ten days are little more than a cloudy blur in my memory. So many things happened, and with such unpredictability, that it remains impossible to sort out any kind of rational account of these events. This is not something that occurred because of my older age or the long time lapse. Indeed, after things quieted down, and I began to think back and piece together what happened—where and when—I was never able to do so. About all I can remember of the attack is having machine gun and rifle fire almost constantly, day and night. Therefore the best I can do is tell what I remember.

The Japanese landed the night of May 3, I believe. They were repulsed a couple of times but eventually established a beachhead. The plateau we were on began with a steep cliff less than a quarter of a mile from the beach. This could only be negotiated through a couple of narrow ravines leading into it. One ravine had a narrow, winding road leading up it. This was the Sayre Highway. Into it several tank traps had been built. The other ravine was long and heavily wooded. On a high point overlooking the whole area, we had placed our only field artillery piece for that side of the island, a 2.95 Spanish American War mountain gun. Also a .50 caliber machine gun had been mounted on a staff car. I know for a fact that this accounted for at least one kill because I saw the plane as it struggled and finally crashed in a canyon. We had no tanks, but there were two old D-8 Caterpillar tractors in the area, which were converted into tanks by mounting .50 caliber machine guns on them and welding some armor plating around the driver. With a top speed of perhaps eight miles an hour, they were no match against Japanese tanks that could do almost twenty miles per hour. I still recall when they lumbered out to meet the Japanese. We never saw those poor fellows again. When the situation became untenable at Tankulan, we were ordered to leave and retreat toward Dahlirig. By now there were only ten of us left from our outfit at Tankulan. We had been selected to stay with the general and keep him and his staff in supplies. Our retreat was halted partway down the canyon east of Tankulan by a vicious attack by fighter planes, but eventually we got out of there.

I have no recollection of when we got to Dahlirig or where or how long we stayed there. All I recall is that at 4:00 A.M. we were told we would retreat to Maluko immediately, so we mounted up and fell in line close behind the general, arriving in Maluko about daybreak.

May 9, 1942—Shelling of Maluko; caught between the lines. At Maluko, we were attacked by dive bombers before we even had a chance to dig a foxhole. I saw a depression in the earth where an outside toilet had once stood and rolled on the ground until I could lie in that. There was nothing to do but lie there and watch the bombs come down. If they looked as if they were headed my way, I would quickly turn over and hide my face in my hands. I guess I didn't want to see myself get killed. The Japanese knew we had utilized schoolhouses throughout the island as storage depots, so they targeted these quite heavily. I had hauled tons of rice for storage in the Maluko schoolhouse, so I figured if they hit that rice, it should at least soften the blow and smother some of the shrapnel. After the dive bombers, they would come over us and drop antipersonnel bombs. These are aptly named because when they hit, they make a small crater, but the shrapnel goes out at ground level and a little above, taking everything in its path. Grassy areas will look like a mown lawn whenever an antipersonnel bomb explodes. In fact, they were sometimes called grass cutters. The planes would also assist their field artillery in zeroing in on us, which worked very effectively. These actions had given the Japanese ground troops time to get in close enough to use their mortars. Mortar fire is the most demoralizing fire there is. One can see a plane and even see the bombs a great deal of the time, and this gives one a chance to seek and often take cover. With artillery shell fire, you can often hear the shell fired before it gets there. And at night it is easy to see the flash of the gun, so you can drop to the ground before the shell arrives. But since mortar fire is at close range and the projectile arcs into its target, there is no warning whatsoever. Truly demoralizing.

These various kinds of fire kept on all day with hardly a break. I don't know when we had last eaten, but during one brief lull, Vincent Didio said, "We're going to eat, and we're going to have chicken." The Filipinos always have chickens around, so he had caught a couple, and two or three more had been killed by the grass cutters, so he got under a native hut, butchered the chickens, got a pan and some water, and built a little fire under this hut, so as to be less noticeable by planes. It was about 3:00 P.M.

Before Didio really got going well with cooking the chicken, a motorcycle messenger came up from the south and went through the little barrio of Maluko. In a matter of minutes, he was back and very excitedly said, " Get the hell out of here. There is a column of Japanese less than a mile out of town!" So Didio put out the fire, we forgot about eating, and prepared to leave. But there were two problems. First, Larsen, who was scared to death of the bombing and shelling, had sneaked down into a canyon against orders. And second, we noticed that there was a flat tire on the truck caused by the shrapnel. So somebody had to go down into the canyon to get Larsen, and we had a tire to change—all before the Japanese got there, we hoped.

In those days the spare was a tire mounted on a spare rim, so all you had to do was change rims. But it wasn't that simple in this case. The rim had rested on the wheel, and with the tools we had to work with, there was no way we could get that rim loose enough to detach it from the wheel. So with the Japanese closing in on us, we had to take the whole wheel off and bounce it on a large rock to jar it loose enough to dismount. As if that wasn't enough, a mortar round came in and hit a gasoline dump so close to us that we could hardly endure the heat. But it is amazing what one can do when one has to. We did finally get the tire changed, Larsen had been found, and we finally got out of Maluko. As we passed the south edge of town, we saw a zigzag trench that had been hit by bombs or shellfire, with several dead Filipino soldiers lying there. We found out later that the general had left either in the night or early morning, but because of a breakdown in communication, had failed to notify us that the front was making a hasty retreat, so we had been caught between the lines for more than twelve hours. When we saw those dead Filipinos, we realized how fortunate we had been. It had been one wild day so far.

The road out of Maluko led down a narrow canyon to a bridge over a deep gorge through which a wild, rushing river flowed. Dive bombers had been working that area over pretty heavy that day, so I was concerned about what we would find on our retreat that day. From my many trips through there running convoy, I knew the area well. Not only was it a deep gorge, but the canyon was so narrow as it rose upward that the road was carved right out of the canyon wall, leaving no room to meet, let alone turn around if the road had become impassable. As we neared the far end of the bridge, horror of horrors, there was a huge bomb crater on the down side of the canyon, just at the end of the bridge. No doubt the pilots had thought they had made the road impassable, but with the Japanese not too far behind us, it was pretty imperative that we make it. Hicks put the truck in low, and we all got on the upper side of the load as he used part of the mountainside to get around the crater. It was a daring, but superb job of driving. (I have since learned that the Japanese very likely divided their southward push, some going south from Tankulan toward Sumilao just south of us a few miles and some coming down the Sayre Highway.)

After we got out of the canyon and onto the level plain, we made really good time until we got to the outskirts of Impasugong. There in a bend of the road stood Major Max Weil with a Tommy (Thompson) submachine gun aimed at us, ordering us to stop. Almost in a frenzy, he informed us that this was where we were going to make our last stand and that every blankety-blank soldier with a rifle should dismount now for further assignment. Not everyone had rifles, but several of the men hid theirs under some of the gear and cargo of the truck. To my great disappointment, one of my friends said to me, "I'm not showing my gun. I'd rather be a live coward than a dead hero." I wish I had never heard the remark because from that day on, I never had the respect for him that I had before or would like to have had. After all, this was not a matter of heroics, it was merely a matter of doing what we were called on to do. Nothing more, nothing less. Only four men got down out of that truck. Hicks was excused because he was the driver. Lt. Ricks had no rifle, only a sidearm, but he volunteered. The only other men to obey the order and get out of the truck were Lucero, a guy attached to our outfit by the name of Emerson, and myself. Lt. Ricks and Lucero were put on patrol duty, and Emerson and I were put in charge of about two hundred Filipino soldiers and assigned a certain segment of the front line on the western approach to this barrio. (I still do not recall when was the last time I had eaten anything.)

The afternoon was relatively quiet. Everyone was digging in and waiting, but when darkness came, it was different. Our patrols were out, probing. Their patrols were doing the same thing. Some were breaking through in places. Flares were going up almost constantly, so some of the time it was eerie and sometimes it would be almost as bright as day. Gunfire seemed to be coming from all over.

Around 11:00 P.M., there was a brief lull. Apprehensive of being by-passed again because of a possible change in plans and another quick retreat, Emerson and I decided after some consultation that rather than wait for word of a change in plans, we should try and find out in advance. And the best place to find that out would be at the general's C.P. (command post), which was right in the middle of the barrio. My post was the closest to that point, so it was determined that I should go. When I got there, I detected an air of hushed, yet nervous excitement. A message was coming in on the radio from General Wainwright on Corregidor, which had fallen a couple of days before, explaining to General Sharp that the Japanese were holding them hostage in Malinta Tunnel, threatening to shoot all of them unless Wainwright directed and persuaded General Sharp to surrender all of the Visayan-Mindanao forces. His last words were, " In the interest of humanity, for God's sake, surrender!"

The immediate consensus was that this was it. After all, Wainwright's plea was desperate. What was to be gained by giving cause for more blood to be spilled at Corregidor? And what was to be gained by continued fighting in our sector against impossible odds?

Faced with the definite probability that our cause was lost and that surrender to the Japanese was imminent, I acted strictly on impulse. For several months, as it had become more and more apparent that our ultimate end was to be killed or captured, we began to think and say that when push came to shove, we would go to the hills if and when the opportunity presented itself. After all, nobody wanted to be killed, and nobody wanted to be captured.

We would much prefer being free to continue the fight against the Japanese as guerrillas.

There was one big obstacle to overcome, however. I had to get through the lines. I came across Odell Hicks wandering around in the middle of town, so I explained the situation to him. He thought the same as I did—"Now is our best chance to try it." We decided that the time to do it was then, there was not time to round up anyone else. It was close to midnight when we ran the gauntlet. The road was fairly straight and level going out of the barrio, and the occasional flares gave us some light, so with lights out and me riding shotgun, we tore out of town and headed for Malaybalay. A couple of patrols fired at us, but we made it.

We pulled the truck off the road and parked it under a huge mango tree. Not too far away was a little nipa hut, which appeared to have a small light inside. Approaching cautiously, we thought we heard American voices inside. Sure enough, there were about a dozen or so fellows of our outfit in there. How or when they got there, I do not know, but to our surprise, they had the same thing in mind as we did, although they were better prepared than we were. They had a surprising amount of food, mostly canned goods, and the most ammunition that I had seen during the whole war. In fact, for the first time since the war began I had a whole bandolier of ammunition. There was only one thing I didn't like. Harley Cromwell, a technical sergeant, and the ranking enlisted man in our outfit, had his Filipino girlfriend with him, and worse yet, she had brought along a young Filipino man, whom she said was her cousin. But we were pretty much committed now, so there was not much that could be done about it.

Our plan was to travel at night, then lie low and rest during the day. So about 1:00 A.M., our little group of about fifteen or sixteen headed north into the hills. We were favored with bright moonlight the latter part of the night, which was nice for hiking, but it made us a little too conspicuous for comfort.

Just after daybreak, we came to a small stream. Not wanting to cut or injure our feet, we crossed it with our shoes and socks on—the rationale being that we had the whole day to dry our footwear but it might take longer for cuts or injuries caused by sharp rocks to heal. Taking good care of our feet was an important consideration.

About a hundred yards from the stream, there was a moderate rise, and just beyond that lay a nice little ravine with gentle slopes, good tree cover, and nice areas for spreading out to spend the day sleeping and preparing for the next day.

It had been a long day and a long time since most of us had had any rest at all, although I had probably slept on the ground for a while after we had left Dahlirig. I have a faint recollection of waking up to the sound of gunfire early in the morning. Other than that, I don't recall sleeping or eating since before we left Tankulan. So the first order of the day for all of us at this point was to take our field packs off, put our shoes and socks out to dry, and find a place to sack out, except for whoever it was who took the first shift of standing guard.

I thought I had found a nice spot, so I stretched out on the ground to sleep. I had just gotten comfortable when I became bothered with ants—big black ones that seemed to be coming right for me. I had never seen that kind before, or have I since. I picked up my gear and moved several feet away. Lo and behold, they started coming for me again, by-passing other men, so I moved again. One of the guys told me to quit disturbing the rest of them. For some reason, no one else was bothered by the ants, but wherever I went and tried to settle down, those pesky ants would come crawling my way. It was almost uncanny.

Finally, I decided to throw caution to the winds and go down to the sandy beach by the stream edge, even if I did expose myself. It didn't appear to be the wisest thing to do, but I was getting desperate. I needed rest, but there was no resting here with those huge ants.

I washed my socks out in the stream, put them and my shoes in the bright sunlight to dry, and spread myself out on the ant-free sand to rest. Just before I went to sleep, however, I heard a plane which seemed to be heading for Impasugong. Then I heard a bomb explode. That got me wondering. Then I heard field artillery. It could only mean one thing. As always seems to happen in such cases, initial efforts to effect a cease-fire as a prelude to surrender had failed, and fighting had resumed. That thought troubled me greatly because if fighting had resumed, I should be there with my troops, not out in the hills someplace. Actually, that made me a deserter, and that thought really troubled me. All kinds of thoughts began to race through my mind. First and foremost, I took very seriously the oath I had sworn when I entered the army— to serve faithfully and loyally, to put country above self. And I thought of the punishment for desertion—possible death. But more important, I thought of the dishonor it would bring to my name, my family. I was almost overwhelmed by these thoughts. What would Fay and my family think of me if I was listed as a deserter?

As I lay there on the beach, struggling with my thoughts, I finally came to the realization that it was too large a problem to figure out on my own, so I turned to God in prayer. I laid the whole dilemma out, confessing the selfishness of the act that had brought me to this difficult point and asking for His divine guidance regarding the action I should take. Like most people, I had prayed since childhood, not always regularly, and probably selfishly more often than not. And like most military men, I had prayed in times of danger. But this prayer was different somehow. It seemed as if I was in perfect communion with God. There was a closeness I had never experienced before, and then I made two promises. First I would abide by His direction, no matter what it was, and second, I would commit my life to Him and to serving Him. (This I have done and have found that making such a commitment makes for good discipline.) After laying it all out and making my promises, I lay back to await His answer, and possibly to sleep.

I'm not sure whether I dozed off or not, but suddenly it was as if I heard a voice, "Go back, go back." That was all I needed. There was no doubt in my mind about what to do. A sense of relief, calm, joy, and resolve seemed to just overtake me.

After putting on my damp shoes and socks, I shouldered my pack and walked up to the ravine where some of the men had already awakened and were moving cautiously about. When I announced that I was going back, I had a few questions to answer, but I told them forthrightly what had happened, and then I started up the hill to leave. All of a sudden, Cromwell shouted to me to "stop right there." As I turned toward him, I saw that he had his submachine gun aimed directly at me. "Take one step more, and I'll drill you," he said. My reply was, "I know you outrank me, Harley, but this time I'm taking orders from a higher authority than you," and with that I proceeded up the hill. In a moment I heard him say, "Where are you going, Lucero?" Then I heard Lucero say, "I'm goin' with Nordin." Others began to follow suit, and before long, every one of the group was following along single file, with Cromwell reluctantly bringing up the rear. I had not asked anyone to follow me. I simply told them what I was doing and why. (Unfortunately, Cromwell did not survive the war.)

Except for being fired upon once by either a sniper or small patrol, the walk back to where the truck was still parked was without incident. But before long we found out that the order to surrender was indeed in effect, and instructions were to proceed to Maramag to dispose of all weapons and await further orders.

I had been to Maramag on numerous occasions when I was in charge of convoy duty during the war. Because of the distance, road conditions, possible delays resulting from air raids, or off-loading part of our cargo at intermediate supply dumps, it had always been dark when we arrived at Maramag. This trip proved to be no exception. Although the day was bright when we started out, there seemed to be a dark cloud, a pall hanging over us. Again, the tropical sun had set, and our arrival at Maramag was marked by pitch blackness.

There was an air of sadness and bewilderment as we exchanged greetings with the troops we had not seen for some time, those who had been sent into the deep Maramag forest to assist at our small base there. By the time we got there, they had received orders as to how to proceed: in essence turn in all arms and ammunition, load up all surplus food for transport, and await orders to proceed to Camp Casising just outside of Malabalay. We had missed evening chow, so we had to wait until morning. By then it was running into days since some of us had had any food at all. Circumstances had been so hectic and uncertain that it was impossible to recall just when we had eaten last.

We had been advised to get rid of all items that would be considered weapons or illegal contraband. This of course meant bolos, so I had the sad duty of doing away with my prized gift from John the driver. I decided that rather than throw it out back of the crude barracks, where some Japanese soldier would later find it, I would bury it in the latrine and its filthy accumulation. So it was with a heavy heart that I took that beautiful bolo with its hand-crafted scabbard of Philippine mahogany and inlaid silver out to the filth of that latrine and there sadly disposed of it. And so ended my last full day of freedom.

Shortly after breakfast the next day, trucks came into our camp to be loaded with food and whatever supplies were to be taken into camp. These were still our own trucks and still our own drivers. The Japanese had not made themselves visible as yet, but had made it very plain that every man, every gun, and every bullet had to be turned in, and that they were in the near background to assure that there would be no escape. When everything and everyone was loaded, we began our slow and sad journey toward Malabalay and eventual imprisonment at Camp Casising. I was one of several men sitting atop some sacks filled with rice loaded on a bomb-service trailer pulled by a four-by-four GI truck. I couldn't help but think how different things were when I was transporting that rice down to Maramag for our troops, as opposed to riding atop it as it was being transported away from Maramag, very likely for their troops.

It was probably about noon when we arrived at a spot just south of Malabalay where the Sayre Highway was intersected by a dusty, narrow road. The Japanese had set up a checkpoint, and it was there that we had our initial contact with our captors. My first impression on seeing them up close was that they were so small.

Since I had not had an opportunity to shave for quite a number of days because of the hectic circumstances of battle and flight, I was concerned that the Japanese may be tempted to remove my whiskers one by one. Happily that did not occur, and after a rather perfunctory inspection, the little men with the guns waved us toward our future home at Camp Casising. From that point on, our lives would be in their hands for no one knew how long. The surrender had become effective May 10, Mother's Day. And on this day, May 12, 1942, our freedom was gone. The next day all Allied communication with the Philippines was severed.

Part II

Captivity

Camp Casising

In the presence of mine enemies.
—Psalm 23

Camp Casising was situated approximately five kilometers southwest of Malabalay on the edge of a great, gently rolling plain that seemed to stretch uninterrupted all the way to Sumilao. This broad expanse, ringed in the far west by low ranges of mountains, provided a vista for some of the most beautiful sunsets one can imagine. Malabalay itself is on the northeastern edge of a high plateau, with mountains of varying heights making up the horizon. It did not seem to be as subject to distinct wet or dry seasons as some of the coastal areas on the island of Luzon. For the most part, the climate was hot and sunny, with occasional showers. But ordinarily, the sky was as beautiful a blue as one can imagine. Days were hot, but not really oppressive, while the nights were cool enough to require blankets.

The camp itself had been a training camp for the Philippine constabulary, a sort of military police force, which was a law enforcement agency in the Philippines. The barracks were very crude, with rather poorly defined bays on either side of a somewhat lower center aisle. The walls rose about three or four feet above the floor of the bay, leaving an open space of about three feet or less below the roof line. Some may have had metal roofs (corrugated steel), but most were either thatched or covered with nipa. The kitchen and dining area was a rather large rectangular building with a metal roof set approximately in the center of the campground. There were several very crude latrines which were essentially long covered sheds with open benches over a long slit trench. In a short time, they became filthy.

Electricity, when we did have it, was usually quite sporadic and quite inadequate, with only one or two small bulbs per barracks and practically no outside illumination at any time. This made going to the latrine in the middle of the night quite an adventure. It would sometimes lead to failed attempts, bumping into others on a dark night, cussing, and disgust.

Since there were approximately eleven hundred American troops in the camp, water became a scarce commodity. For that reason, each man was limited to one canteen of water per day. This had to suffice for washing, brushing teeth, cold water shaving, bathing, laundry, and, of course, drinking.

Whenever a rain shower came up, which was not often, there would be a scramble to get outside for a shower and to try and rinse out clothes at the same time. Also, men would set out mess kits and canteen cups to catch some extra water. There was a small creek about a half mile or more from the camp, and on one occasion some guards took a group of us down there to bathe, but to my recollection, that only happened once. I suspect they thought it was too risky. Perhaps one reason for that assumption was that on the way back to camp, we came across a great hoard of rather large locusts. Realizing these locusts could provide quite a delicacy, plus some much needed protein, quite a few of the men began scrambling after them. They were so thick that you could almost pick them out of the air. A couple of the men had access to some cooking oil in the commissary, so the locust gatherers had some nice, crisp locusts as an extra that night. As for the Japanese guards, I presumed they were glad it only amounted to a food hunt, not an escape attempt.

As is always the case in a capitulation of that magnitude, the conquering force will have little or no opportunity to make arrangements for provisions. Consequently, one of the directives by the Japanese had been to bring all of our remaining food supplies into camp to be used for our own sustenance. So for a while at least, we had some flour, sugar, coffee, pineapple products, and even some powdered milk. All of these were rationed quite sparingly because no one knew how long the duration would be. Even the rice we had brought in was a great help to us and to the Japanese, because it relieved them of having to provide it immediately. So for a while at least, we were able to eat somewhat traditional American fare.

Another element of relative good fortune at this, our first cantonment as captives, was the fact that we had reasonably good guards. They were among the same troops who had been fighting against us just a few days and weeks before, and it seemed to us that even though we had been enemies, there was a certain amount of respect or understanding on their part for the fight or resistance we had given them. After all, they had suffered some of the same privations, dangers, fatigue, and uncertainty that we had. In a way, it could be likened to the feeling between two athletic teams who have been engaged in a bitter struggle. When the struggle is over, the winner has a certain amount of respect for the vanquished and for the resistance put up. It is worth noting that at a war college sometime prior to World War II, American military strategists had determined that if and when Japan made its move to try to conquer the South Pacific, the Philippines would be sacrificed in a delaying action, providing time to fortify Australia and its periphery. At that time, a delay of three months in the Japanese timetable was thought to be sufficient, and that being with the aid of the U.S. Navy. As it turned out, the Fil-American forces held out for five and a half months, even though our navy had been destroyed at Pearl Harbor. The most valiant resistance put forth was on

The pump at Camp Casising near Malaybalay. This pump was the sole source of water for about 1,000 Americans and 11,000 Filipinos. (Photo by Glenn Nordin, 1955.)

the island of Luzon, particularly on Bataan and Corregidor, but the Japanese learned that a number of other islands were part of the package.

As far as resistance on Mindanao is concerned, it has already been chronicled briefly in the narrative from the first bombing of Davao only one day after Pearl Harbor, the first land invasion only eleven days later, two subsequent landings, resistance, air and sea raids, plus offensive actions by planes and motor torpedo boats operating from Mindanao. There was another activity worthy of note which went on in the defense of Mindanao, however, that can best be described by excerpts from a letter written by Col. Ray I. Elsmore, commanding officer, Fifth Air Base Group:

> Other tasks were undertaken and accomplished. Within thirty days after Pearl Harbor these men, regimenting and working hand in hand with Filipino native laborers ... selected and prepared for use seven additional airfields within a twenty-five mile radius of Del Monte, complete with hideouts in native cover and camouflage nets for concealing all aircraft thereon; constructed twelve-foot-by-twelve-foot timber shelters under from ten to twenty feet of earth, sufficient to house the air base personnel and carry on essential activities within a few yards of the Del Monte Air Field, two of these underground shelters being more than two hundred feet in length; dug two tunnels into hills overlooking the airfield large enough to house both base and group officers; commenced (and completed) a tunnel into a hill or an underground hangar large enough to house five P-40s, and a runway so that the P-40s could be flown directly from the tunnel mouth. In short, these men labored

long, hard and tirelessly, without complaint, to prepare their new home for combat conditions.

Nor did they stop when their air base had been so prepared. General MacArthur had issued a general directive to build fields with all haste throughout the Philippines. This directive was not received at our base, but was seen at the headquarters of Major General Sharp, Commander of the Visayan-Mindanao forces, and was taken as a cue and work started. Our air base personnel, augmented by some of the 19th Bombardment Group awaiting evacuation, was fanned out for hundreds of miles in all directions over the island of Mindanao, to select new sites, regiment native labor and construct new landing fields.... In less than five months we had twenty-two airfields constructed and completed suitable for operation of both bombers and fighters. Each of these fields had hideouts prepared in native cover with camouflage nets, and at some of them blast pens and underground storage space had been constructed.... Sites were selected where they would be most inconspicuous and capable of camouflage.... Every officer and enlisted man cheerfully responded to every call made upon him and worked long hours in order to accomplish each task assigned. They served unselfishly, without praise or glory to the end, and of their devotion to duty, I as their Commander, am proud.

Another interesting passage comes from Appendix I of "A Brief Chronology of the Philippine Campaign." "May 10, 1942—Major General Sharp surrendered his forces after the enemy had gained control of Davao, Catobato and Lanao Provinces. The small units in Zamboanga and Agusan, he said, would have been unable to hold out against a hostile superior force; and the Bukidnan Plateau had become indefensible after defensive lines both north and south began to crumble. The U.S. Headquarters were at Malabaly in Bukidnan. Major General Sharp also directed the surrender of all other forces operating in the Philippines. His order was issued after a conference with an officer of General Wainwright's staff." Thus about five months after the invasion at Davao and two days after the fall of Corregidor, Mindanao capitulated. Because Bataan had fallen in April, the Japanese now had total control of the Philippines. But the campaign had probably been far more costly and had taken them longer to accomplish than they had once anticipated. Their timetable had been upset, and we had bought time for America to begin fortifying the southern rim.

Out situation as prisoners changed before long because the combat troops guarding us were needed to continue the advance southward in an effort to secure forward positions in Indonesia and Malaysia, with the ultimate goal of capturing Australia. Eventually, they were all replaced with occupation troops composed of Japanese and Formosans. We were told these troops had been instructed to hate Americans and to administer punishment and torture. When these new troops came, we definitely could tell the difference. But for the moment, we were pleasantly surprised at our treatment.

One of the most noticeable things after the surrender was that all of a sudden it was so quiet. The peacefulness and days free of danger seemed like

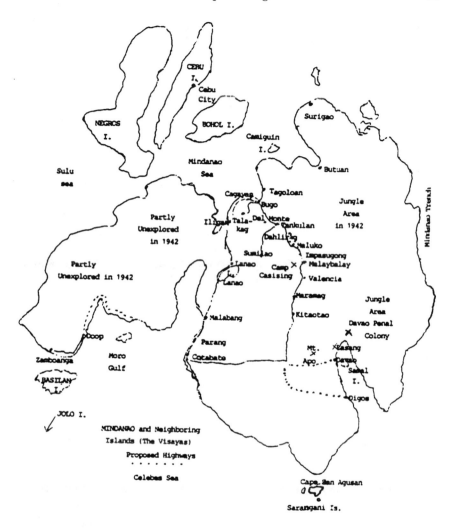

Map of Mindanao and neighboring islands (the Visayas).

a welcome respite at first. The change in our situation had happened so quickly that we had not yet come to the full realization that we had lost the most precious thing of all—our freedom. It wasn't long though until we wished we could be back there fighting for freedom rather than in this prison camp longing for it.

Somewhere along the line, I had heard the old saying, "A good soldier will get a corner bunk and nail it down." I don't know if there is any truth in this saying, but Bob Dennis and I got a corner bay in a barracks at Camp Casising and kept it all the while we were there. There was really not much more than space in the corner of the barracks, but in that space were all of our meager earthly belongings, and with boards for a bed, this was home.

We had known each other back at Fort Douglas, but not too well. It wasn't until our nearly three weeks aboard ship on the way over that our acquaintance really grew and developed into a wonderful friendship that lasted until he died over fifty years later. Bob had a lively wit and a likable personality. He was also as proud of his Irish heritage as I was of my Swedish background. We shared a mutual liking of history, geography, and literature. He was more interested in sports than I was, but I was more interested in hunting and fishing than he was. Another interest that we shared was that both of us had sweethearts back home. He and Velma had gone together for several years in college, despite the fact that their relationship had had its ups and downs. It was in a down state when he joined the army, so he had gone home the previous Christmas to restore that relationship. He wasn't sure, however, how successful he had been, so that was of considerable concern to him. I of course had shared with him the dismaying news of my aborted engagement to Fay. We had made a couple of convoy trips before I had been assigned to take charge of the operation, and he had also been among those in our detachment who had been assigned to our sub-base in Maramag sometime before the invasion at Bugo-Cagayan.

It was only natural then that after we got somewhat settled at Camp Casising we began telling each other what had transpired since we had last been together. In relating to him the dilemma I had found myself in at the time we had started for the hills, I told him of how my decision was the result of answered prayer. That opened up a whole new area of discussion we had never touched on before.

As we delved into the topic of religion in the days that followed, I realized that on that particular subject, we were poles apart. For a starter, he really didn't believe in God, or at least he said he didn't. On occasion, I would steer our discussion to the matter of creation. He was quite versed in the theory of evolution from college days but wasn't able to equate that to a viable beginning or creation theory. Since it was before the time when the Big Bang theory had gained much prevalence in the nonscientific world, he was pretty much bereft of any plausible answer to that question. This issue did lead into another area of religion, however, that is of greater consequence—the area of faith. Just as he was unable to offer any tangible proof regarding the matter of creation, or a beginning, neither was I. That opened up a whole new dimension in our discussions. I explained that while I liked to have proof for, or a reason for most of my beliefs, there are certain things that I accept in faith. Why? Because it is the word of God—the Bible. This in turn led us back to the subject of God. I proceeded to explain to him that for the Christian, there is no escape from God. He is, He always was, and He always will be. It was only natural that our discussions would lead into the topic of Christianity.

At that point, I was able to show him from my weather-beaten New Testament some of the promises and teachings of Jesus. Naturally he questioned much of what I said and what I showed him, but this only led to more opportunity to explain God's plan. One of his criticisms was that if it's such a sure thing and if it's relatively so simple, why are there all these different denominations? I tried to explain that there are many reasons for that such as interpretation and tradition. When asked why I was Lutheran, I replied rather honestly that perhaps the main reason was that my family and their forebears were Lutheran. But I also tried to explain some of the Lutheran belief and tradition. I made it very clear that Lutherans do not stand in judgment of the efficacy of other Christian faiths, but they do hold that there is but one God and that salvation is through Christ alone, who atoned for the sins of mankind (including our own) through His death on the cross.

In all our discussions, I did not at any time criticize nor berate any other religion, or any other denomination, nor did I try to make him a Christian or a Lutheran. I believed that it would have to be his decision, and his alone. I said that as a Christian, it was my hope that he would take it seriously, think it over, and not close the door. There was one thought which I left him with, and that was the question of eternity and the soul. I said, "It's too serious a thing to take any chances on." We never had any deep discussions about religion after that, partly because we had pretty much exhausted the subject and partly because we were subsequently moved to another camp and split up into different barracks. But I came away with the feeling that Bob was not an atheist, as he thought he might be, but rather an agnostic, and if such was the case, there was room for the Holy Spirit to work. (He became a Christian later, but that's another story.)

Our first link with the outside came when the Japanese allowed a few native vendors to set up a sort of canteen for a few hours every Thursday. The merchandise was quite limited in variety and quantity, but it gave us an opportunity to get a few extras occasionally. In considerable demand were basic toilet articles, but the supply was short-lived. The two best-sellers were native tobacco and a sort of candy made out of brown sugar and chopped coconut. Depending on the quality, the local tobacco went for 1½ to 2½ pesos ($.75 to $1.25 American) per hand. (A hand would average 150 leaves.) Good Sumatra leaf would run a little higher. Since paper for rolling cigarettes was a scarce item, a lot of the men took to making cigars, using native tobacco for filler, and the much better Sumatra leaf for the outside. Some of the men got pretty adept at making cigars. Once in a while there would also be curry powder and a few other local spices available.

One of the side benefits was that the natives could sometimes slip us messages from the outside. They were watched pretty closely, but we always figured out a way to make contact.

After a couple of weeks, we were surprised to see that one of the new vendors was none other than Rosalie (Rosie), who had sort of been Sgt. Cromwell's girlfriend back in Tankulan. This gave the guys in our outfit somewhat of an inside track, as she knew all of us and liked us because we had been good to her. She had been a seamstress and had her own shop in Davao. When the Japanese had landed there, they had engaged in a program of plunder and rape. Before she was able to escape, she had been raped sixteen times. But now at Malaybalay, she was beating them at their own game. She had become infected with syphilis and seemed pleased to inform us that she was giving it to every Japanese soldier that she could.

The canteen facility became an added boon to me with Rosie there— someone I could trust. I had smuggled my camera into camp and had taken a whole roll of film. I was not particularly interested in prints because they could be incriminating. But I thought that the best way to preserve the films until later was to have them developed into negatives. Sure enough, Rosie was able to find a photographer in Malaybalay who could do the work, so I slipped her the film on the sly, and in a week or so, I had the negatives back. We almost got caught making the exchange when she handed me the negatives, but she made it look as if she was handing me something else.

After we had been interned for a while, some of our officers wisely decided to make arrangements for various classes to be conducted by qualified teachers, usually officers. This not only provided an opportunity to learn new skills or broaden our knowledge, but it also was a good way to make use of our time, and we had plenty of that. Included in the curriculum were classes in commercial arithmetic, bookkeeping, English, astronomy, and Spanish. Classes were held in the forenoons five days a week and were staggered so a person could take more than one subject. I signed up for bookkeeping and Spanish and really enjoyed these classes. The roll call in Spanish class provided a humorous note each day. The names were arranged alphabetically and preceded by the rank, so the roll call in that class went like this—"Pvt. Church, Pvt. Couch, Pvt. Davenport, Pvt. House."

One of the immediate by-products of these classes was that they provided access to blank sheets of typing and notebook paper. I had given some thought to keeping a diary while in prison camp, but had no materials with which to do so. I was able to garner seventy-five or more sheets and thus began my diary. From then on, I made daily entries until the paper supply was exhausted, which was over two years later. These entries included not only some of the hideous things that happened later on, but also some of my thoughts and impressions relative to our treatment and our captors. It was potentially dangerous, but it was a factual account and something I thought might prove valuable in writing a book.

When Staff Sgt. Ernest Parry of our unit found out I had access to paper, he asked me to write up an account of my action in the campaign. After we were captured, he had devoted considerable time to learning where each of us had been and when. From his conversation with me, he had determined that because of coincidence or circumstance, I had seen more action than anyone else in our outfit, and he wanted to document it. I had been up on the hill when that was being bombed and strafed. Things were quiet in Bugo then. When the shelling and bombing had hit Bugo, I was there, but it had been quiet up on the hill. My convoy duty had subjected me to considerable air attack, and I was one of the ten selected to stay with the retreating front lines following the final invasion. He made three copies of the account, but my copy was with my ill-fated diary, and Sgt. Parry did not survive prison camp. So much for history.

At one point, two Americans came to the gate of the prison compound and asked to be admitted. They had been in a group of about fourteen men who had taken off for the hills just prior to the surrender. Coincidentally, their group was similar in size to the one I had joined briefly, and they had headed in the same general direction as we had. When they got back into the jungle, they had been ambushed by unfriendly natives who killed all but those two men. They were dirty, almost starved, and their clothing had been reduced to rags. After that horrifying experience, they were glad to be in the relative safety of prison camp. This event rather vindicated my decision to abide by the answer I had received through prayer. Although I had not asked anyone to return with me, there had been some feeling of resentment toward me now that we were prisoners. My companions on the escape attempt had a hard time understanding that type of religious conviction. I didn't hear much about the issue, however, after those two men turned themselves in. The possible dangers to be encountered in the hinterlands were only corroborated by what Mr. Albarece had told me concerning the potential danger of taking supplies for storage to that out-of-the-way schoolhouse I had considered, where even thirty-five years later, teaching was considered hazardous duty.

July 4, 1942—Some of the men celebrated Independence Day with rice wine. During the course of our internment, we were to witness numerous demonstrations of ingenuity, as in the case of the rice wine. Some men had found an old keg with a capacity of about five gallons. First they went up to the kitchen and got enough water to fill it in order to soak it and be certain it was leakproof. Then they procured rice, brown sugar, and pineapple juice to add to the water. This did not pose that great a problem because they were all members of the Quartermaster Corps, which had charge of the commissary. The end result must have been what they desired because the participants really did frolic around for a while. It had rained in the night, so there were puddles, some an inch or more in depth, all around the barracks area. Some of the guys took off their clothes and pretending the puddles were swimming pools, would make a running dash, plunge right in, and slide on their bellies to the other side. Luckily, another rain shower came along so they were able to clean themselves up somewhat before lying down and waiting for the inevitable hangover to overtake them. Needless to say, it was not a very noble display of patriotism. Fortunately, it was the only such display.

Our interest in our country found a more positive outlet. We were fortunate in that some officers had been able to bring in a radio of sufficient quality and power that we were able to get KGEI, a short-wave station in San Francisco. From its daily broadcasts, we were assured that even though we were in a helpless situation, momentum was building back home. Even the sound of American music was uplifting. Of particular interest to us was news of the beginning of campaigns in the southern Pacific to eventually retake the Philippines and other fallen bastions. This began with important sea battles—the battle of the Coral Sea, the battle in the area of the Solomons, and the battle of Midway, which proved to be the turning point of the war.

News of these battles was of particular interest to George "Rugged" Guernsey, a member of our unit who hailed from Iowa. He had a brother in the navy who served on the cruiser USS *Houston*. While we were still at Fort McKinley, the *Houston* had sailed into Manila, and George had been able to get a pass to spend the day with his brother aboard ship, so he knew the *Houston* was in the area. About two years later, George received a letter from his mother with information that his brother had gone down with the ship in the Java Sea on March 1, 1941. In less than a year, George also perished when the hell ship he was on was sunk.

July 9, 1942—I had my head shaved. Not too long after we had settled into our barracks, we began to be afflicted with bedbugs. In all probability, they had been secluded in the cracks between the boards and began to surface when new warm bodies to feed on arrived. We would shake our blankets, leave them out in the sun, and examine them closely in an effort to reduce the population. At the same time, we would kill all that we could find in the floorboards. This would help, but we never could get rid of all of them. They would prove to be a perpetual nuisance for the next three and a half years.

Then one day, as I was going to the latrine, I met a guy named Willis Wright, who had a disgusted and anguished look on his face as he exclaimed to me in passing, " Damn it—I've got me a case of crabs. Now where do you suppose I could have gotten them except from these filthy latrines?" I felt sorry for Wright, but hoped it would be an isolated case. In a short time, however, we began to hear of more and more men going to sick call to get blue ointment, the traditional military medication for the treatment of pubic lice.

Finally, I noticed that I had more than bedbugs crawling on me, and sure enough I had crabs too. When I went to sick call to get the blue ointment treatment, however, I wasn't quite as fortunate as the other men. I was informed that because of the amount of hair on my body, it would take so much ointment that there wouldn't be enough left to treat future cases.

Instead, they recommended that I go down to the motor pool and get some distillate, a type of motor fuel, and apply that.

Since I had no alternative if I was to rid myself of those pesky little bugs, I went to the motor pool and got my distillate. Then out back of the barracks, I proceeded to apply the cure, being sure to do a good job of it. The problem, though, came when I tried to rinse off the distillate. I could only get one canteen of water a day for all my needs, so I really did not have nearly enough to rinse the oil off properly. Complicating the matter was the fact that the water was cold, thereby negating its ability to rinse at all. After a few days, I began to suffer serious consequences. A film of oil had remained on my skin, and in that hot climate, it began to cause burns. This was especially true in the area of the scrotum and between my upper legs—the area of least ventilation that received additional irritation from friction caused by walking or almost any movement. I developed huge, open, burn sores. These later scabbed over and healed, but it took a long time. These areas still bear the scars from that treatment.

I decided at this time that by having my head shaved, I would deprive other vermin of a home, as well as reduce the frequency of having to get a haircut. (Opportunities for haircuts were not too plentiful.) It was a practice I maintained for the duration of my internment.

Execution by Firing Squad

We were rudely jolted out of our reverie one day when we were informed that there was going to be an execution that afternoon and that we all had to witness it.

It so happened that two of the Filipino soldiers had been caught sneaking into the camp toward morning. Their wives either lived nearby or else they had come to be close to the camp, and these two men would sneak out of the camp, spend most of the night with their wives, and then sneak back in toward morning to be there for morning roll call. Camp Casising was by no means a maximum security compound, so getting through the fence was not that difficult. But this time they had gotten caught. They had been summarily tried by the Japanese and sentenced to execution by firing squad before sundown. The American camp commander had tried to intervene in their behalf, but it was a futile attempt. The accused men had to dig their own graves and the holes for the execution posts to be set in, which they were to be tied to just outside the fence. Shortly before 5:00 P.M., we were all herded down to the execution site. The Filipino men were already lashed to the posts alongside their respective graves. The Filipino who had been their commanding officer was stationed near them, just inside the fence. At exactly 5:00 P.M., the firing squad commander gave the order and the first volley was fired into the men, causing them to slouch down. Immediately their commanding officer shouted, "You are in the American army—die like Americans. Attention!" With that, they jerked their heads up in an attempt to come to attention, just as the second volley hit them. After this, there was no movement. They were cut loose, were rolled into the graves they had dug, and were covered over with the dirt they had thrown out of those holes. They never got to see the sun set. And the Japanese had made a point.

The atmosphere in camp was more subdued after the execution. We were suddenly made aware that this was no summer camp venture we were experiencing. The first glow of relief from daily danger and fighting was over, and the men were becoming somewhat restive. Likewise, our own individual idiosyncrasies were beginning to surface. While Bob Dennis and I had our differences of opinion and occasional disagreements, we always were able to settle them amicably and even seemed to be better friends for it. There was one area of contention we hadn't settled, though. I am the sort of person who likes to greet others cheerily in the morning, while this was far from the case with him. His morning grouch seemed to get worse as time went on, so one day I decided to meet the situation head on and asked him, " Bob, what on earth is eating you, anyway?" He just growled back, "Nothing!" "Well," I said, "if it's nothing, why do you act this way?" Then I found out. "Look," he said, "if you want to get along with me, just don't say anything to me until after I have had breakfast—nothing." "OK," I said, and that's the way we operated from them on, and it went fine. It was just an idiosyncrasy.

Internal guard duty had been increased after the execution. Previous to that, our own guards' duty had been mainly to see that the prisoners did not rob the commissary, kitchen stores, or other areas, but now they also were on the lookout to prevent any actions that might provoke the Japanese into another drastic gesture. Like all military guard duty, it was a thankless, lonesome job and obviously not conducive to cheerfulness. Men coming off the graveyard shift would also be hungry and cold, so it was commonly understood that they would automatically go to the head of the chow line. This particular morning was no different from any other. The sun had not been up long enough to warm the air to a comfortable level. Bob Dennis and I had observed our regular ritual of silence. On the way up to the mess hall, Clucas had joined us, and after saying, "Good morning," he too walked along in silence because he was aware of the fact that until after breakfast, silence was golden in the presence of Dennis. The chow line was not very long when we got there—perhaps four or five men were ahead of us. Just about then, the men who had been on guard duty began filing in ahead of the line, and as they did so, several men started protesting about bucking the line. This drew the ire of the internal guards who were coming off duty, one in particular. He apparently thought I was one of the men who had complained because he approached me menacingly and told me to "knock it off or I'll knock your block off." I honestly told him I had not said a word to anyone yet that morning, and Clucas bore me out on that. But the man still wanted to fight, so I said, "Listen, you're bigger than I am and very likely a better fighter. You can whip my ass. You know it, and I know it, but I'll tell you one thing—when you finish, you'll still be wrong and I'll still be right." Then I just stood my ground. If he still wanted to fight, that was his option. I wasn't going to start it , and I wasn't going to back down either. Recognizing the impasse, he let the matter go and joined his colleagues at the head of the chow line.

I did not see the man for more than a week after that. We happened to cross paths on the way to the latrine, but nothing was said by either of us. After a while, he would give me a nod or slight wave if we happened to meet, and I would reply with a similar gesture. And then one day, he said, "Hi, Nordin." I'm not sure that I knew what his name was yet, but I made it a point to find out so that I could respond with "Hi, Imlay." Finally one day he greeted me with, "Hi, Carl." Naturally, I had been becoming increasingly aware of the fact that there was no enmity between us, but now I realized that I had gained a friend. It seemed to be the norm of military practice to address another person by his last name. It is only in the case of close friendships or people who know each other extremely well that a person is addressed by his first name.

Nothing was ever mentioned of this first encounter in the next two years that I would be privileged to count him as almost the best and truest friend a person can have. As our friendship developed, I learned that he too was from Wisconsin, he too had a sweetheart back home, and he too came from a Christian home. His name was Maris "Jug" Imlay.

August 15, 1942—All generals, full colonels and their "dogrobbers" left Malaybalay. (*Dogrobbers* is a term given to orderlies, and others who do menial jobs for higher-ranking officers.)

Up until this time, there had been quite a number of full colonels, plus five generals in our camp. That was a relatively high number of generals for a group of officers and men of that size. One of the generals happened to be General Manuel Roxas, who after the war became the first president of the Philippines when they won their independence from the United States on July 4, 1946, as previously promised. General Roxas would stroll through the camp occasionally, often pausing to visit for a few moments with both officers and enlisted men. I had the pleasure of being in such a group on an occasion or two. He was a fine man, an excellent general, and a very capable president. The other generals were General Sharp, General Fort, General Vachon, and one whose name escapes me. We learned later that this group of officers ended up in camps in Manchuria, Korea, and Formosa. Their lot had also been difficult.

October 3, 1942—All specialists left Malaybalay. The term *specialists* in this case was more or less a misnomer. It was actually a ploy to woo labor forces to Japan. There were two hundred who volunteered to go. Three of them— Vincent Didio, Pablo Gonzalez, and Roderick McKay (who had been in charge of the pier at Bugo)—were from our unit. After the war we learned that they had received no special treatment or any more desirable jobs than we, who came later on, had received. In fact, Didio was only a few miles from Hiroshima when the atomic bomb was dropped. (He suffered no injury from the blast.) The only advantage they may have had was that their hell ship ride was not as dangerous, or as bad as subsequent ones. The one disadvantage in going that early was that they had to spend two more winters in the cold and miserable winter climate of Japan than we did.

October 18, 1942—All remaining Americans left Malaybalay (Camp Casising). How different it was to be riding the familiar road from Malaybalay to Bugo in an open flat bed truck, this time as guarded prisoners of war. I had previously moved up and down those roads as a free man with a purpose—a dedication to do my job in the war effort, no matter how humble that job might be.

When the convoy slowed as it climbed up out of the canyon just east of Tankulan, I wondered if any of my former Filipino friends were still there or if they even knew we were approaching. I was apprehensive also about what their reaction might be or what they might think of us. After all, we had lost the war up to this point, we the Americans, whom they had thought were so mighty, had failed them. Because there is a sharp turn in the road just at this edge of Tankulan, the convoy slowed to a snail's pace, which enabled everyone to get a good look at the roadside. There, lining the road on both sides, stood the local townspeople, waving and cheering us on. As I scanned the roadside, looking for familiar faces, I suddenly heard someone shout, "There he is, there's Carl." And then I saw them—Salvador and Mrs. (Marcelina) Albarece and a nurse whom I had given a ride in the cab of the truck in which I rode shotgun in order to help her get to her work in a hospital beyond Maluko. (We were not supposed to give rides to locals, but Salvador had requested it for her.) As we drew closer, I saw their smiles through their tears and saw that they were wiping their eyes with the white handkerchiefs they were waving. The sight really filled me with mixed emotions. I was happy to see them again—happy to know they still liked us—but I was sad for their sadness, sad that there was nothing I could do about it, and sad that I might never see these fine people again. They had been so good to me, and I had grown to cherish their friendship. It all made me more aware than ever of my impotence as a prisoner. I was slowly beginning to realize what loss of freedom entails. I could not even go and shake the hand of a friend or comfort them or say farewell. There would be many more difficult lessons to be learned regarding loss of freedom in the months and years that lay ahead.

The remainder of our trip to Bugo was uneventful, and there, a little over eleven months after disembarking from the Philippine motor ship *Legaspe*, we embarked on the Japanese troop ship #760.

Our trip around the northern and eastern sides of Mindanao was uneventful and quite pleasant, considering the circumstances. Evidently American submarine activity had not become a major threat that early in the war, so the Japanese let us spend most of the time on deck. The weather was warm and sunny, and with the gentle South Sea breezes blowing, we were really quite comfortable. Viewing the island from the deck of a ship is a most pleasant experience. Our twice-daily meals of mostly rice alone were barely adequate, but we kept thinking it could only get better. We slept on the steel decks, but they were relatively clean. After rounding the northeast tip of Mindanao at Surigao, we proceeded south along the eastern side of the island. This took us in close proximity to some of the islands that George Plowman had in mind for a joint lumbering venture after the war. Also, we saw a part of Mindanao we had not seen before because in 1942 there really were no through roads from the interior to the area in the middle of the eastern side of Mindanao. That part of the voyage also took us over the deepest water in the world—the Mindanao Trench, or the Mindanao Deep, with a depth of 35,400 feet, almost seven miles. On October 20, 1942, we arrived in Davao Harbor.

Davao Penal Colony (Dapecol)

October 23, 1942—Disembarked and walked twenty-five kilometers to Davao Penal Colony, where we were interned. Some men passed out. Many were unable to carry their packs all the way. I had my negatives in my field pack—I carried it all the way. A favorite trick of the Japanese seemed to be to march prisoners during the hottest part of the day. This day was no exception. At high noon, we disembarked and began our walk through the hot streets of Davao and on up the road toward the Davao Penal Colony. By 2:00 P.M., the hottest part of the day, we were drenched with sweat and some men were beginning to weaken. This dehydration had caused us to use what little water we had left in our canteens. At approximately 3:00 P.M., we came to a place where there was a slow-running spigot of water. The Japanese gave us less than ten minutes to fill our canteens, but considering the slowness of the water flow and the size of the group (about one thousand men), this was not near enough time. I was about fifteen men away from having a turn at the spigot when the guards ordered us to fall back in line and continue our march. Fortunately, I still had a swallow or two left in my canteen. As the afternoon wore on, the hot, tropical sun continued to bear down on us, and naturally it began to take its toll. Some men passed out as they walked. Others would begin reeling, catch themselves, continue on for a ways, and then plop over. Some just went as far as they could, then would sit down, but would be unable to get up again and move on. Fortunately, there was one truck to pick up stragglers, but when space on that became limited, the Japanese did not look kindly on stragglers. Some of the men were forced to throw their packs, barracks bags, or whatever they were using to carry their belongings by the side of the road in order to continue.

About 6:00 P.M. a chow truck caught up to us, and we got a fifteen-minute break. All we received was a little rice, and for the first ones in line, there was a little tea. By now we were entering quite thick jungle country, so the guards kept a very close eye on us as we trudged along that lonely little road, with every kilometer taking us further from civilization.

I don't know what time it was when I walked into that godforsaken camp, but I recall that there was a water spigot just inside the gate, and I didn't go

Davao Penal Colony (Dapecol). Note the old ditch. Photo by Glenn Nordin.

another step until I had satisfied my thirst and filled my canteen. I also recalled that it was a beautiful—almost white—moonlit night. The brilliance of the moonlight had not been that evident as we had marched up that corridor, which was a narrow road with high trees and heavy jungle on either side. But when we broke into the huge clearing in which the compound was situated, it seemed almost unreal, it was so bright. There was no particular order or organization that night; each man simply found a spot and lay down.

Davao Penal Colony occupied thousands of acres set in a very dense, almost impenetrable jungle of the most malaria-infested area in the Philippines. Before being used as a prisoner of war camp, it had been a maximum-security prison for some of the most hardened Filipino criminals. It was not unlike our former Alcatraz Prison in that its very setting was considered a deterrent to anyone thinking of escape. The Filipino prisoners who had been there prior to 1942 had been moved to the Philippine leper colony on the island of Palawan, except for a few who were retained for a short time to assist in getting us started with the general farm work.

The colony itself had been designed to be self-sustaining. Just inside the main gate on the right side of the road was a large coffee and avocado plantation. Behind that was a coconut plantation. There were about two hundred hectares in each of these plantations. (A hectare is 2.2 acres.) On the left were two large parcels for growing vegetables with a combined area of approximately five hundred hectares. On the extreme western edge of the colony was an abaca plantation and an abaca mill. On the extreme eastern edge of the colony was an area known as Mactan, where three hundred hectares were devoted to the growing of rice. A narrow-gauge railroad ran through the colony from east to west. There was also a banana plantation next to the jungle on the north side of the railroad. Just southwest of the main compound was a chicken farm, and close to that was a pasture area for the Brahma steers that were used in plowing and cultivating the vegetable plantation.

Set just about in the center of this huge complex was the main compound, which was triple-fenced with barbed wire, the strands being less than six inches apart and the fence being about four meters high. A company street ran from east to west, lined on one side by the kitchen and eight barracks. Back of the barracks and about five meters from the fence on the back side of the compound were three latrines, each one having about twenty holes for sitting on. In the corners of the main compound were guard towers that were manned with armed guards twenty-four hours a day. The area was floodlit during all periods of darkness. To the east of the kitchen was the hospital area, with a few shade trees. In addition to the main building, the hospital area contained several outbuildings, including the isolation ward. Just outside the fence on the north side of the compound was a huge parade ground. Just beyond that and across the tracks were a couple of bodegas (warehouses) and other buildings occupied by the Japanese. The Japanese camp commandant occupied a house just east of the parade ground. It was set back a ways from the street separating the two. This was the street that led to the main entrance of the compound. The Japanese had a guardhouse on the east side of this street just outside the guardhouse at the compound entrance.

Each of the eight barracks would accommodate approximately 250 men. On either side of the center walkway was a raised platform extending from the center aisle to the outer wall. The wall extended up about four feet, leaving about a three-foot opening between the wall and the roof. This opening ran horizontally the length of the building on both sides and served as a window. It was completely open, as there was no glass. Each side was divided into bays, or sections. Each bay accommodated eight to ten men and had its own bay leader. Except for metal roofs, the buildings were constructed of wood throughout. Each building had one low-wattage light bulb, which provided minimum illumination.

The building that housed the kitchen was the same size as the barracks buildings and stood right next to the first barracks. Its sides were open. It contained two long rows of huge iron kettles (or quallies) in which the cooks prepared our rice, soup, and tea. Each kettle was heated by a wood fire. One detail, the firewood detail, did nothing else but bring in firewood from the jungle. This was done in the most primitive manner.

Just opposite the kitchen and quite close to the entrance gate was the camp's only source of fresh water, a single spigot. As I recall, there was a hose running from this water line to the kitchen. This water spigot was also known

Two views of barracks at Dapecol. At top, note one of the few benches available for 2,000 men. At bottom, note tree at far right: Protestant church services were held under this tree. Photo by Glenn Nordin.

as the mess-kit cleaning area. We had nothing other than a stream of cold water flowing from that spigot for washing mess kits. To avoid diarrhea it was important to wash your mess kit as thoroughly as possible, but under the circumstances this was difficult to do. We had no soap, so we would try to clean the kits out with gravel before rinsing them. Having only one spigot

Kitchen area at Dapecol. Note the cast iron cooking kettle. The mesh runway matting was added after the war. Photo by Glenn Nordin.

for two thousand men made for long lines for filling our canteens. In fact, you would see men going down to fill their canteens at all hours of the day or night. We could use this water, unheated, of course, for shaving, but not for bathing, as there was not enough for that. So to provide bathing facilities, we dug several holes about three feet in diameter in front of the barracks between the company street and the fence. The holes filled to a depth of about two or three feet of the surface with muddy surface water. At each hole was a five-gallon bucket attached to a rope for drawing the bucket of water to the surface. This we would simply dump over ourselves and call it a bath. It also had to suffice for washing out what few clothes we had.

Roll call, or *tenko*, would be held just after sunrise and just before sunset each day. Everyone able to stand would stand at attention in front of his barracks and count off when the roll call party approached. The barracks leader then gave the report. Lights out was at 9:00 P.M. Not only was our floodlit compound watched by guards in the guard towers, but at different intervals all through the night, guards would patrol both the front and back of our barracks.

When we arrived at Dapecol, we had a new group of guards—men who had been trained to hate Americans, especially prisoners of war. Some of these guards acted as interpreters as well. One of them was a man who had gone to school in the United States and had taken a dislike to Americans there because he had experienced racism; we nicknamed him Simon LeGree.

He had the looks, mustache, build, puttees, and whip-cracking character of the slave driver from *Uncle Tom's Cabin*. His English was fair, but he had a hatred of Americans that was clearly evident at all times. He loved to slap them around, make them bow, and castigate them at the slightest provocation. A rather short, somewhat stocky man by the name of Mr. Wada had an equal dislike for Americans. Although his command of English was barely passable, he acted as an interpreter. He always seemed to be in a hurry, and no matter where he went, he seemed always to be running. So of course we nicknamed him "Running Wada." Another guard named Takiyama was feared by all because he could be particularly mean, but he could surprise you, as a later incident will show. There was also a Lt. Yuki, who spoke English but was not used as an interpreter. He was a very decent man and did not seem to have ill-feelings toward us. On the whole, however, the guards were a hard, embittered group of men. One of the worst things about them was that they were so unpredictable. We never knew what might come next. They could go from a smile to a violent rage in an instant, with little and sometimes absolutely no provocation. We were never at ease. Our camp commandant, Major Maeda, was also an enigma. He was a portly man, probably in his fifties, who didn't show himself much, but when he did, he was exceptionally stern and bellicose. We found this out shortly after our arrival, when we were first called out on the parade ground for a lecture, some stern warnings, and an admonishment to work hard. One of his most cherished speeches to the Japanese occurred each year on Pearl Harbor Day. On that day, the whole camp would be summoned to the parade ground. There would also be a large contingent of Japanese soldiers in attendance. Then Major Maeda, dressed in full military regalia, medals, samurai sword and all, would read the emperor's Imperial Rescript. Following the reading of the Imperial Rescript, the guards would raise their rifles with bayonets attached and make three short fake charges, yelling "Banzai" each time.

The Imperial Rescript stated:

> We, by grace of heaven, Emperor of Japan, seated on the throne of a line unbroken for ages eternal, enjoin upon you, our loyal and brave subjects; we hereby declare war on the United States of America and the British Empire.
>
> The hallowed spirits of our ancestors guarding us from above. We rely upon the loyalty and courage of our subjects in our confident expectation that the task bequeathed by our forefathers will be carried forward, and the forces of evil will be eradicated.

Inside the camp, our American camp commander was selected according to rank. At one time we had a U.S. naval officer for camp commander who during his tenure established the naval tradition of giving the time of day with the traditional bells system. Even numbers signified a particular hour and uneven numbers signified the half hour. One bell was 12:30 A.M., two bells was 1:00 A.M., and so on to eight bells, which was 4:00 A.M., signifying the traditional navy watch. Then it started over again, so the next eight bells marked the watch that ended at 8:00 A.M., and the next one ended at noon. Then the cycle would start all over again. It really was a pretty useful system because by the time it was established, the Japanese had relieved all of the men of their watches.

Our own officers or officials within the camp included a provost marshal, who among other things kept order in the chow line, seeing to it that there was no line bucking. Another unenviable position was that of mess sergeant. There were few supplies for preparing meals, and as time went on, with the men becoming hungrier and more irritable, there was much criticism, doubt, and envy directed toward this man.

Completing the internal governmental structure or chain of command were the barracks leaders (one for each barracks) and the bay leaders (one for each of the bays of eight to ten men into which the barracks were divided). All in all, it made for a pretty smooth-running arrangement.

Quite soon after we arrived at Dapecol, the Japanese let us know in several ways that we were indeed prisoners. First they took away our mess knives and forks, because they were considered weapons. From now on, they would be classified as contraband. This left us with only a spoon, plus our mess kit, canteen, and cup. Next they asked us to turn in all Bibles because these were also declared contraband. Anyone caught with a Bible would be severely beaten. My big Bible had been buried with my clothes and my footlocker at Tankulan. I decided that since Nathan Peery had made a protective pouch out of shelter half (canvas) for my New Testament while we were in Camp Casising, I would keep it hidden or buried rather than turn it in and probably lose it for good. This way I could read it on the sly (there came a time later on in Japan when I thought this decision would cost me my life.) Rules for work were also prescribed. All able-bodied enlisted men would be assigned to the various work details, with only two days a month off. The normal day began with rising at 5:30, breakfast at 6:00, tenko, or roll call, at 6:30, and fall out for work at 7:00. There would usually be forenoon and afternoon yasume, or rest periods, of fifteen minutes each, plus sometimes as much as an hour off at noon. This noon period, however, could include time needed to march to and from the place of work, which could sometimes be a considerable distance. Details would normally be back in camp at 5:00 P.M. with supper at 6:00, evening tenko at 7:00, and lights out at 9:00.

The standard ration of food at Dapecol was rice, Kang Kong soup, and tea, morning, noon, and night. Kang Kong is a tuberous plant, somewhat similar to a water lily, that grows wild in ditches and in the jungle. It was simply boiled and served up as soup, usually with nothing added. On very rare occasions, there might be something else added, as when a carabao, beast of burden, went *jurmantadu*, crazy from the heat. The Japanese would then have to shoot it. After butchering it, they would take the good cuts of meat for themselves and give our cooks the entrails to pep up our soup. It had a meat smell and taste, but divided among two thousand men, a person was lucky to get even a sliver of meat. Similarly, even though the Japanese are a fish-loving and a fish-eating people (our guards had fish several times a week). I can recall getting fish only about three times in our two-and-a-half years at Dapecol. Other extras might include camote (a type of sweet potato) greens in our soup. The Japanese got the camotes. Camote greens are strong tasting and not at all good. Although we raised hundreds of acres of vegetables, we never received any except cassava once or twice. The Japanese surprised us by bringing in two thousand eggs on one occasion and a thousand on another. But how do you prepare two thousand eggs in iron kettles, other than to mix them in with the soup? So all things being equal, I figure that in 3½ years, I got 1½ eggs. The staple of our diet of course was rice, sometimes in the form of *lugao* (a watery, cereal type of preparation) but generally steamed. I must say that considering the primitive means for cooking, the men in the kitchen did a superb job of preparing the rice. Our beverage was always green tea, with the Japanese giving us the stems, and the poorer, rougher leaves. So basically, it was rice, Kang Kong soup, and tea that was supposed to nourish the bodies of hard-working men. The standard rice ration at Dapecol was 600 grams per man per day for heavy duty, 500 grams for light duty, and 350 grams for nonworkers. Sometimes the men of the rice field detail, who performed extremely hard work, received 640 grams per day. Someone devised a rather clever method of ladling out the rice in the proper quantity. Different-sized cans such as sardine cans or other cans were attached to handles which the cooks used in dishing out the rice. For instance, the heavy-duty ladle tightly packed was supposed to be the 640-gram ration for the rice field detail. Men queued up in line for the size ration to which they were entitled, and the cooks dished it out accordingly. It was as fair a way of dispensing the proper amounts of food as one could imagine, but of course there were always complaints, and as the men became hungrier, the complaints increased in number and in seriousness.

We were deprived of so many necessities that it may seem foolish to complain of smaller losses. Nevertheless, we discovered that after several years of deprivation, small comforts one normally takes for granted assume a much larger dimension.

For instance, there is just the simple matter of sitting down. Most people listening to accounts such as these are sitting down, either in a classroom or a similar situation. The same is very likely true for the person who reads this story. For illustration purposes, I have asked students to try to imagine having almost no place to sit down from the time they enter high school until just before they graduate. That includes all vacation time also. The eight barracks in Dapecol each had one bench on the front which would accommodate about six or seven people at the most. To sit on the platforms where we slept was uncomfortable in both Camp Casising and Dapecol because they were too low above the center aisle. In Japan, they were too high to be comfortable if one sat on the lower level, and of course the upper level was even worse. Even if they had been comfortable, the space was hardly adequate to accommodate two thousand men. Therefore we usually always just stood, or we would sometimes squat until our haunches got tired or cramped.

Then there was the matter of beds—the softest material I slept on for all that time was boards. At other times we slept on concrete, rock piles, or the steel decks of ships. Adding to this discomfort were the ever-present bedbugs and lice. By the time we got to Dapecol, the bedbugs were so bad that we used to count the number we had killed between our two thumbnails before drifting off to sleep and then compare the numbers at roll call the next morning. Many times I had killed over fifty before falling asleep. They just kept coming out of the cracks in the wood floor. One night I had evidently gone to sleep while saying my prayers because I had my hands clasped together on my chest when I was awakened by a sharp bite on the wrist. When I awoke with a start, I was looking right into the eyes of a big rat who gave a squeal as he let go and left. We would subconsciously be aware that rats were scampering over our blanketed bodies in the night. It got to be commonplace but never comfortable.

We had the added difficulty of shaving with cold water, old blades, and little or no shaving soap, often without benefit of a mirror. Soap, toothpaste, and toothbrushes eventually became premium items also.

In an attempt to comprehend living under these conditions for such a length of time, one must also take into account the hard labor, the drastic scarcity of food, the constant threat of reprisal for little or no reason, the complete severance from civilization, and most of all, the complete loss of one's freedom to the point of always either being fenced in or accompanied by guards. Just as it had been our unfortunate lot to fight for over five months knowing that in the end, we would either be killed or captured, so now it became our lot to live under these conditions, and worse, for no one knew how long.

By now it had been over a year since the ill-fated telegram had arrived at my parents' home back in Wisconsin canceling my furlough and directing me to return to Fort Douglas immediately. It was almost impossible to conceive of all that had happened in that space of time. I had been rudely snatched from my dream of spending fifteen days with Fay and my family, from whom I had now already been separated for thirteen months. In the lonesome weeks and months that followed, I had been unceremoniously uprooted not only from the security of Fort Douglas, but also from our beloved United States. We had all been catapulted from the safety and joy of life being lived in peace into the horrors and daily uncertainty of war. We had been forced to fight that war with our hands tied behind our backs, symbolically speaking. We had suffered the anguish of having to make do with insufficient food, ammunition, and other war materiel for many months, only to be sacrificed to the enemy in the end. And now we had lost our peaceful American way of life with its ample material comforts, and we had even lost our freedom. And as the days and months went on, we were to find out that losing our freedom was the most bitter pill of all.

Although there had been many circumstances and incidents in the months of fighting and early days of captivity that were associated with just the basic fact of survival, there were not many days when I would not have thought of Fay and my family, if at no other time, at least in my prayers. But now, even they were beginning to seem farther and farther away, and I found that to be very discomfiting. This was such an unnatural, unfulfilling way to live.

I was quickly and brusquely reminded of what my new circumstances were on my first work detail at Dapecol, however. It was a rainy, cold day—and days can be cold in the tropics, especially when your clothes become soaking wet and you are in a rundown condition. We had been in the tropics long enough that our blood had become thinner, and because of reduced rations during the war and months of prison camp rations, our systems were already beginning to deteriorate.

To reach our work site, we had ridden on flatcars on the narrow-gauge railroad that ran through the colony out to the western edge of the cleared area. The first thing we were told to do was to remove our shoes and socks. Then we were ordered to follow a little stream back into the jungle to where there was a gravel deposit in the stream bed. All that day we carried gravel in five-gallon buckets hung from the traditional siggi poles slung over our shoulders. The gravel was brought out to the edge of the clearing and deposited in a pile close to the railroad tracks. Our feet were tender from not having gone barefoot, and our bodies were soft after months of relative inactivity. The guards had boots on, wore rain slickers over their very adequate outer clothing, and had protection on their caps. But we endured bone-chilling cold and torture to our feet as we walked either in cold water or on gravel or on the rough jungle floor, carrying heavy loads of gravel on our soft shoulders. The guards who stood by either smirking or shouting "Speedo" were a grim reminder of who we were and what our new lot in life was. We were next to nothing. We were next to nothing—prisoners who from now on would do only what the Japanese wanted us to do, when they wanted it. They would give no quarter, and we were taught that from the very beginning. It was a long day, broken only by a short lunch hour of plain rice eaten out in the rain. At the end of the day, we were brought back to the main compound, barefoot, cold, hungry, disillusioned.

One of my next work details was on what was called "plowing and field detail." It usually consisted of hoeing the various crops. They could be carrots, camotes, cassava, corn, onions, or whatever needed hoeing. It was exceptionally hard work because most hoes in the Orient are about eight inches long and four or five inches wide: they are not very sharp and are made of heavy metal. Moreover, the ground had been poorly tilled and was hard and weedy. Even though we were working among vegetables, we were forbidden to eat any of them. I recall one time when I was working among the cassava, I kept hacking away until I was able to liberate a piece of root. Cassava root is practically tasteless, but it is starchy and sometimes bulky to chew on, a rare treat in prison camp. I got a few chews out of it before a suspicious guard caught me in my reverie. Then he had his field day, working me over. But at least I had had my cassava while it lasted. After we had been at Dapecol for a year or so, I was on a detail coming in from plowing a field. I was hot, hungry, weak, and nearly delirious when we reached the main intersection where the road from Davao came into camp. Almost in a daze, I half imagined I saw a group of officials coming to inspect conditions at our camp. And there in my delirium, I imagined I saw my father as one of the officials. I had presence of mind enough, and had been a prisoner long enough, that I knew not to make a sound or a move of recognition. As quickly as this mirage had appeared, it disappeared, and reality took over. But after arriving in camp, that picture would not leave me, and it brought many thoughts. Would he know me? What would he think of my weakened, unkempt condition? Would he tell Fay, and what would she think? And after that, whenever I passed that spot coming in from work, although I did not see the mirage again, I was graphically reminded of it and of the same attendant questions.

Sometime after we got settled in at Dapecol, we began to come across some of the men who had been in the Lake Lanao and Malabang area at the time of the surrender. Although they had not been separated from us by a great distance in miles, the terrain and lack of communication and connecting roads had set them quite apart from where many of us were. Most of us had had little or no knowledge of what their plight had been during and after the fighting.

When it came to bringing these prisoners out to the camp, the Japanese acted as usual by not beginning the march until the heat of the day. To compound their misery and to prevent any escapes, the men were lined up and tied together at the wrists with wire. Then they were forced to march in a column of fours, unable to use their canteens. When a man staggered, stumbled, or passed out from thirst or exhaustion, he was bayoneted, cut loose, and left by the side of the road to die. After learning of these atrocities, I became intensely interested in trying to find Lt. O'Brien, the man from Madison, Wisconsin, who had asked us to join him as he celebrated his birthday with a veritable banquet in the hotel dining room in Iligan just before the war had started. I was horrified to learn what his fate had been. It seems that he became terribly exhausted but was trying with all his will to make it because they were close to Iligan. Then as he broke over the hill, he caught a glimpse of the harbor, the supposed end of the march. In desperation and joy, he began to shout at the top of his voice, "There it is, there it is," whereupon the guards shot him in order to stop the disturbance. They cut him loose and left him to die by the side of the road, he who loved life so much.

On the Slopes of
Mount Apo

November 6, 1942—Two hundred of us left Davao Penal Colony and worked at a lumber mill, after which we loaded the Sakito Maru with lumber. We had been confined behind barbed wire long enough that it seemed good to in some sense breathe the air of freedom, though the constant presence of armed guards reminded us that a sense of freedom was only an illusion. Piling lumber was relatively clean work, but it was hard work, and especially hard on our hands without gloves to protect us from the slivers. It was even worse down in the hold of the ship, with the sun beating down and not the faintest sign of air movement. But it was a change, and we welcomed that. We were angered though by what we observed going on in Davao harbor—beautiful lumber being taken out of the Philippines one shipload after another. The same went for carrots, camotes, corn, beans, papaya, and bananas. Meanwhile the Filipinos and we prisoners were going without. This had been one of their main reasons for going to war—to get more raw materials for a population that had outgrown its bounds at home and for an industrial and military complex that had developed an insatiable appetite. Now we could see with our own eyes that they were accomplishing that goal with a vengeance.

November 12, 1942—Two hundred of us arrived at a Japanese plantation to stay and work. Actually, it was an experimental farm of the Philippine government, but because of the strong Japanese influence resulting from the proximity of the large prewar Japanese population of Davao, it was often referred to as the Japanese plantation.

Mt. Apo, the highest mountain in the entire Philippines, rises almost immediately back of Davao City to a height of 9,690 feet. The plantation on its eastern slope offers a commanding view of Davao Gulf, Samal Island, and even the ocean beyond the mainland. It was not difficult to stand on its slopes and, gazing east, dream of the land that lay half a world and a whole hemisphere beyond—America, home, loved ones, and freedom. The view would occasion many a daydream.

The experimental farm itself was really quite nice and a rather interesting place to be. It was situated on a fairly level plateau approximately two-thirds of the way up the mountain, so at roughly six thousand feet above sea level, the air was generally dry and clear. Escaping the mugginess so prevalent at lower levels made the heat much more bearable. After all, we were less than five hundred miles from the equator. During the months we stayed there, we had relatively nice weather, but when a tropical storm did come up, we would often have quite a view of the electrical display as the lightning danced from the peak of Mt. Apo to other peaks in the area and across the water to peaks on Samal Island in Davao Gulf. The rainbows afterward would be just as breathtaking. A variety of crops were raised: hemp, ramie, cassava, various fruits and vegetables, and ornamental shrubs and trees, including fan palms.

Living facilities for us prisoners at the experimental farm were crude and substandard by just about any measure. As usual, we slept on the floor, with little room for each person. Toilet and bathing facilities consisted of a slit trench and an outdoor water spigot. The kitchen consisted of crude, broken-down fire trenches for the iron kettles to rest over that were set in a deteriorated, ramshackle building that appeared ready to tumble down at any time. There were a few, but not enough, tables with rough benches to sit on while eating.

November 26, 1942—Had a half day off for Thanksgiving. Also had beef in our soup. Our meals consisted of rice and a watery stew of onions. Camotes were added later, as well as some sugar. One of my first details at the plantation was working on the road. The task consisted mainly of pick and shovel work—picking out protruding rocks and trying to level the hard dirt with shovels. The day was exceedingly hot, and the sun not only beat down on us without mercy but also reflected right back at us from the parched, reddish roadbed. By this time I had become very good friends with Jug Imlay, with whom I had had the confrontation in Camp Casising at Malaybalay. On this particular day, we were working about thirty yards apart—close enough so that one guard could keep us both covered. Finally I noticed that the guard who had been hollering "Speedo" at us every so often started sauntering up to me, eyeing my left wrist in particular. Then he stopped me and pointed to my wrist watch, saying "Savicu" (pronounced saw-vi-soo), which means "give" or "hand over." Why I had worn it to work that day, I don't know, but I knew right then it would soon be his—after all, he had the gun. But I hated to give it up. It was a seventeen-jewel Bulova, that kept near-perfect time, which was saying a lot for wind-up wristwatches of the 1930s vintage. I had bought it from the local county agricultural agent for $17 (a lot of money at the time). It was a replacement for my good pocket watch, which had received a mortal dent in it after a hockey puck made a direct hit as I skated into a midair pass. Besides, that Bulova was the first wristwatch I ever owned.

I wanted to ignore the man and his insistent demands, but of course that was out of the question. Just then the noon whistle blew, so I hurriedly said, "Tenko, tenko," indicating that I had to go for roll call now, knowing full well that he dared not hold up roll call. Once back in camp, Jug wanted to know what the commotion between the guard and me had been all about, so of course I told him. Then we began to strategize as to what would be the best procedure for the afternoon. We finally decided that after all, he knew I had it and would get it sooner or later, even if he had to make an excuse to search my belongings later on. Furthermore, if he didn't get it now, sooner or later I would lose it to another guard, one way or another. After all, I was about the last guy to still have a watch. Besides, if they should do a search of my belongings, they might just find my good Shaeffer pen and pencil set and my diary.

When it came time to return to work, I went knowing full well that I would be one watch poorer by nightfall and the guard would be one watch richer. But I had no idea that it would develop into such a significant transaction. He passed Jug on his way to me, whistling as he sauntered along. Jug recognized the tune he was whistling and hollered up to me, "Listen to the tune he is whistling." Then I heard it and recognized it. To my utter amazement, he was whistling "Jesus Loves Me." Then he was there with his insistent "Savicu." I immediately pointed my finger at him and asked, "You Christian?" I had caught him off guard and he responded, "Hi" (Yes). The ensuing conversation went something like this, me in my pidgin Japanese and Spanish, and he in his limited English:

> NORDIN: Me, Christian too.
> GUARD (with a big smile): Oh, ah so.
> (I felt I was ahead.)
> NORDIN: Christians love, you know, don't hate.
> GUARD: Hi, me no hate, me like.
> NORDIN: Christians pray. (I fold my hands and look heavenward.)
> GUARD: Hi, me pray. Mother pray, too.
> NORDIN: I pray for you, for everybody.
> GUARD (somewhat taken aback): My mother say in letter she pray for everybody. She pray for you.
> NORDIN: Christians good.
> GUARD: Hi, Christians good. (All smiles.)
> NORDIN: Christians no steal.
> GUARD: Hi, Christians no steal.
> NORDIN: You take watch. (I point to my watch.) That is stealing.
> GUARD (smile vanishes): Savicu ... now.
> NORDIN: No, that stealing. That not good. That not Christian.
> GUARD: Savicu, now.
> NORDIN: You want watch?
> GUARD: Hi, now.
> NORDIN: OK, you buy, not steal. Buy OK, buy Christian.
> GUARD: OK, OK. How much? Pesos, cigarettes?

Whereupon we began dickering in the same pidgin English, Japanese, Spanish, whatever seemed to work. The final upshot was that I got ten packs of Filipino cigarettes, two packs of Japanese cigarettes, and two hands of tobacco. Then I noticed he had a Wesclox pocket watch that he probably had lifted off some American, so I said, "You take watch. Me no have watch. Changee, changee." So I also got his watch (which I later sold to another guard for two-and-a-half pesos).

After we had closed the deal, my guard informed me it would take a while to get all the payment to me because he had to be very careful that his superiors didn't catch him fraternizing with the enemy, so to speak. We set up a signal system, and every few nights, I would meet him down by our kitchen area to receive partial payments. In the end, he came through with everything I had bargained for, so I was satisfied, and he was justifiably proud of his Bulova. I traded the native tobacco and the Japanese cigarettes to other prisoners for rice. I kept the Filipino cigarettes because they were of better quality, and I shared them with five of my buddies, Bob Dennis, Bill Lowe, Don Vance, Charlie Goodliffe, and Glen Bailey, as I recall. Jug Imlay didn't smoke. In those days we had what we called butt-shooters, which was a cigarette holder made from a piece of bamboo. This enabled us to smoke the entire cigarette, making them go farther. At first, I gave each man half a cigarette each evening as we sat on the floor for our daily smoke and bull session. Eventually, as my supply dwindled, I resorted to cutting one cigarette in sixths with a razor blade each evening. On special occasions, I gave each man a whole cigarette. Looking back, it wasn't much, but years later, guys have told me how much they appreciated that bit of generosity. It does indicate how different things were then as compared to peacetime.

After my bargaining episode with the Christian guard, life at the plantation developed into a pretty ordinary routine, except for an episode in the ramie field one day.

Ramie is a fibrous plant in the nettles family which grows to a height of nearly five feet and is seeded so that the individual plants are only a few inches apart. It is used in making a very nice fabric for clothing. A field of ramie is a beautiful sight of tall, even, sturdy stalks that are almost impenetrable, at least visually. Harvesting is done with hand-held sickles, a tool similar to the old-fashioned corn knives used in America in earlier times. After it is cut, the ramie is laid in bundles or sheaves that are picked up later for further processing.

It was a hot day, and the Japanese did not give us much time to look up, so our eyes were pretty much fastened on the work at hand. All of a sudden the yell went out—"Corpsman." I looked up and saw the medical corpsman on duty charging up to a spot about thirty or forty feet from me, pushing workers out of the way as he approached his patient. Then I saw him lay the man down as he knelt alongside him. From where I stood, I could see he was working feverishly over the man for some time; he later assisted him off the field to a shady spot.

When we got into camp that noon, we learned that a cobra between four and five feet long had bit the man in the upper leg. The corpsman, acting quickly, had properly sliced the wound crosswise and had proceeded to suck out the poison. The man suffered some shock and had a sore leg for a while, but fortunately, he lived to tell about it.

The whole incident turned out to be a valuable lesson for all of us in the days and months to come. Cobras are far too plentiful in that part of the world and often run from four to six feet long. They do not rattle or give any warning. When they strike, they have only one-third of their length on the ground, thereby using two-thirds of their body length to reach out and strike their victim. They are lightning-quick in their move. It was not the last cobra strike in the ramie fields, and there were many later on in the rice fields. But thanks to the good work of corpsmen and the instructions they gave to the rest of the men in the days to come, we never lost a man to cobra bites—and the dead snakes provided more than one good meal to those who had a chance to smuggle some in.

December 25, 1942—Had a full-day holiday. Also had beef in our soup, and papaya salad in addition to regular chow. January 1, 1943—Had a three-day New Year holiday. Also had pork in our soup and papaya salad. January 2, 1943—Japanese allowed Filipinos in camp. Music and songs were in order. January 3, 1943— First church services were held in our new camp. Even though we worked during the period between December 25 and January 1, the Japanese did not work us quite as hard as usual. It may have been that they knew it was sort of a holiday season, but I tend to think that they were sort of coasting toward their three-day New Year's holiday. We later learned that to the Japanese, the New Year holiday and celebration is one of their special times of the year.

At any rate, it was all very relaxing and enjoyable, especially the singing, the mixing with a few Filipinos, and of course the extra food.

Although they did allow us to have church or religious services, they did let us know that these services were not to be the highlight we associate with the season. They accomplished this by forbidding us to have a church service or regular worship on Christmas. Rather, it would be done on their terms, at a time designated by them—their holiday. Despite that sort of unkind twist, however, our Christmas service was a special and a meaningful observance for us, even though it was ever so humble. Captain Keeley, a Fifth Air Base medical doctor and our camp commander, led the service. It was held in our crude barracks and began with the singing of familiar Christmas hymns and carols. Then Captain Keeley gave the message. Since there was no Bible at hand, he read us an article from a 1939 *Reader's Digest*. The article dealt with the work of Dr. Alexis Carroll, a scientist and an agnostic who was searching for an answer to the beginning of things. He was working on splitting the atom, one of the smallest and most basic elements of energy, and possibly of life. When it was finally split, he realized the atom wasn't the base of matter because now he was dealing with protons and neutrons. According to the article, this discovery caused Dr. Carroll to realize that creation was something bigger than man's understanding or ability. Ultimately he became a Christian. That night Dr. Keeley reinforced our hope in the unknown and helped us to realize that, as insignificant as we individuals are and as hopeless and helpless as we may feel we are, there is a God who is greater, stronger, and more compassionate than we are able to imagine. It was an unforgettable Christmas.

I had a stroke of good fortune after the holidays in that I was assigned to a detail right on the grounds. Part of the time we were tidying up the grounds, flower beds, and hedges. It was easy and relatively clean work. Besides that, we did not have to work hour after hour in the hot blistering sun, but were in the shade a great deal of the time. Another advantage was that there were few military guards around. Instead, we were watched over and directed by a civilian Japanese who had been signed on to take charge of the plantation.

After we had the grounds looking in tip-top condition, the Japanese set us to moving trees. This was a difficult task because it involved pick and shovel work. In order to accomplish it in the primitive way employed by the Japanese, we had to dig out an area all around the tree to a depth of four or five feet and bind the bottom tightly with burlap, making an earth ball. Then, guiding it with ropes and moving it with pries and cables, we would move it through a predug trench to the desired spot, sometimes twenty or thirty feet away. It was hard, coolielike labor and disconcerting in that it seemed as if they were spoiling already beautiful settings for the sake of experimentation. The first tree we moved was a deciduous tree of some kind that must have been at least twenty feet tall. Next we tackled a fan palm nearly that tall. Fan palms are rather delicate and difficult to move, at least by the primitive means we were employing. I would be surprised if any of the trees survived, but we were not around long enough to know.

January 23, 1943—Left Bogo (Filipino name) plantation and returned to Davao Penal Colony. The move was an abrupt one. We had no advance notice that we were to move, nor did we ever find out why. Maybe we had done all that was needed at that time. After all, there was no need to keep two hundred men there on a permanent basis. We did not know it then, but that was to be our last decent detail for the duration of our prison camp experience. For the most part, from now on work, rations, health, and treatment would continually get worse to the point that it was a miracle that we survived at all. Many did not.

At any rate, immediately after breakfast, we slung our packs on our backs and began marching down the mountain toward Davao. They tried to keep us in a column of fours, but with rocks and holes in the road, that proved rather difficult. As we marched through the city to the waterfront, however, they tried pretty hard to make us look good. We really didn't care. There were very few Filipinos allowed on the sidelines, and we weren't fussy about whether we impressed any Japanese, civilian or military.

The weather had been nice when we started out, and the first part of our march had been relatively pleasant. The farther down the mountain we went, though, the more oppressive the air and the heat became. In a short time, we saw storm clouds gathering behind Samal Island, indicating a storm moving in from the ocean. At the waterfront, we were loaded into boats, around fifteen or twenty men to a motor-powered boat, and just after we got a mile or two out in the bay, it began to rain, and it rained and it rained.

The deluge continued all the while we were in the open waters of Davao Gulf, accompanied by a stiff breeze. It was a miserable combination which resulted in two hundred cold, wet, miserable, and hungry men. By the time we reached the mouth of the Lasang River and headed into the jungle, the rain had eased up some, but as the monkeys scampered through the treetops overarching the river, aroused at the approach of these boats into their inner sanctum, the shaking of the trees made it seem as if it were raining just as hard as ever. The screaming of the macaws and the chattering of the monkeys as we slowly wound our way up the river made us feel we were invading a world where we were not supposed to be. The jungle seemed more inhospitable than ever.

Finally, we arrived at the eastern terminus of the narrow-gauge railroad that traversed the Davao Penal Colony from east to west. There we boarded flatcars and rode through Mactan, a little settlement of bodegas, barracks, and other buildings in the colony's rice plantation and on to the main camp of Dapecol.

A number of things had happened in camp in the two-and-one-half months we had been gone. A cemetery for American prisoners had been established, and one thousand prisoners from Cabantuan Prison on Luzon had been brought down, swelling our ranks to two thousand men. This was when we found out firsthand about the battles of Bataan and Corregidor, the Death March, and the horrors of Camp O'Donnell and the Cabantuan prison camps. It was also a time of reunions for many of us who had been separated by the war. On the pleasant side, Red Cross packages, some bulk supplies, and medicines had been brought into camp.

The next day those of us who had been at the plantation got our first taste of Red Cross food. For breakfast, they made the rice into lugao, a watered-down version that very closely resembled a stateside hot cereal such as Cream of Wheat. Then, wonder of wonders, there was sugar and milk made out of Klimm, a brand of powdered milk, and coffee. Talk about seventh heaven—we were in it. We could scarcely remember how good real American food was. At noon, we got another surprise—rice and fish-head soup. That wasn't quite as good. The Japanese had taken the fish, naturally, and given the cooks the heads to try and make something out of. So they had boiled them first to make them somewhat malleable and then added pow-dered milk to make a sort of cream broth. I recall getting the rice on my tray, tea in my cup, and fish-head soup in my mess kit. Then I sat down to eat and saw those fish eyes looking at me from a puddle of milk. It was not easy to proceed, but I knew there was much-needed protein nourishment in that mess kit, so I started first by sampling the milk broth. Not too bad—sort of tasty—fishy yes, but tasty. Finally I began to nibble on a fish head. Not too good, and yet, not too bad. But then I got to the eyes. Rubbery, chewy, taste-less. I tried at first to eat around the eyes, but that was messy. Then I tried to pick them out, but with only a spoon, that was next to impossible, so I finally resorted to closing my eyes and chomping away at the whole heads, eyes and all. Maybe they were healthy for us, but they weren't what one would call good.

Mactan

January 27, 1943—Was sent to Davao Penal Colony rice field. If there was any area or department of the Davao Penal Colony that should be given special consideration or treatment, it would certainly have to be Mactan and the rice field operation. It was the largest and most important crop of any in the colony, and cultivating it was by far the hardest, dirtiest, and most disagreeable work of any at Dapecol. Plowing and harrowing were done with carabao, the local beasts of burden. They are in the water buffalo family and are among the orneriest animals in the world, I believe. If they become too hot, their brain melts and they go *jurmantado*, or crazy. When that happens, there is nothing that can stop or tame them. They just charge in a wild rage until they drop or are shot. In order to keep cool, the carabao lie in wallows, huge, wet, stinking mud puddles. When they are being worked in the rice paddies, the animals would just lie down in the rice paddy any time they chose to, and when they did, there was no way to get those beasts to move until they were good and ready to do so. It could be disgustingly frustrating.

Other types of work at Mactan were planting, weeding, and harvesting. Planting the seedlings was done by hand, as was the weeding. Harvesting was done with a sickle, and the rice sheaves were carried in huge baskets to the railroad to be hauled to the threshing bodega. The harvest season was the only time the rice paddies were drained down to a point where they were relatively dry. The rest of the time they were partially flooded, so we continually wallowed in water and mud halfway between our knees and our hips. This made the work doubly hard. The old stubble, poorly grubbed stumps, and all sorts of foreign matter were hard on our legs and feet also. Months later, it got to the point that every time I stepped down into the mud, it felt as if my toes were going to break off because they were being constantly bent beyond their normal position. Perhaps the only good thing about working at Mactan was the opportunity to get some extra food occasionally. Sometimes they would have us clear out the canals, and as we were wading through the muddy bottom, we could feel what were called mud fish wiggling under our feet. They moved slowly enough so that we could reach down and catch them with our hands. We would slip them in a pocket or an empty mess kit and bring them into camp to be cooked up later over a little guan stove. Other sources of food which we came across when weeding or cleaning the canals were shrimp, which we ate raw on the spot, and birds' eggs, which we broke over our hot rice. One other advantage to working at Mactan involved defecating. Toilet tissue in prison camp is a scarce commodity, and what little the Japanese did issue was of very poor quality. So, when nature's call came upon us out at the rice field, we simply fertilized that spot, moved over to some clean water, and washed ourselves off.

Mactan itself was almost like a little settlement. There were several bodegas (sheds or warehouses), usually with open sides, and most of them quite large. One large one housed the stationary threshing machine and large diesel engine. There was also a family residence, where Mr. Asuncion and his family lived, along with several outbuildings, including a chicken coop. Mr. Asuncion was in effect the supervisor for the whole Mactan operation and lived there with his family. Then there were the barracks for the workers, or in our case, the prisoners. These buildings were low, dark, and gloomy. The grounds were low, so there was usually water, or at least extreme dampness around, that permeated the dirt floor of the buildings. The men slept in double-decker, screened-in mosquito cages. Each compartment was approximately six feet by thirty inches, with a sliding door for entry. If a person got one with a reasonably good screen, he was lucky, but there were not too many of those to be found. It happened to be an important item of consideration because the mosquitoes at Mactan were really a serious matter. There was no electricity, so the only light we had came from a little kerosene lantern. Our toilet facilities consisted of a slit trench. The mosquito cages were terribly infested with bedbugs, no doubt because they had been inhabited by the criminals who had been sent to Palawan. At any rate, this was our home for the time being—a bedbug-infested cage 6' long, $2\frac{1}{2}'$ wide, and $2\frac{1}{2}'$ high, with no facilities. This was Mactan.

January 31, 1943—Received our Red Cross packages at rice field. Since our group of 200 men had been at the plantation on Mt. Apo and then had been at Dapecol only a few days before going to Mactan, we were approximately a month late in receiving our Red Cross packages. Although the facilities at Mactan were not very cheerful or conducive to deriving the most out of a special treat, we were almost like kids with a new toy. Each man received an eleven-pound box containing such items as Spam, corned beef, tinned jelly and butter, chocolate bars, toothpaste, soap, shaving cream, toothbrush, cigarettes, instant coffee, Klimm powdered milk, and even chewing gum. We felt like millionaires. We had almost forgotten that such good things even existed.

There was a great temptation to gorge ourselves on all the goodies those boxes contained, but our better judgment told us that our systems would not be able to handle too large of an infusion of this rich food all at once. Those who did yield to temptation found out to their dismay that restraint was the better course of action. A few dozen unscheduled trips to the slit trench in the middle of the night proved to be a good teacher. Then there was the question of future deliveries to consider. We had been informed that according to the Geneva Convention, each man was supposed to receive an eleven-pound box of Red Cross food and supplies each week. Some of us reasoned that because Japan was not a signatory to the Geneva Convention and because we had already waited almost a year to receive this one, we would probably be better served by rationing it out over a reasonable length of time. In this case, discretion was the better approach because it turned out that we averaged one eleven-pound box per man per year, rather than one a week, during our incarceration.

Within a day or two of receiving our Red Cross packages, a system of barter developed out of a need to exchange items according to the individual's particular likes or desires—cigarettes for food, food for cigarettes, Spam for jam, or jam for Spam. It didn't take long to develop a rather standard value or rate of exchange to be used in consummating deals. It was a rate that would last for three years and went something like this: Spam and corned beef were exchanged for five packs of cigarettes per can; butter and jelly went for three packs of cigarettes per tin, and so forth. Those who didn't smoke would also sell their cigarettes for cash if they couldn't get food or other merchandise for them. The going cash rate was about one peso per pack, or fifty cents U.S. This way they would have money for food if they should happen to find a deal. Later on, when we had occasional short-term canteen privileges, they might be able to purchase curry powder or some other condiment for cash.

One of our concerns at Mactan regarding our Red Cross food was how safe it was when we were out in the fields working. I suppose one reason we worried was that the guards would wander into the barracks out of curiosity about what we had and what we were doing with it. The fact that they would wander into our living quarters at all during off-work hours did make us somewhat suspicious because that normally was not done. I'm not sure that anything was taken during the day, but it was a worry.

One of these guards, Takayama, entered the barracks more often than any other guard and seemed a little more brazen. He was also known for being more volatile with the prisoners out on the work details. What began to concern me was that he seemed to be looking me over more than any one or any thing else. Finally, one evening as I came in from the latrine, he met me in the corridor and began laughing and pointing to my chest and then the top of my head, saying, "Changee, changee." It soon dawned on me that since I had very little hair on the top of my head and more than a lot of men had on their chests, he was trying to tell me that the situation should be reversed. He also made quite a fuss about my beard, pulling it some, partly in jest, I guess. This went on for a few evenings, longer than I thought was necessary. Finally, one evening when he was trying to make out that I was different, I thought to myself, "I'll show you something different," so I reached in my mouth, removed my lower partial denture, and stood there holding four teeth in my hand. That really threw him because dentures were practically unheard of by the average Japanese back in those days. He just stood there and gaped. Then I opened my mouth and showed him two big vacant spots, one on either side where the dentures fit in. He was really nonplussed. After staring at the teeth in my hand, then at my mouth, he walked away, shaking his head. And that was the last time he came to me in the barracks. I was to have a much more serious encounter with him a year or more later, however.

It was a good thing the Red Cross packages had come when they did to help sustain us as we labored mightily in the rice paddies. First we weeded and cleaned out the canals, which was back-breaking work. Then we put in the seedling beds, lifting the tender six-to-eight-inch seedlings out of the heavily flooded paddies (flooded in order to prevent root damage), tying them in bunches, which were then carried away in huge baskets slung from a siggi pole on the shoulders of two men. The bunches were then heeled in for a few days until the planting detail finished off that part of the operation.

Planting was the only thing done at Mactan that had any semblance of being scientific. First, twine strings or small ropes were strung across the paddy from one dike to the other. The distance between each string was six inches. Then the planters, usually officers, would each have bunches of seedlings in a sort of pouch or bag as they stepped into the paddy. Each planter would do about two rows, setting the seedlings in the mud at six-inch intervals. While doing this, they usually recited some academy marching chorus or other ribald verse in unison at the top of their lungs. With about fifty planters to a paddy, planting and chanting in unison, it was an interesting operation to see and hear. It was also an exceptionally pretty sight to see a finished paddy done so perfectly.

It was up to us, the coolies or peons, to prepare more paddies for planting. Plowing was done with a one-handled steel plow with a six-inch lathe drawn by a single carabao. Rope tugs extended from a yoke to the implement being pulled. Carabaos have large, spreading horns, so a guide rein extended from a ring in a carabao's nose over the top side of the right horn and back to the driver. To turn right, the driver would pull on the rein hard enough to exert some pain on the animal's ringed nose. To turn left, the driver simply slapped the right side of the carabao's body hard enough with the reins so he would attempt to turn away from the discomfort. To halt the animal, the driver would simply shout, "Ha" rather than "Whoa." Most of us met with limited success in getting the animals to start. Once started, the success rate in getting them to stop was about the same as for starting.

The next part of the process in paddy preparation was harrowing with heavy, clumsy, unwieldy implements drawn by the carabao. All the harrows I ever saw appeared to be handmade. The main frame was a heavy plank of

Philippine mahogany about 3 or 3½ feet wide. Inserted in this heavy bar were sharpened, rounded wooden pegs six or seven inches long that were set about six inches apart. A couple of uprights extended from either end of the bar to a height of about three feet. A bar across the top connecting these two uprights made the handle the driver used to guide it through the mud. A tug hooked to either end of the harrow. It was about as primitive as you can get.

Those kinds of implements, with carabao as the power unit, made farming just about as hard and uninteresting as it can get. And yet, with all the bad and derogatory things said about carabao, there were a few good ones. Being out there as long as some of us were, we got to know which ones they were. We even got so that we could usually spot a good carabao in the herd. So when those of us who would be driving carabao that day were released from morning tenko, we tore off on a run to where the animals were being pastured to try and pick out a good carabao for the day's work. Sometimes we had to run for a mile or more to get to the herd. Then we would climb on their backs and ride them bareback to the place of work. It wasn't that we were eager to do a lot of work for the Japanese, far from it, but there are few things worse than struggling with a lazy, ornery carabao all day, with a guard shouting "Speedo" at you from the dike.

That was exactly the situation I found myself in several months or maybe a year later. Bob Dennis and I were plowing the same paddy one day on contract. Putting us on contract was a devious method the Japanese would resort to when they thought we were deliberately stalling, or goldbricking, which was usually the case. At this time, our contract was two men to a paddy, and when you had finished two paddies with six-inch plows, you were done for the day.

On this particular day, I had the misfortune of getting one of the laziest, orneriest carabaos in the lot. Besides that, the rope tugs I had were half-rotten and in poor shape. The part of the paddy where I was plowing also happened to have some hidden stump roots. On top of all of that, the guard we drew was Takayama. I hadn't been plowing long when the point of the plow lodged in a stump or root. I finally got the plow dislodged, but by this time that beast of mine had lain down in the mud and was contentedly chewing its cud. After finally getting the carabao up and moving, I stubbed my toe on the hidden root. Meanwhile, Dennis was steadily plowing along, and it looked as if we should be able to finish two paddies by 2:00 P.M. This would give us over two-and-a-half hours rest in the shade of the bodega. Then I hit another stump and a tug broke. I tied the two ends together and pulled the plow loose. The carabao was down by this point. Takayama was sweating in the bright sun and pacing the dike, yelling, "Speedo, speedo." Dennis quietly asked, "Are you having trouble, Nordin?" Then he sort of smirked, "Mine is going good." I finally got the plow loose, the tug fixed, and the carabao up and moving. The retied tug was too short, however, and pulled the carabao's yoke sideways. So I stopped the carabao and evened-up the tugs by tying a knot in the other tug. The carabao was down again by this time. By now the sun was getting high and was bouncing off that mud and water something fierce, causing the perspiration to stream off me in rivulets. I stubbed my toes a few more times and snagged the bottoms of my feet on sharp objects. But I finally got the carabao up and going. We made a few more rounds, and then the carabao got hot or lazy or ornery and lay down again. Takayama was still hollering "Speedo." I finally got the carabao up and going, but before we had gone fifteen feet, we hit another submerged stump. Both tugs broke this time. The carabao lay down again, of course, and there was Takayama on the dike only about fifteen feet from me, yelling, "Speedo, speedo—Nordin, you no good, speedo, speedo." Just then I snapped. Where I summoned the strength, I have no idea, but I grabbed that steel plow with both hands, and bringing it back over my head, I hurled it at Takayama and blurted out, "You son of a bitch!" It landed right in front of him, splashing mud and water all over him and his gun. Off to my right, I could hear Dennis murmur, "Oh my God, Nordin, now you've done it." I just stood there trying to collect myself as I watched Takayama clean the mud from his face and eyes. After brushing off his uniform, he dipped the muddied stock of his gun in the canal, took out his handkerchief, and wiped his gun as clean as he could. Then he called to me and motioned for me to approach him. I went a few feet and stopped. But he wanted me closer, closer. Finally I was right next to him at the edge of the dike. I thought this was it. His gun was clean, ready for firing, but at least the bayonet was not attached, so it wouldn't be quite so messy. "Do it quickly, and get it over with," I thought. But wonder of wonders, he didn't shoot me. Instead he looked me straight in the eye and said, "Nordin, you mad?" I said, "Hi (Yes), I'm mad." He said, "Me bad?" I said, "Hi! You bad." Then he reached in his pocket, took out his cigarettes and, after shaking one part way out, he said, "Sauvicu" (take one, or, I give you). I about dropped in my tracks but regained my composure quickly. Then after I thanked him, he lit up, and we had a smoke together. I have never seen or heard of anything like it before or since. In fact, Dennis, awestruck, said later that he never would have believed it if he had not seen it with his own eyes. He also said he was glad he was a witness because no one else would believe a story like that if there had been no one to corroborate it, especially since it was Takayama—the feared and hated Takayama. I don't recall for sure how the rest of the day went, except that it was almost ethereal because I felt that I really had been snatched from the jaws of death.

There was a further benefit: from then on Takayama always went out of his way to be good to me, sometimes to the consternation of his colleagues, as well as my own. I had heard about the unpredictability of the Oriental mind; now I experienced it firsthand.

The time had come at Mactan when we could have gone back to Dapecol on an exchange of details, but Jug and I and a few others decided to stick it out a while longer. For one thing, the extra rations were inviting, even though we probably more than burned up those few extra calories. But that little extra bulk did help to fill out an empty corner of our usually empty stomachs, or at least we thought so. Then too, except for Takayama, we had some halfway decent guards, and by remaining at Mactan for at least another hitch, we delayed our return to the arena where Simon Legree, Little Caesar, Running Wada, and Aroo Men were flaunting their authority. (The Japanese had difficulty pronouncing l's, so "all" became "aroo." About the only English one guard knew was, "all men," so he was almost constantly going about yelling, "aroo men.")

We began to notice after another few weeks, however, that our legs were beginning to swell, especially from the knees down. They turned red and became blotchy and scratched-looking. We thought it was from the wet mud and the stubble, but we wondered why this hadn't happened earlier. We were to learn much later that it was probably the first symptoms of a dreaded tropical disease, schistosomiasis (Japonica). It caused us some discomfort, but we continued to work, probably too long. We had no doctors at Mactan to put us on light duty or declare us unfit to work at all, so we labored on.

March 13, 1943—Came in from the rice field; went to the sick compound. This was a separate compound on the other side of the tracks, almost a mile east of Dapecol. It was near the site where the old saw mill used to be. There were several barracks, a kitchen, and a couple of latrines, as I recall. It could easily accommodate several hundred men. It seemed to be older, or at least more run-down than Dapecol. There were hardly any medical facilities there. It seemed instead to be a place to recuperate. It also turned out to be a place to reunite.

I was sitting one day on the edge of the bay, with my feet in the shallow aisle, not very comfortable, when, to my utter amazement, who should come up to me and call my name but Howard Lang from Webster, Wisconsin. He was the KP pusher who had stalked me while I was doing KP duty on the *Hugh L. Scott* out in the middle of the Pacific Ocean a year and a half earlier. After we had had coffee, cake, and ice cream that day and I had finished my KP duties, he and I had gone our separate ways to where our respective units were billeted on the ship, and we hadn't seen each other since. We reminisced and I learned Bud Lang's story.

Upon arrival at Manila on November 20, 1941, his outfit (192d Tank Battalion) went to Fort Statsenberg (next to Clark Field) on Luzon. This was the same day I went to Fort McKinley. When war broke out, the 192d fought valiantly on Luzon, later retreating to Bataan, where they fought against horrendous odds under unforgiving jungle conditions. Howard was a tank commander. The enemy included not only the Japanese but also disease and starvation. After the fall of Bataan, Bud had made the infamous Bataan Death

March and was one of the unfortunate thousands who fell ill with malaria, dysentery, and tropical ulcers, but he is the only person I have ever known that returned from zero ward at Cabantuan Prison Camp—twice. Because the men were dying so fast and because there were so many other sick ones to try to care for, when a man's condition was considered terminal, he was removed to zero ward to die. Twice a day an orderly would come to slosh away the feces, put out the dead ones and, if any men were still alive, offer them food and drink. The first time Bud was in zero ward, he remained for thirteen days until it was finally determined that he might live. The second time he was there, he spent seven days before finally beating the odds. When I first met Bud, he was a big, strong man, tipping the scales at around two hundred pounds. But now this six-foot frame carried less than one hundred forty pounds. His full, round face was gaunt, and his formerly lively eyes were dull and sunken under graying eyebrows. He had been through an awful lot and he would go through much more, only this time I would suffer it with him.

One day when Bud and I were talking and reminiscing about a variety of things, I happened to mention a fellow whom I had met in boot camp in Fort Snelling, Minnesota, back in September of 1940. In fact, he had gone downtown in Saint Paul with Kenny Carpenter and me on my birthday. I guess one of the reasons that we fell to talking about him is that he used to stop in my hometown of Siren en route to one of his fishing lakes between Siren and Spooner. Bud and I often talked about fishing. At any rate, I told Bud that when we were offered destinations to be shipped out to, this guy had selected Corregidor and the coast artillery. I sort of wanted to go there, expressly for the opportunity to travel far and see unusual places. But Kenny Carpenter didn't want to go that far and we both wanted to be associated with the air corps, so we compromised; we took the air corps opening farthest from home in the States at that time—Fort Douglas, Utah. Ironically, and unknown to me, Kenneth Carpenter had died a year and a half earlier in Cabantuan in the Philippines. Finally I mentioned the name of my boot camp companion to Bud—John LaVoie. "John LaVoie," Bud said, "Do you know John LaVoie, Frog LaVoie?" "Yeah," I said, "the good-looking Frenchman, Frog LaVoie." "Well," Bud said, "I've got good news for you. He's right here in this compound. He came down from Cabantuan with us!"

It was probably the next day that Bud and I happened to be coming out of the latrine at the same time when he said, "Carl, I want you to meet someone," and that's how my reunion with Frog LaVoie took place. His voice sounded the same as always—cheerful, pleasant, but not quite as strong as it used to be. If I hadn't heard his voice, I would never have picked him out in a crowd. He was so thin, and so much older-looking. But it was a great reunion. I think his surprise was greater than mine though because I at least knew that he had gone to the Philippines, whereas the last knowledge he had of me was back in Fort Snelling two and one-half years, one war, and a couple of prison camps earlier. John and I saw each other quite regularly after that. I did not learn for many years that he went down with the hell ship carrying the Lasang detail when it was torpedoed.

I spent the next couple of years trying to find out more about a man from Grantsburg, Wisconsin, whom Bud had told me was in the Philippines. His name was Vernon Johnson, and I had met him a time or two at the Grantsburg bowling alley back in the 1930s. He was also in the 192d Tank Battalion. But I never caught up to him over there. It wasn't until I was at an American Legion function while I was home on furlough in Siren after the war that we came face to face. Later that month, we rode the same train together to our respective hospitals in the Chicago area.

There was really no one else that I knew or had known of who had been on Bataan or Corregidor, but I kept up my search for someone who had known Kenny Carpenter or had details of his death. It wasn't until a year later that I finally came across a sergeant from his outfit who had taken it upon himself to develop a sort of unofficial record of his outfit. He hadn't seen Kenny die, but he had a date he thought was reasonably close to the date of his death. Ironically it was the same date given when his next of kin were later notified of his death. At that rate, the sergeant's other figures were probably close to the mark also. If so, that meant that as of that time, there were eight survivors of the original company of close to two hundred men. It wasn't until two years later, in Japan, that I came across a man who was in Kenny's outfit and had seen him the day he died. According to this man's account, he had looked in on Kenny earlier in the day and when he came off work detail later on, his body had been removed for burial. Kenny and I had enlisted together, even before the draft program had begun, and thus were among the first to go to the service from a small rural area in northern Wisconsin. Because we had both ended up in a strange land so far from the close-knit community we had left, I made it a one-man mission to find out all I could about Kenny's action in the war and his subsequent captivity and death, hoping that some day, somehow, I could bridge or personalize the gulf that existed between him and his family as a result of his tragic suffering and death. He had died of cerebral malaria—a horrible death. My search for information was a sad and lonely mission, filled with countless dead ends, but it was worth it because even now, more than fifty years later, I have been able to give answers to questions members of his family still have.

March 15, 1943—Got paid 7.43 pesos ($3.67 gold) for working at Bogo plantation. This was the first of the few and rare times we were ever paid for working while prisoners of war. It was nowhere near what the Geneva Convention mandated. Furthermore, it was paid in occupation money, which was not even worth the paper it was printed on because it had no official monetary backing. Later, in Japan, we got paid in Japanese wartime money, which was worth even less. About the only thing this play money was good for was that it served as a medium of exchange on the rare occasions when we would have limited canteen privileges in camp. It was all almost laughable, when you considered the rate of pay we received. Seven pesos and thirty-five centavos, or $3.67 U.S., for the three months of manual labor at the plantation. In Japan, prisoners who were privates received ten sen a day, and noncommissioned officers got fifteen sen a day. At the 1944 exchange rate, that amounted to two cents U.S. for privates and three cents for noncoms per day, if and when we got paid, which was rare.

Back to Normal in Dapecol

God is our refuge and strength, a very present help in trouble.
—Psalms 46:1

It had been over four months since I had left Dapecol. Jug Imlay and I were among the last of those two hundred men to be assimilated back into the daily life and routine. It seemed good to get back with some of the guys of our respective outfits, to meet more of the men who had come down from Cabantuan, and to learn more firsthand from those men about their war, their fortitude, and their personal victories, even in defeat. We seemed to be mutually strengthening each other in our adversity. More and more, I was beginning to realize that it's a pretty sorry person who doesn't gain strength in adversity. If you don't, you're eventually lost. There is no way of just staying the same. It never got better, and it didn't stay the same. We had to cope, and this strengthened us.

Underlying this need to cope was another important dimension—determination. It takes determination to get out early in the morning, every morning, and face a day of hard labor with your stomach calling for food. It takes determination to stand at attention and never wince while being beaten. It takes determination to bow to your tormentor following a beating and say, "Arigato" (Thank you). It takes determination just to live sometimes. While there was humor in camp, with some of the best instances of humor that I have ever witnessed, nevertheless there was a growing element of determination among us that was even beginning to change our visages. In fact, before it was all over, our very looks had hardened to the point that some were barely recognizable when compared to their old selves. We just had to steel ourselves to never ever let the Japanese get the better of us.

In spite of all this, there was help and hope available in camp. Although Bibles were contraband in camp, we were not prohibited from having religious services in camp on our day off—twice a month. Protestant services were held under a tree next to the noncoms' barracks. Another source of encouragement was an occasional lecture by a Dr. Brown, a botanist who was caught in the Philippines as he was returning from Africa. With a booming voice and an outstanding vocabulary, he would give lectures on science, history, or philosophy, but always with a Christian connotation. There was one lecture on overcoming challenges in life as a way of becoming stronger that was especially meaningful. Comforting also was the privilege of prayer, one thing the Japanese could not take from us. Thus I could talk with God about home, family, hopes and dreams concerning Fay, my country, my health, my buddies. It was a great source of strength.

March 18, 1943—Came down with dengue fever. March 24, 1943—Turned to duty again. An infectious disease transmitted by mosquitoes, dengue fever is often called "break-bone" fever, which aptly describes the effect it has on its victims. Weakened by loss of appetite from the dengue fever, I also had difficulty eating because of open sores on my tongue and inside my mouth. I needed ascorbic acid, so Dr. Keeley saw to it that I got on the Davao Road detail, where a lemon tree grew on the right-of-way. Shortly my scurvy was gone.

Working on the Davao Road detail often entailed hauling gravel in buckets suspended from poles. We had to be especially watchful going back into the jungle to get gravel from stream beds, as pythons lying on branches overhead might be waiting to seize some prey. Possibly the largest snake in the world, they kill their prey by squeezing it to death. One time a python was just starting to cross the road as our truck approached. Unable to stop, the truck rolled over it just as the tail was emerging from the jungle on one side, and the head was entering on the other—a distance of close to thirty feet. It was about seven inches in diameter.

April 4, 1943—Eight officers, two enlisted men escape from Prisoner of War Camp #2 at Dapecol. Neither the Japanese or anyone else in camp knew the men had left, and the escapees already had a twelve-hour head start by tenko time. For such a large party to escape with success, the escape had to have been brilliantly planned and well executed. By gaining the confidence of the Japanese, these men on the coffee detail had been able to smuggle Red Cross supplies and medicines to a hiding place and had fortified themselves with chickens they stole from the nearby chicken farm and cooked on the job. They had also been able to bring two Filipino prisoners into their confidence by promising to secure pardons for them from President Quezon, who was residing in the United States at the time. (They did, in fact, secure their pardons.) These natives had assisted greatly in the jungle, especially by obtaining a carabao for carrying gear and supplies. It is a story in itself, with at least one book having been written about it.

While we were happy for those who had escaped, the rest of us in camp had mixed feelings—even fear about what would happen next. We had already been put in "death squads" of ten, but none of us knew who the other nine men in our group were. If one of your group escaped, the other nine would be executed. In a group of two thousand men, this gave one pause. There was no execution on this occasion, however, but the men from these squads, along with Colonel Olson, our camp commander, were held in an isolation compound for "contemplation" for several weeks.

Other punitive treatment adversely affected everyone in camp. Our already meager rations were drastically reduced, salt was taken away, and many privileges denied us. Shakedowns and beatings increased in frequency and severity. Dapecol, which had been one of the better prison camps in the Philippines, was never the same again.

The Japanese decided to increase the security of the camp by erecting yet a third fence around the compound, using kapok for posts. Although the fruit of the kapok tree is extremely light, the wood itself is very dense and heavier than most woods. Cutting these twelve-foot posts of trees over seven inches in diameter and carrying them out of the dense jungle on our bare shoulders was extremely hard work. It was almost torture because they have sharp spines on them that gnaw into the skin. Our bare feet also suffered considerably. It was all the more difficult for me, as I was losing my appetite and getting weaker each day. I had developed a fever of 102.5, but I was told I could not get off work until it got to at least 103, so back to work I went. I barely remember going into camp that night. By then it had risen to 104.5.

April 29, 1943—Had my first attack of malaria. I don't remember much about this illness. The hospital was full, and they were low on quinine. I was in the same bay as Jug Imlay at the time, so he took care of me as best he could when he wasn't out on detail. I just sort of drifted in and out of consciousness. I recall Jug trying to feed me once and also trying to get some medicine down me. About all I know about it is what he told me. He did say I had had a pretty close call. I know it left me awfully weak.

Since it was now close to Mother's Day of 1943, I decided to have my beard shaved off in honor of my mother. It was the longest beard in a camp of almost two thousand men. I used it as a pillow by rolling it up and placing it on my canteen; it almost covered my dog tags. When I had been on various side details, it had not always been easy to find opportunities to shave. After it had sort of got away from me, it had turned out to be a project in itself, so I had been letting it grow since November.

Somehow Donald Jensen, a commercial artist, heard of my decision, so he asked if he could capture my beard by sketching a portrait. I had no idea there was paper in camp, but since he did some sketching for the Japanese he had no problem with that. As he put my name and address on the finished product and noticed that I was from Siren, Wisconsin, he asked if I knew Frances Christensen from Milltown. "Know her? She married my best buddy, Harold McBroom from Siren, shortly before I went overseas," I said. It turned out that Don and Frances were relatives. I was able to keep that picture rolled up in a bamboo tube all through my prison camp experience.

Haircuts were getting hard to come by, so most of us had our hair all cut off each time. With my new shave, haircut, and a new T-shirt I had received in the Red Cross package, I felt pretty dressed up for Mother's Day. Someone stole that T-shirt after I laundered it later. At the time I thought it was a terrible loss. It was the first one I ever owned, and so much better than my other clothes. By this time most of us had been able to rig up some kind of G-string to wear during working hours. It didn't protect much more than our modesty, but it was cool and easy to launder, especially when we worked at Mactan.

Speaking of Mactan, it was here that I was initiated into personal discipline, Japanese style. We had a chance to take a quick swim in a stream before going back to Dapecol. I had gone upstream a ways when I heard a guard screaming at me. I hurried back but had trouble negotiating the slippery bank. When I finally got to him (I was naked), he gave me the command "Koitski" (Attention), whereupon he proceeded to beat me severely. As soon as he finished, I had to bow solemnly and say "Arigato" (Thank you). It was very humiliating, but I had seen men beaten almost to a pulp for not doing so. On at least three occasions, I had seen men beaten so badly they had gotten on their knees and pleaded with the guards to kill them. For me and for others, there would be more beatings, but like some other things in life, it's the first one you remember.

June 26, 1943—Second attack of malaria. After being off seven or eight days with this attack, I finally asked to be reassigned to duty ahead of time— anything so I could qualify for more rations. I was very hungry! Fortunately, I was assigned to the fence detail. We worked next to the jungle, which gave us an opportunity to grab some extra fruit once in a while. Being in the shade part of the time was an added benefit for someone recovering from malaria.

One day while I was hoeing onions in the bright sunlight, I began feeling rather strange. Thinking the heat was making me woozy, I stopped for a moment, and as I looked out on the row, I saw it was moving. The whole field was moving in waves. "Earthquake!" someone shouted. It was my first such experience, but it would not be my last. There is no sensation quite like it.

Several months later as I was harrowing out on Mactan, the whole rice paddy started undulating. My carabao fell in a heap, and the dikes resembled snakes ambling along as water washed over them in waves. Guards had trouble negotiating the dikes as they tried to escape the sloshing water. Some fell in the paddy, some in the canal. It was another earth-shattering experience, so to speak. But there were no buildings to fall, at least not this time.

August 8, 1943—Speech by Major Maeda, telling us to work harder and longer, and that we would suffer drastic cuts in our rations. Any time we were called out en masse for a speech by Major Maeda it was not a good sign. Even the interpreters seemed to take delight in delivering the ultimatums. We did work harder because we had to, and our rations were cut drastically.

Things were getting pretty serious by now. Our deficient diets and unsavory living conditions were resulting in open skin ulcers and other infections. There was more and more beriberi (both wet and dry), more paralysis, pellagra, and vision problems, such as Ben LeBeau, Bud Lang, and others had.

Carl Nordin with a 5½ month beard (Dapecol).

The men with beriberi were becoming more fatigued since the dry beriberi cases had to walk night and day because of the pain, and the wet beriberi cases were constantly going to the latrine to rid themselves of the excess fluid, which had a serious swelling effect on them—even extending to the genitals. Just a few vitamins could have prevented all of this. Yet despite our pleas for unpolished rice with the vitamins still in it, the Japanese continued to give us the vitamin-deficient polished rice. One of the worst diseases was cerebral malaria, because the afflicted brain often reduced a man to an animal-like condition. As conditions worsened and men became more hungry, they resorted to all sorts of schemes to smuggle in food. Three illustrations come to mind.

I recall Sergeant Jacques, a tall, slender man, grabbing a rather large papaya off a tree one noon and slipping it in his jacket. "You're not going to smuggle that in, are you?" I asked. "Watch me," he said. During the shakedown inspection, he simply rolled his jacket from side to side. After the guard passed him, Jacques winked at me and said, "No pain, no strain."

Then there was the guy with the chicken. Every once in a while a guy would grab one of Mr. Asuncion's chickens out at Mactan and wring its neck before getting on the train to go back to Dapecol. This particular time the guy thought the guard had seen him, so he stuffed the chicken inside his jacket without giving it the coup de grace and hopped on the flatcar. To his horror, the guard happened to get on the same flatcar and stood very close to him. At the gate we formed a column of fours (four hundred men) for the shakedown. Those of us who were aware of the situation were as apprehensive as the guy with the chicken was. When the guards were almost to where he stood, someone aware of the situation cackled just like a chicken. Back they went and started all over again, when he cackled just like a chicken again. When it happened a third time, the frustrated guards uttered some expletives and motioned us through the gate. We all had a good laugh, and the chicken was not discovered.

Food was involved again in an incident at Mactan. In lighter moments there would be bantering between the Americans and the Japanese as to the merits of the martial arts—jiu jitsu vis-à-vis boxing. Scroggins, who had gone as far as the Golden Gloves contest, bet a man a bowl of rice that before the day was over he would knock a Japanese on his can. The man took him up on it because, after all, who would do a silly thing like that? Later that day while working in the paddy next to Scroggins, I saw him in an animated conversation with a guard. Suddenly I saw Scroggins come from the bottom with an upper-cut like I'd never seen before, catching the guard on the chin and sending him flying headfirst into the rice paddy with his rifle landing a few feet away. The guard brushed himself off after he got out and glanced nervously to see if his superior had seen him get caught in such a vulnerable situation. Upon seeing he had not, the guard was glad to leave things just as they were. Scroggins got his bowl of rice that night.

Working in the machine shop provided Fitzjohn with an opportunity to fashion a pair of clogs, ostensibly to keep his feet clean. These were higher than usual, however, with a hollow space and a trap door under the feet, allowing room to smuggle in a cup or two of rice from the bodega. All went well until one day when he caught his foot doing the goose step in front of the guard station and spilled rice all over. He was severely beaten on the spot and put in the guardhouse, where he was beaten almost to a pulp. When released over a month later, he looked terrible and had no hearing in one ear.

Morale and
Morale-Building

The word *quan* is much used by the Filipinos and twice as much abused by the Americans. I learned from Mr. Albarece that it is a catch-all word, similar to our "whatchamacallit" or "thingamajig." Our abuse of the word was twofold. Whereas the Filipinos pronounced it with a shortened soft sound, as if the "a" were silent (qu-n), we Americans gave the "a" an expanded broad or hard sound. Our second abuse was the many ways we used it. For instance, "I quanned up some coffee," or "I quanned a papaya off the tree." In fact, the official publication of the American Defenders of Bataan and Corregidor is titled *The Quan*.

And so it was that stoves the ingenious POWs made out of smuggled materials came to be known as "quan stoves." By using a round gallon can with a grate in it for the hot embers or charcoal, one could produce an intense heat when air was pumped in from a bellows made out of shelter-half (canvas). Since there were no flames or smoke associated with its operation, it became the ideal way of cooking on the sly.

It was about this time that I met Dan Stoudt, who had been Bud Lang's tank driver on Bataan. Since Dan had only one eye as a result of a battle injury, he got a job in the bodega rather than being sent out on heavy work details. Thus he had an opportunity to smuggle in some coffee occasionally. In order to get the most flavor out of the coffee beans, Dan would put them in his sock and beat them against a rock to pulverize them. Then he would boil them on his "quan stove." I still have pleasant memories of being invited to Dan and Bud's barracks when they had enough coffee for a third man. Those were big treats and great morale builders.

Considering the deprivation and degradation under which we lived, the incessant hunger, and the daily uncertainty of life in general, it's amazing that morale remained as high as it did. Very likely several factors came into play. I have already mentioned one—our determination not to let the Japanese get us down, no matter what. That determination eventually became a common bond, uniting and supporting us against a common foe. Another factor was that we were Americans, and we knew that ultimately we would win the war. Even though America had been weak when we went to war and our fighting had been from a position of weakness, in our innermost beings we knew that America had unlimited potential and that given cause and time, it would rise to whatever heights were necessary to achieve the victory and to avenge its conscience of Pearl Harbor, Clark Field, and other defeats. We were sure that those sneak attacks had aroused a sleeping giant and that in the end we would prevail. Another factor in maintaining our morale for many of us was our own personal faith, of course.

But there was another dimension in morale building at Dapecol that became very important to us and was very successful. A man by the name of Corporal Biggs had gotten up a little entertainment troupe. He even talked the Japanese into letting the group have a few musical instruments. These men would develop nightclub style programs and put them on for camp entertainment at certain intervals. Some of the songs were the ones that were popular when we had been taken out of circulation, some were military songs, some were written by the troupe and might be either ribald or sentimental. There would be the customary joke-telling, of course, and then there would be specialty numbers, like Corporal Ken Day singing "Old Man River" in his deep bass voice (one of the best renditions of that song I have ever heard) and whistling solos by Robert (Goat) Jaeger, the only man I have ever seen who could whistle with his mouth open or while smoking a cigarette. Then to really please the troops, they always closed the program by all of us singing "God Bless America." Part of the bargain was that the Japanese would have one or two representatives present to preview the first performance, which would be held in the shade of the hospital area for the benefit of the patients. The main performance would be in the hot sun of the parade ground, the only area large enough to accommodate several hundred men. The few guards on duty guarding the performance would be way back in the shaded area.

These programs had gone on for several months, to the satisfaction of the Japanese, because they figured that allowing us some entertainment and contentment would make us less restive, and after all, they were monitoring the programs in the preview, so there could be no contraband content. On this particular day, just as we were singing "God Bless America" at the tops of our voices, Chief Reagan, boatswain on the 41 Boat of the Motor Torpedo Squadron 3, the boat that had brought General MacArthur from Corregidor to Mindanao, reached inside his denim jacket and pulled out an American flag. This flag was the official flag of the squadron, and Reagan had been chief boatswain on the flagship. Another man took the other end, and there it was, bullet holes and all, the flag of the United States—our flag, which we had not seen in almost two years—the most visible symbol of freedom there is. As they stood there holding that forbidden symbol, we sang "God Bless America" as we had never sung it before, and I dare say there was not one dry eye in that crowd of hard-bitten men. Even to this day, more than fifty years later, when any of us get together, we speak of the incident, and remember it with emotion. And it seems that everyone who was there that day and has written any account of anything at Dapecol always includes that incident. It symbolized something we had lost and almost forgotten the reality of, the most precious thing to mankind—freedom. I have no idea how Reagan had smuggled that flag in or how he had kept it secret, but it was by all odds the greatest morale builder that I experienced in all those long years of captivity. To this very day, the sight of our flag, and what it stands for, is a source of a special joy and pride. The song also came to be especially meaningful, partly because of the very singable melody and partly because the lyrics speak so eloquently of "home, sweet home."

Despite our outward bravado and various morale-building acts and activities, an insidious force seemed to be numbing our senses and drawing us further and further from reality. Home and loved ones slowly seemed farther away. That we had actually been free at one time seemed difficult to comprehend. I would dream of home, family, Fay, pleasant situations, and they would seem so real. But then would come the dawn and the awful reality of the fence, the guards, the empty feeling in the pit of the stomach, as we moved into one more day of hard work with not enough food.

There were unsettling dreams also, like the one I had of my father being near death in a hospital. It turned out that he had been in the hospital at that time and that he had nearly died.

At the opposite end of the spectrum, however, was a dream that was almost euphoric in nature. In this dream I was suddenly airborne, so to speak, and floating up over the fence. It was as if I were experiencing the "rapture" as I seemed to be propelled toward a great bright light which seemed to be emanating from Jesus clad in white, a presence, as it were. When I momentarily took my eyes off Him to glance at those below, the Presence vanished. It was as if to say, "Never take your eyes off Jesus." The thought of that dream remained with me for days and was a tremendous morale builder.

There were deliberate attempts by the Japanese to demoralize us as well. They showed propaganda movies depicting Japan as the high-principled nation that was going to lead Asia into a sort of never-never land with the establishment of the Greater East Asia Co-Prosperity Sphere. There were also films with footage of the raid on Pearl Harbor and films or leaflets indicating the Japanese were winning all the battles. Some of this propaganda was too blatant to have any credibility at all. About the only useful purpose these leaflets served was as toilet paper.

A few of the men got a boost in their morale as a result of receiving an occasional letter or package from home. There might be a pair of socks or some food item, which would probably be spoiled, but it was from home and it could be eaten, even if it was spoiled. I was becoming fearful that something must have happened at home because in Fort Douglas I had the reputation of receiving more mail than anyone else in the outfit and now I received nothing.

September 13, 1943—Had my third attack of malaria. With my temperature reaching 105 again, this attack was almost as severe as my first one had
been. I recall becoming lucid enough one day to realize it was my birthday.
I later learned that it was on that day that my folks had received official word
that I was now listed as a prisoner of war. Up until that time I had been listed
as missing in action (MIA).

Some time earlier our camp had been visited by a Swiss and a Swede as
neutral observers from the International Red Cross in Geneva, Switzerland.
While at our camp, they gathered information about us to be relayed to our
government and to our next of kin.

These neutral observers also provided the opportunity to take out
National Service Life Insurance (GI) and set up a correspondence process
which helped some, but was frustrating because we were only allowed to use
the prescribed postcards with three multiple choice statements and a message limited to ten words. Even that would have helped if the Japanese would
have given us a reasonable amount of opportunities to use them.

Since we had no contact with the outside world, some of us made up calendars. We had to give this up, however, when paper became nonexistent.
From then on, calendars were entirely mental in nature, but to our surprise,
when we were liberated, we found we were right on target.

In the early fall of 1943, Mack Davis came to me after tenko one evening.
He wanted to talk to me alone. Early in our conversation, he confirmed what
some of us had suspected for some time. He was a "big dealer." He was not
only dickering for food and tobacco for himself, he was in it big time with
the Japanese, which was potentially explosive. The need for utmost secrecy
was understandable. He asked if I still had my beautiful Schaeffer pen and
pencil set and if I wanted to trade it for some food—good food. When I told
him I was hungry for some pork and beans, he said he could get me some.
So we agreed on a price: twenty-five cans of pork and beans, with Mack getting twenty percent, or five cans, as his commission. Somewhat apprehensive, I let Mack have the set so he could show it to the Nip. If Mack lost it
or if the Nip was using him as a ploy, I would have no comeback. But I was
ravenous for food after my last attack of malaria and was more than willing
to take the risk. As it turned out, the Nip liked the set, but would go no higher
than twenty-three cans, fifteen of which would be fish. Mack's take would
still be five cans. The first installment was three cans of pork and beans. From
then on I only got fish in installments of three to five cans at a time, which
was fine, because hiding it was a problem. In fact, the whole clandestine operation was a problem.

Once I got the stuff into camp, I had an even bigger problem. How could
I eat this stuff without somebody knowing it and becoming too inquisitive
or looking up my hiding place? I thought I had solved that by going out to
an old, unused, bedbug-infested mosquito cage between a couple of barracks,

IMPERIAL JAPANESE ARMY

1. I am interned at __Philippine Military Prison Camp No. 2__

2. My health is — excellent; <u>good</u>; fair; poor.

3. I am — injured; sick in hospital; under treatment; <u>not under treatment</u>.

4. I am — improving; not improving; better; <u>well.</u>

5. Please see that __Please write to me at above address__

-- is taken care of.

__I think of you and pray for you always.__

6. (Re: Family); __Don't worry, because I am all right.__

7. Please give my best regards to __Fay Lewis, other friends, and relatives.__

~~l-2 2~~ IMPERIAL JAPANESE ARMY

1. I am interned at __Philippine Military Prison Camp #2__

2. My health is — excellent; <u>good</u>; fair; poor.

3. I am — injured; sick in hospital; under treatment; <u>not under treatment</u>.

4. I am — improving; not improving; better; <u>well.</u>

5. Please see that __my insurance payment__

-- is taken care of.

6. (Re: Family); __Greet the entire family for me.__

7. Please give my best regards to __Fay Lewis and H. C. McBroom__

IMPERIAL JAPANESE ARMY

Two of the three International Red Cross postcards author sent to his parents. The three cards were the only mail his parents received from him in nearly four years.

and closing the screen behind me. Clifford Ketner, a good friend of mine, became suspicious and wanted to know what was going on. Did I have some extra food, or what? When I confessed, his interest was aroused, naturally. I would have liked to have shared with him, but I was hungry and needed that food to build myself back up. After some dickering back and forth in which he offered me cigarettes and then some money, we finally struck a deal. He would give three dollars for the oil every time I opened a can of fish. I wasn't interested in the money, but he wanted to show his gratitude and insisted that I take it. Interestingly, we met a couple of times in later years, and he never failed to tell me how much he appreciated the fact that I had not turned him down.

Obviously, food and water are the two most basic needs people have, but it was interesting to note that another need became apparent—the need to have the company of others, to have companionship. So in addition to the basic chain of command, a sort of social fabric began developing in camp. One of the manifestations of this was the development of state clubs. Getting to know people from closer to home was good therapy. The Wisconsin Club met once a month. One of the more interesting persons I met was Raymond Zelinski, who had been a captain in an observation outfit. After their planes had all been shot out of the air, he was assigned to General MacArthur's staff in Malinta Tunnel on Corregidor. He shared with me what an interesting assignment it had been. He was from Tony, Wisconsin. (After the war, a nephew of Fay's married a girl from Tony whose family had known Captain Zelinski.) Sadly, Zelinski did not survive. He, along with Mark Lemke of Oconomowoc and Kenneth Squires and James Schultz of the Janesville area, were all sunk on the same hell ship.

October 25, 1943—Pease and Brown escaped successfully. They were on the Mactan detail at the time. I could hardly believe my eyes. The train carrying the details out to Mactan had stopped to let the harrowing detail off from the left side of the flatcars before proceeding about a half mile to let the plowing detail off. All eyes were focused on the left side of the train momentarily. Just then I noticed Pease (whom I had met at the Wisconsin Club) and Brown jump off the right side of the flatcar and quickly head for the tall kogon grass alongside the canal. They had almost-new khakis, good shoes, a couple of canteens, and first aid kits attached to their web belts. (Nobody went out on detail that well equipped.) It looked suspicious. The extra equipment had not been obvious on the train because we were crowded together so closely. Now my first thought was that it was an escape attempt. But Pease and Brown? No way. Of all the people in camp, they were the last ones you would expect to pull off such a brazen, daring attempt. I got off to harrow. Then the train moved out.

After a while the roll call guards came hurrying back for another count. They were two men short! They spent several hours going from group to group counting, but always came up two men short. Finally, in a low voice I said to a friend, Ralph (Doc) Howland, "Just between you and me, I know who it is—it's Pease and Brown." "Pease and Brown," he exclaimed. "You're crazy." After telling him what I'd seen earlier, he said, "If it hadn't been you who told me, I never would have believed it." Since I think I was the only one who had witnessed it, I had wanted to tell someone.

After counting and conferring between the two groups, the harried guards ordered everyone back on the train and brought us all back to Dapecol. By the time we all got back and a search party was arranged, Pease and Brown had a good half-day's start.

For the next few days, there was little activity at Mactan because a large contingent of the guards went out each day to search the jungle for Pease and Brown, to no avail.

Following the escape the Japanese introduced sterner measures for Mactan details which, though harsh, resulted in at least one humorous incident. The order went out that from now on men going to work at Mactan would be allowed no jacket to guard against the morning chill, no hat, and no canteen. Thus the uniform of the day would be no hat, no shoes, no jacket, no canteen—only a G-string. The first day out after this new dress code was in force, as we all fell in for roll call after getting off the crowded train, there in the front rank stood Sergeant Thrasher, naked as a jaybird. After he was cuffed around by the guards for "indecent exposure," they learned that poor Thrasher didn't own a G-string, a fact I can attest to because the only thing I had ever seen him wear at Mactan had been a blue fatigue hat and jacket.

Humorous incidents like that did a lot to take our minds off our miserable circumstances. Another illustration also took place at Mactan and helped lift us out of the mundane. Most of us rode our carabao bareback to the main bodega at the end of the day. Many of us became quite adept at being able to stay on the animal's back as it swam a stream in back of the bodega. We enjoyed doing it because it was fun, a challenge, and we came out all cleaned off and cool as the carabao sank down so far that only his nose was above water.

On this particular day, we finally persuaded Kenneth B. Larsen, a big man, to try it rather than to walk all the way back to a small footbridge and cross on it as the carabao swam at his side. So into the water he and his mount plunged. About midstream it seemed the carabao suddenly swam faster, and then it quickly scrambled up the bank without Larsen. All we could see was his hat, a great big, ten-gallon, Stetson-type hat that was his trademark. The hat floated peacefully in midstream as Larsen came splashing and thrashing up the bank. Of course, he was bareheaded, and yes, of course, he had to go back out there to retrieve his hat, and yes, of course, he was late again.

December 25, 1943—Had one-and-a-half days off for Christmas. Got extra chow and cigarettes from the Japanese. Biggs' troupe gave a nice program Christmas Eve. It was as if I was having a bad dream when I realized that two years had passed since I had attended mass for the first time in my life that midnight back in Tankulan. It was even harder to think back three years when Sergeant Parry had invited Kenneth Carpenter to spend Christmas with him and his widowed mother in Salt Lake City. Although we didn't know it then, Kenneth Carpenter had already been dead a year and a half, and Sergeant Parry would be dead in nine months. And what seemed like an eternity ago was the last Christmas I had spent with my family four years before.

I wanted to put the best light on a bleak situation, so I dressed up again, only this time in my khakis because my prized T-shirt had been stolen. Even though my feet had spread out still more, I was determined to wear my shoes and socks that day. It was then that I discovered to my horror that my shoes were starting to rot from the damp tropical climate.

December 29, 1943—Started in as detail leader on plowing and field detail. There were a few advantages to this detail. It was cleaner and lighter work than Mactan. Once in a while you were able to get a vegetable or a slice of one cut by a hoe. We could wear shoes occasionally. Also, I got to see my buddy Odell Hicks almost daily because he had worked himself up to being sort of in charge of the Brahma steers used in working the fields. Being a very conscientious man, he took as good care of them as he had our company truck when he was our driver during the war.

There were no particular advantages to being a detail leader. You transmitted the requests of the Japanese to the rest of the detail and maintained a link of responsibility between the two. This could also be a disadvantage because the Japanese thought that even an insignificant detail leader was responsible for the actions, good or bad, of those in his charge. This could and did have serious ramifications at times.

January 1, 1944—Had a three-day holiday for New Year's celebration. This year's celebration was not marked with extra food as it had been the previous year at the experiment farm on Mount Apo, but the three days of rest were welcome. We used this rest to replenish our tired bodies.

By now a new pastime had developed in camp. Since food was always on our minds, we started coming up with recipes. Some were real and reasonable, while others were almost outrageous. But all of them were the figments of a mind that was trying to respond to a starving body.

When we weren't thinking about food, we would often be thinking about what we would do if we ever got out of this godforsaken place. One day Corporal Kenneth Day and I were working alongside each other on some detail. He was always an interesting man to talk to. Suddenly he said, "You know, Nordin, when we get back we ought to start an organization, sort of like the American Legion or the Veterans of Foreign Wars, except that it would be for former prisoners of war." I thought that was a good idea, and told him so. Interestingly enough, just such an organization, the American Ex-Prisoners of War, was started after the war, and Kenneth Day was its second president.

He later became adjutant of a similar organization, the American Defenders of Bataan and Corregidor, and editor-in-chief of its official publication, *The Quan*.

It was about this time that I received another lift that brought me out of the mundane at Dapecol. Meeting me at the gate one evening was Bob Dennis. He had been on camp duty, so I hadn't seen him for a while. "Carl," he said, "I have been wanting to tell you something for some time."

"Yeah, what is it?" I asked.

"I've become a Christian," he said.

"Great!" I told him. "Glad to hear it."

Guardedly, he then said, "But that's not all. I'm afraid you won't like the rest. I've become a Catholic."

"Great!" I said again. "I'm overjoyed."

"You are? You really mean it?"

I assured him that the most important thing of all was that he had become a Christian. He had taken instruction from Father LeFleur, a fine Catholic chaplain who had distinguished himself during the bombing of Clark Field. Bob had feared I would be disappointed that he had not become a Lutheran, but when I assured him I had no problem with his choice, he seemed pleased. That night I thanked God for Bob's decision.

January 20, 1944—All Americans at the Davao motor pool were brought back to the penal colony at about this time. We didn't know what triggered this. Could it be that now, in the third year of the war, the tide was turning? We were hearing rumors about Africa. Why Africa, we wondered?

The Japanese made occasional disparaging remarks about Mussolini. In addition, names like Borneo, Bouganville, Rabaul, and Celebes were being mentioned in the rumors floating around camp. One thing was certain. They were unhappy about Mussolini. Was there beginning to be a crack in the porcelain, we wondered? If so, could we sit it out? We had to.

January 23, 1944—I went to quarters with cellulitis on my feet, stomach trouble, and high white or abnormal blood count. Many of us were becoming weaker, listless, and nauseated, and we were suffering with mild headaches constantly. Normal white blood count is around 10,000. When it goes above that, it indicates some type of infection. Mine went to 17,000, then to 19,000, and up to 23,000. Dennis had a count of 43,000, and there were reports of even higher readings. Doctors were at a loss to identify the cause. All they could say was that medical science would never believe these reports. Five years later I had to have brain surgery as a result of schistosomiasis (Japonica) on the brain. It is caused by a bug found in fresh water that enters the pores of the skin and circulates in the blood until it finds a place to lodge, usually the liver, intestines or spleen, but in my case, the brain. Then it breeds and lays its eggs. They do not hatch there, but leave the body through one's excreta and go back into the water, where they develop a flipper to propel themselves to a certain type of snail called the host. Attaching itself to the host, it feeds from the host and develops into a fully sexual bug, and the process begins all over again. Since this insect must have this particular host snail in its development, the associated disease is sometimes called "snail fever." We had seen these snails in the rice paddies, but didn't know they were in league with a killer.

February 11, 1944—Went back to duty. Being round-faced and having a ruddy complexion, I usually look healthy even when I don't feel well. This became my nemesis in prison camp because I was often returned to duty when I was sicker and weaker than I appeared to be. After all, I was starving too.

Sometime toward the end of January or the first part of February, the Japanese had informed our American camp commander that another shipment of Red Cross supplies was on the way. The camp commandant and the senior officer of the army and navy decided that there should be a special committee set up to handle the distribution of these supplies. Making up the committee would be three officers to be selected by the camp commander and the ranking officers of the army and navy, plus eight enlisted men. Since the distribution of anything that valuable was serious business and it was important to avoid any semblance of favoritism, it was decided that the fairest way to select these eight men was by a camp-wide election process.

Bob Dennis was on camp duty at this time, so he was privy to the latest developments in camp and was one of the first to hear of this plan. He already had his own plan pretty well formulated in his mind and was eager to tell me about it. In a nutshell, he wanted me to run for a position so to speak, on the committee, and when he saw me hesitate, he said, " I'll be your campaign manager." I thanked him but sort of dragged my feet. Then he gave me a little snow job about being honest and about how important it would be to have dependable men on the committee. He told me to think it over and let him know after evening tenko. Before we split up to go to our respective barracks, though, he made one final plea that I should run.

During the supper hour and the time remaining before evening roll call, I mulled this new proposition over in my mind. The more I thought about it, the more I realized that I was hard-put to find reasons not to run and there were reasons to give it a try. I began to realize that because of the severe conditions that existed in camp by now, it was imperative that the distribution of Red Cross supplies be as fair and impartial as was humanly possible, and if elected, I would obviously lend my best efforts to achieve that goal. So I decided to allow my name to be submitted and allow the voters to decide.

When we got together after roll call, I told Bob to count me in with one proviso: that nothing derogatory be said about any other candidate. He gave me his word, and I knew he would keep it. Then came the preliminary plans— he would put my name in nomination at our local caucus (the Detached Second Quartermaster) and we would go from there. The person who was successful in the caucus would have his name on the ballot in the primary election.

The caucus was held one evening about a week later. Harley Cromwell and I were the two contenders in that contest. Since he was a technical sergeant and I was only a corporal, I thought the race was already over for me, but when the vote was taken, I had prevailed. Now Bob went into action. Each evening he would seek me out and apprise me of the progress being made in the campaign. He was relishing it. It was serious business around camp, too. After all, the fair distribution of extra-special food for two thousand starving prisoners was at stake. His efforts paid off because when the results were in, I had won in the primary. Next was the general election.

The two high vote-getters from each category were placed opposite each other on the ballot for the general election. My opponent was a Sgt. Simkins, who had been in a unit on Bataan. Again, more campaigning. Simkins and I had a good private talk one evening. We had never met before, but we emerged as very good friends, with a no-animosity pledge.

I was tense the day of the general election. Now that we had gone this far, I didn't want to lose. In addition, it is only natural to want to be approved by one's peers. Everyone whose name appeared on that ballot had already won a fair amount of approval. Now there was one more test. To my great joy and satisfaction, when the results were tallied, I was one of the eight men selected by the entire camp to serve on the Red-Cross committee. The first man to congratulate me was Bob Dennis; the second was Sgt. Simkins.

There is an interesting footnote to this illustration of democracy at work in a prison camp. It illustrates how big an event that election was to us over there. Fay and I were at a reunion of Fifth Air Base prisoners of war at Twin Falls, Idaho, in 1989—forty-five years after the big election. A man whom I had known in Dapecol but was not from my outfit came to that reunion—his first time. We had not seen each other since 1944 because he had survived the sinking of a hell ship later that year and I had gone on to Japan. When he spied me at the gathering that day in 1989, his eyes lit up, and his very first words as he pointed his cane at me were, "I voted for you." Then, and only then, did we get down to visiting and filling in the forty-five-year gap.

The next few entries that come from my notes give a brief chronological account of the distribution: *February 16 and 17, 1944—Red Cross supplies unloaded at Davao. February 22, 1944—I was on detail that went to Davao to load Red Cross supplies on barges. February 23, 1944—Red Cross supplies arrived at Anabogan. February 24, 1944—Last of Red Cross supplies arrive at Dapecol.* After the committee of officers and elected personnel had been fully formed and had its first meeting, we realized what a serious, no-nonsense group of men it was. And the man heading up the group was the epitome of those characteristics—a navy Lt. Commander by the name of Allen McCracken. He was not a large man, but he had a jaunty air about him that seemed to exude confidence. With his neatly trimmed black mustache and quick, piercing eyes, he reminded me of a bantam rooster who wasn't afraid of anything and would be quick to act if necessary. And he was fair to the nth degree.

February 29, 1944—Two boxes of Red Cross supplies issued to each man in camp. I will not go into great detail regarding the distribution, but rather give illustrations of how fairly we approached our job. For instance, when there were not enough items of any one kind to issue one to each man, we would put them in groups or piles to be issued by lottery. This would apply to such items as razor blades, combs, toothbrushes, etc. The same was done for loose cans of food or whatever might have been retrieved from damaged boxes. When doing this, we tried our best to make the piles or groupings of as even a value as possible. When that was not possible, we devised a scheme of making different-value lottery tickets, so that if a man drew something of poor value one time, his next drawing would be for something of better value. In the case of shoes, nine of the hundred-and-twelve crates of shoes listed on the bill of lading had been damaged and four pairs of shoes plus one odd shoe were missing. The remaining shoe was not only the right size, but for the proper foot of a man who had had one foot amputated some months earlier. When it came to partially spoiled cans of meat, a man could exchange a spoiled can for a good one from a supply we had from damaged cartons. The spoiled articles were then turned over to a veterinarian who, in the presence of at least one committee member, would cut away the offensive part and give the rest to the cooks to mix in with the rice. All in all, the committee endeavored to do what was necessary and fair to the very best of its ability. I am proud to say that we did not take one cigarette, one spoonful of powdered milk, one stick of gum to which we were not entitled, the same as every other man in camp. The only unfavorable comment heard was that since there were three different sizes of dippers used to ladle out the rice according to the size ration to which different groups were entitled, those receiving less rice did not receive equal distribution of spoiled scraps.

Lasang

March 2, 1944—Six-hundred-man airport detail left for Lasang. I was among the 600. Former fifty-man driving detail came back from Davao. "Duty," the Japanese doctor said, as I went through the examination line. Two days before he had pronounced me "light duty," as they were trying to put together a six-hundred-man detail to perform heavy-duty building on an airfield. The Japanese doctor was really a pretty nice man. He was sensitive, humane, and at times gave the impression that he almost felt sorry for us. But he had a job to do—find six hundred able-bodied men capable of sustained hard labor to go on this side detail. So they ran us through inspection again, only this time the doctor was accompanied by a superior officer who would question him if he thought the prisoner looked strong enough to work. So my status was changed to "duty."

I was disappointed. I didn't want to go to a strange place, especially not to carve an airport out of the jungle for the Japanese. I was secretly dreaming of building my body back up now that we had Red Cross food to supplement our meager diets. I even dreamed of reversing the dry beriberi that was bothering me more and more. Unlike wet beriberi, which causes grotesque swelling, there is not much visual evidence of dry beriberi. It's the incessant pain and burning, especially of the feet, that causes most of the suffering and loss of sleep. In my case it was the usual "you look good" syndrome that was my nemesis.

I had another symptom that wasn't visible, but nevertheless was a physical deterrent. I seemed to be uncommonly weak in the knees. I had noticed that after my first attack of malaria, I felt drained. That in itself was not uncommon, but it seemed that in this case, I never fully regained my strength, especially in my knees. Within myself, I knew that I had been very sick, and I also thought that I had been returned to duty before I was fully recuperated. Our bodies were also undoubtedly weakened by whatever it was that had elevated our white blood cell counts. (In an article about snail fever, I later read that it is considered one of the most debilitating diseases one can get. Interestingly, my feeling of weakness in my knees never completely left until I had received treatment to kill the schistosomiasis bug in 1949.) At any rate, I didn't feel strong enough to help build an airport, but I looked OK.

When we arrived at the Lasang Airport, we instinctively knew it was a bad situation. The four barracks were of crude construction. Privates were assigned to barracks one and two, officers to barracks three, and noncommissioned officers to barracks four. Thus Sgts. Cromwell and Parry, and I as a corporal, were separated from the other fifteen men from our detachment who were sent to Lasang. Because of the smell and flies emanating from the two latrines, the Japanese moved from near the latrine area to a position between a couple of the American barracks. There was one open well to draw surface water from for bathing and laundry purposes. The kitchen facilities were inadequate, and the food was substandard, even by prison camp standards. We had two chaplains, three doctors, and one dentist, which was a pretty decent complement of professional personnel for that size detail. Our American camp commander was Lt. Col. Rufus Rogers, a soft-spoken, kindly, yet courageous, Texan who had been with the cavalry and had fought on Bataan. The Japanese contingent at Lasang left a lot to be desired, but worst of all, we had inherited Running Wadda, the mean-spirited, hateful interpreter and sometimes self-appointed disciplinarian for whom everyone had developed a strong distaste, with good reason.

One of my first details had to do with filling potholes and performing general repair work on the parking ramp. It was pick-and-shovel work, and any dirt that had to be moved was transported in large baskets by means of a pole passing through the basket handles and resting on the shoulders of two men. The men would sometimes have to carry this heavy load a considerable distance. It was difficult, demeaning work, and it was contrary to the rules of the Geneva Convention governing the work of prisoners of war. We did as little work as possible and worked as slowly as we could. True, the Japanese were not signatories to the Geneva Convention, but America was, and we were American prisoners of war.

Work on the parking ramps had its advantages, though, especially after a rain, when they were soft and spattered with potholes. I don't know what the Geneva Convention says about sabotage, but it is acknowledged as a clandestine activity of war. And out there on the parking ramps, we availed ourselves of every opportunity to commit sabotage. I'm not sure that it had a great deterrent on the Japanese war effort, but it definitely made us feel good. Our first experience at this tactic came one morning when a group of us was asked to help push a couple of fighter planes out of the soft ground at the edge of the ramp. We could easily have pushed the planes to solid ground in a matter of seconds, but rather than do that, we only pretended to push. In the meantime, we poked as many holes in the fabric as we could, while at the same time bending and kinking the wire cables to the tail assembly, hoping to weaken or damage them enough so that they would eventually break in flight. On another occasion, a two-motor transport plane had brought an inspecting general down from Luzon the day before and had parked on the ramp. It had rained during the night, and one wheel in particular had sunk down considerably. At about 9:00 A.M., the pilot went out to warm up the engines prior to takeoff. Seeing the predicament he was in, he asked our guard to have us provide assistance. Again, we did all we could to be counterproductive by holding back while pretending to push, tramping around the mud hole, causing the wheel to sink even deeper, and in no way giving assistance. In the meantime, the Japanese became more and more concerned because a flight of three fighter planes that had gone out on patrol earlier that morning were due in any minute, having used up their range of fuel. The nose of the stuck plane protruded out dangerously close to the path of the incoming planes, so there was cause for much anxiety among the Japanese. Likewise, there was cause for that much more delaying action by the Americans. Finally, the three fighters returned. Recognizing that they had a hazard with which to contend, they circled the field a couple of times, looking things over. When the first one came in, he came in a little kitty-cornered in order to give a wider berth to the stalled plane. In doing so, he ended up slightly off the left side of the runway. By this time, it was easy to see that the two remaining pilots were getting concerned about fuel, as they waggled their wings quite extensively. The second one came in straight, but way too hot, and went clear off the runway and into the jungle at the far end. Seeing this, the third one came in ten or twelve yards short. This would have been all right, except that right at the end of the field the runway dropped off sharply by several feet because it had been built up to provide a more solid base. Unfortunately for this pilot, the wheel slammed into this sharp incline a foot or so below the crest, causing the plane to bounce upward about twenty or thirty feet in a sort of spiraling motion. It came to rest with a loud crash across the field from us, decapitating the pilot, whose head rolled along the edge of the runway. Part of the plane burned. Other parts flew into some Japanese, causing numerous injuries. There were also a few Filipinos doing some clearing in the area, but none of them were injured. Our guards hurriedly marched us back to camp, and as we passed where those wheels had hit the ground, we had to work hard at containing our glee. We had not intended that anyone should get hurt or killed, but sometimes that is part of the package. We had won this round. That was one less plane to shoot at Americans.

For me, the hardest and most disagreeable work at Lasang was the coral detail. Most of the coral that was used to surface the runway came from a small hill of almost solid coral located several miles away from the camp. Our job was to hack the coral out of this hill with pickaxes and then break it into small bits and pieces to be shoveled into the truck and brought to the runway for use on the surface. The coral was white, so it reflected the sunlight right back at us with unusual intensity. Standing there in the hot sun with the temperature usually around 100 degrees anyway and then having the sun bouncing off that white rock as you worked with a pickax or a maul was about as taxing as anything I have ever done. At least in a rice paddy part of the body is either in mud or water. In the coral pit, the only water was the perspiration running off our bodies. To make it even more disagreeable, dust got in our eyes, caked our bodies, and stuck in our nostrils. Adding to our misery were the sharp, jagged edges of the coral. The only thing good about that detail was quitting time.

March 6, 1994—Major Maeda left Dapecol. I learned of this after I returned to Dapecol from Lasang. Another detail that proved to be almost as difficult and disagreeable as the coral detail was one in which we were clearing inroads of the jungle away from the edge of the field, burning the brush and smaller trees and then leveling the ground by carrying the dirt in baskets. There seldom was much, if any, breeze in the tall brush, and there always seemed to be a lot of flies, mosquitoes, and bugs. The more open areas would often be excessively hot as a result of the brush fires that were often burning. One reason I remember this being such a difficult detail is that I became very ill with diarrhea. At first, I thought I could fight it off, and when I did finally go on sick call, I didn't yet have the required 103-degree temperature, so I was denied being put on quarters. That night I made over twenty trips to the latrine.

I went to work in a sort of a daze the next day out on the job; I kept on making trips back in the bush. I told the guards that I was bioki (sick), but they just said, "No, you singoto (work)," so I would try to go through the motions. About 10:00 A.M. Jug, seeing how sick I was, tried to convince the guards I was sick and should be allowed to rest. All he got for his efforts was a good, sound beating. I continued to alternate between a semblance of work and making trips back in the bush.

Mercifully, the noon hour finally came, and with it the chow truck from the main camp with a tub of cooked rice and another tub of some ugly-looking soup. At best, mealtimes were never very pleasant on that detail. There was not much shade to be found anywhere, so we either stood or sat on the ground covered with brush stubble with little or no relief from the sun. Flies swarmed around our food and faces, and different kinds of bugs crawled on us. Then there was always the danger of being bitten by a centipede or a scorpion. I had very little appetite by this time, but I tried to eat a little anyway. That effort was frequently broken up by trips back in the bush. I must have passed out as I was returning from one such trip. All I could recall later was that the sun suddenly turned black. When I came to, Jug was fanning the air around my face and talking to someone. When my mind cleared further, I heard the word "bioki," and then I saw the guards glowering at us. "Bioki, nai" (not sick). My head was swimming, my insides hurt, my rectum felt raw as I lay there for a few moments trying to rally enough strength to get on my feet. After a brief pause, I made an attempt to get up, but I went reeling. Jug caught me before I fell. Just about then, the chow truck was about to return to camp. Jug hollered at them to wait because he wanted to put me on it. This enraged the guard. Jug did not mean to intentionally by-pass the guard's authority; he merely meant to halt the truck before it moved away. A shouting match ensued in which the guard kept saying I wasn't sick, but that I should work, while Jug kept saying I was his "tomadactchi" (friend) and that I was "tak-san bioki" (very sick). When the guard threatened to kill Jug, he told him to take me back to camp first. Things were getting pretty tense by this time, but finally when the guard realized Jug was not going to back down, he uttered what I presumed were some choice Japanese expletives and told the drivers to take me away. Rolling around as I lay on the bed of the truck going over that rough ground was probably the only thing that kept me from passing out again.

March 18, 1944—I was put on quarters with trichinosis dysentery. There were six or eight of us lying on our board beds in the barracks where I lived. In all there must have been thirty or more sick men in camp, some with malaria, but a greater number with dysentery. Jug came to check on me morning and evening. Mac Davis also stopped by once when he heard I was sick. Little did I realize when I saw Jug the morning of the twentieth that I would never see either of them again.

The Lasang detail, along with another detail of 150 men, were put aboard a hell ship on August 20, 1944, for shipment to Japan. On September 7, it was torpedoed and sunk by an American submarine. Those who did not perish immediately had to make it to shore by whatever means they could. Many in the water drowned, and many were gunned down by Japanese in lifeboats. Some were picked up and then used for target practice, as they were forced to jump back in the water again. There were countless tales of heroism and pathos. A case in point: It wasn't until 1993—forty-nine years after the fact—that I heard what had happened to a friend of mine, Jim Light. I was talking with John Playter, one of the survivors, and learned that he came across Light struggling in the water. Playter had a bullet hole in his hip, but Light had a big one in his shoulder and upper body. An artery had been severed, so every time he took a stroke, a stream of blood would shoot out. Playter tried to help Light, but between the two of them, they were getting nowhere, and Light was weakening fast. Realizing the futility of his situation, Light finally said, "There's no way I'm going to make it, and you won't either unless you let me go." So Playter had to watch Light go down. I had first heard of the plight of the Lasang detail a year later in Manila. When Fay and I attended a convention of ex-prisoners of war in Kansas City in 1956, I came across the first survivor I had seen up to that time, Cletis Overton from Arkansas, whom I knew from Dapecol days. From Cletis, I learned that of the 750 men on that ship, there had only been 82 survivors. Each person's account of survival and rescue is a dramatic story in itself. From everything I have been able to determine in the intervening years, the torpedo must have entered the area of the ship where the men in my detachment, and very likely Jug also, were lying. If such be the case, their deaths were instantaneous. Of the seventeen men from my outfit who were assigned to the Lasang detail, I am the sole survivor.

It is dangerous to speculate too deeply into why fate sometimes deals with us in inexplicable ways. We can't help, however, but wonder sometimes as I have in the case of my escaping the tragedy that marked the Lasang detail. It all seems to go back to Col. Rogers. I had not known him prior to going to Lasang, but after we had been there for a while, he began greeting me by name, if we should happen to meet on Company Street or if he happened to see me pass the office on my way to the water spigot. In return, I treated him with the respect that was his due—nothing more, nothing less. But there are times when a person can sense that someone likes or respects you for what you are. Such was the feeling I received from Col. Rogers. Perhaps he sensed my respect for him also. At any rate, I have been unable to figure out any other reason why he selected me along with one other person to return to Dapecol, when the truck could have taken at least twenty men and there were more men who were sick. It is for that reason that when I try to figure out why I should have been one of two to return to Dapecol that day, in good conscience, I have to give all the credit to Col. Rogers. That act saved my life. The sad irony is that he lost his life on a ship that turned out to be a hell ship because it was not properly marked.

March 20, 1944—I was sent back to camp at Dapecol and put in isolation at the hospital. About 9:45 A.M. a messenger came to my bunk with orders to gather up my gear and report to the head office by 10:00 A.M. No reason was given, but Sgt. James Schultz, who was ill also and had a bunk only three spaces from mine, said, "If you have orders to gather up all your gear, that can only mean one thing: you're going back to the main camp." Gathering up my gear only took a couple of minutes, after which I walked over to where Jim lay to bid him good-bye. Something touching happened at that moment that I shall never forget. As he raised up to grasp my hand, there was a tear in his eyes as he said, "Carl, I'm afraid I won't make it back. If you get back, will you bring a greeting and my love to my sister? She is the only one I have left." Then he gave me her name and address. Sadly, Jim did not make it back. He was so young and such a nice person. Unfortunately, of all of the next of kin I have tried to locate and give information to, Jim's sister is the only one I have not succeeded in contacting. I left in such a hurry that I did not write down her name and address. It was also many years before I knew for sure that Jim had not survived.

The truck taking us back to Dapecol was waiting when I got to the front office. To our surprise, there were only two of us going back, although the truck could have taken many more. I have often wondered about this but have decided that the Japanese commander at Lasang would not allow Col. Rogers to reduce his complement of men by any large numbers. Dapecol was not that much to look forward to, but it was great to leave Lasang.

Isolation at Dapecol was aptly named, as it was a building set completely apart from any other building in a rather remote corner of the hospital grounds. The building was shaded by large trees, so it was relatively cool even in the middle of the day. Adding to our comfort was the fact that we slept on canvas cots, instead of on boards, and we had mosquito nets. Wardmen mopped down the wooden floors each day, so it was a pretty plush place to sleep and recuperate as prison accommodations go.

Most of the men in that ward suffered the same affliction, and more cases of a similar nature were brought in while I was a patient there. Not knowing what was causing this malady for sure, these cases were assigned to isolation ward just in case there was a danger of contagion. It was learned later that the cause in a great number of the cases was malnutrition because many recovered once they received proper food and nourishment.

Even though we were isolated, we were kept pretty much up-to-date about goings-on in the camp. That was why concern about the Mactan detail became a topic of conversation in the ward when the train that was supposed to bring the detail back to camp after a hard day of work in the rice paddies failed to show up shortly after 6:00 P.M., its usual time of arrival. Seven o'clock came, then eight o'clock, then nine o'clock. With no telephone line to Mactan or any other form of communication, the whole camp was concerned with what could have happened to the thousand or so men who had been out there since early morning. To make matters worse, a hard tropical rain had been falling for several hours by then. Ten o'clock came and still no detail, but then we began to hear something in the night. It grew louder and louder, and even though the point of origin was several hundred yards away, we could begin to make it out: it was our men singing. And the sound coming through the rain and the blackness of the night became louder still, with an unbridled bravado that set the whole camp cheering. What happened that night is best described by a member of that detail, Kenneth W. Day, past national commander of American Ex-Prisoners of War, who wrote an account of it entitled "Night Train From Mactan," for the *Ex-POW Bulletin.*

> No one knows how or why it happened, but the train wasn't ready for the return trip at 6:00 P.M. Nor did it show up at 7:00 or 8:00. Darkness fell, and the Japs lit bonfires inside the bodego for light. There was no rest, because they decided to count us again. Counting a large group of men is not easy under the best of conditions, and for the Japs it was always doubly difficult. They simply can't count. A thousand half-naked men were formed into long lines which twisted around and around the large floor in the flickering firelight. Half a hundred guards did what they could to keep order and take their count, screaming insanely in Japanese all the while. They never did find out how many prisoners there were.
>
> Finally at about 9:00 P.M., the train came. Utterly exhausted, we climbed on for the long ride back to the barracks. A heavy tropical rain had started, which meant still more trouble. Each of us took off his clothes—maybe a

shirt and a pair of pants for the lucky ones—and rolled them into a tight ball to hold in folded arms. The rain poured down on our naked bodies, but our clothes were kept reasonably dry, to be put on after we got out of the rain.

But the train would not start. Our weight was too much for the little locomotive on the slippery rails. Her drive wheels would spin, but would not grip and pull. So we got off and pushed. When the train picked up a little speed, we got on, and it stopped again. Get off and push, get on and ride, get off and push again. And so it went, for five miserable miles, muscles aching, toes stubbed on the ties, Japs screaming, rain thundering down in the tropic night.

There was a level stretch of track as we approached the compound, and at last we all got to ride. It was still raining, and by now our clothes were wet. It was after 10:00—sixteen hours after we had left for our day's work.

Someone toward the front of the train started singing. It was not a gay song, nor one of the dirty parodies so popular in our camp at the time. It was not an army marching song to lift our spirits, nor a pretty melody to make us forget. Not by a damned sight, mister. It was *God Bless America!*

Swiftly it swept along, car by car, until a thousand throats shouted it in unison. And when we got to the end of the song, we sang it again and again. Major Herman A. Little, boss man of the whole detail, stood near the engine and shouted at us between phrases: "Louder! Louder!"

As the train rolled past the Jap commandant's house, that portly officer stepped out on his porch to see what it was all about. We saw him and sang louder still. Was it to be a riot? Would the guards start shooting? We didn't care one way or the other. At that moment we would have taken on the whole Jap army, as indeed we had once before.

Finally the ride was over, and we were herded through a wide area. It had been an awfully hard day and a terrible ride, but there were some compensations. For the first time in years, we felt like men again. The Japs sensed our ugly desperation and chose to back away. As we passed through the gate, each pair of men was given a coconut.

That incident was a testimony to the indomitable spirit of the American prisoners-of-war and an indication of our determination not to allow our wills to be broken.

March 24, 1944—Vitamin pills, adebrain, cigarettes, and notes found in bodega at Mactan. When the rice detail came in from Mactan that night, there was a mixture of excitement, optimism, and frustration. As the detail had left the train at Mactan that morning to go to the bodega and line up for roll call and assignment to duty, the first two or three men were attracted to a bamboo tube lodged in the corner of a couple of the bodega trusses. What really got their attention was a couple of packages of Lucky Strike cigarettes protruding out of the end of the tube. Naturally, the men dashed over to retrieve the tube. Their fast action got the attention of the guards, who went over there and quickly took it away from them, but not before they noticed that the tube also contained adebrain (used to fight malaria) and, most important, a note. When news of this incident got around camp, there was excitement because it was an unusual development, optimism because it signaled contact from the outside, but frustration because we wanted to know what message the note had for us. Now only the Japanese knew.

I eventually did learn more about the contents of the bamboo tube. About a year after I returned to America, I was back at my old job as clerk in the Siren Post Office. One day, as I momentarily had my back facing the service window, I heard someone say, "Hi, Nordin." I turned, and there facing me was Pease in full uniform with infantry insignia on his lapels and captain's bars on his shoulders. He had been home to visit his family near Cumberland, Wisconsin, which is about thirty miles from Siren, and was on his way to Fort Ord, California. After a few phrases of introductory conversation, he suddenly asked, "Didn't you guys get our 'plant'?" "What 'plant'?" I asked. Then he proceeded to tell me they had placed a bamboo tube in the east bodega at Mactan with cigarettes and adebrain showing to make it noticeable and that contained in the tube were instructions to us regarding their plan to "spring" us after their earlier escape from Dapecol at Mactan. He and Brown had made it to the guerrillas in the Surigao area, although Brown had been pretty badly wounded in a skirmish with the Japanese and had had to be left in the care of some Filipinos while recovering.

At any rate, Pease had received a field commission upon integration into the guerrilla organization on the island of Mindanao. According to him, seventy guerrillas had come back to the Dapecol area, where they had the camp under surveillance in order to establish guard routine and strength. It should be mentioned that surveillance of a cleared area from the cover of the jungle is not difficult. The instructions to us were that, at a given time, we were to seize the guns of the guards at the front gate, kill them and the guards in the towers, and secure their weapons. While that was going on, the guerrillas would have been sneaking up on the main Japanese contingent from their rear. He said the operation was so well planned that it would have been over in a matter of minutes because of the element of surprise and the cooperation of those of us within the camp. When I asked about the sick, he said they had carabao to carry them and friendly Filipino rest houses along the way. When we didn't respond to their signals, they finally had to abandon the plan after over ten days of waiting. Would it have worked? No one knows. Was there actually such a plan? I suppose it is open to question, except for one thing. How did he know about the "plant"? It had been over six months since he had escaped from Dapecol. Yet he described the location, contents, and time.

March 27, 1944—Escape of seven men on the fence detail. Coming so close on the heels of the discovery of the plant at the bodega in Mactan, I could imagine that the Japanese might have thought there was some collusion between these seven escapees and guerrillas in the near vicinity. There is no evidence, however, to support that conjecture.

After the war it was learned that there were two groups of men who had been giving some thought to escaping, each group making its plans with no knowledge that the other group existed until the last moment. The night before the escape a man from one group confronted a man from the other group, saying that the men in his group were planning to pull off their escape the next day. He told the other man that he knew of his plans, but to forget about them and join his group. The second man, Captain Wohlfield, left the latrine in consternation but decided that if secrets were no better kept than that in his own group, he had better take advantage of this opportunity and go with the other group, allegedly led by Lieutenant Hadley Watson.

At roll call the next morning, Wohlfield found out that there were eleven men in the group and that it comprised the entire fence detail. The first break period that morning was used in formulating plans, but there was already dissension within of the group, so there was complete lack of coordination.

With no further planning, Wohlfield, Watson, and a man named Carmichael, spying an apple tree at the edge of the jungle, decided that this was the ruse they would use to make good their escape. Obtaining permission from the guards to get themselves and the guards a treat, they convinced the guards that they would need a shovel to knock the fruit to the ground. When they got to the tree, Watson knocked the guard unconscious with the shovel, took his gun and shot the other guard who was between him and the fence, and then disappeared into the jungle.

The three remaining guards had emptied their clips shooting into the jungle where all the commotion was, so Wohlfield and Carmichael were busy fighting off these guards with shovels and the butts of guns that they had managed to wrest away from them. In the melee that followed, guards from nearby details also began firing, but to little avail.

In the wake of the whole wild affair, three officers failed to escape, five guards were either dead or wounded, and of the eight men who escaped into the jungle, one was caught and killed the next day and one remained unaccounted for. The remaining six eventually got to guerrilla headquarters and fought again in various parts of Mindanao, Leyte, and Luzon; Wohlfield even went Japan with the army of occupation. But their trek through the jungle to safety had been long, lonely, and dangerous. They had been fortunate to make it at all with so bad a start and so little planning.

As usual in the case of every escape, rations were cut again in camp, and the guards became jumpier.

March 31, 1944—I was moved from isolation to the main ward at the hospital. April 1, 1944—I was moved from the hospital to barracks #8. Although I was still very weak from the siege of severe diarrhea of the previous two weeks, there were those who needed closer supervision than I did at this stage, so I was sent back to quarters to regain my strength. On sick rations, which were further reduced after the last escape, gaining any weight would be a slow process, but it was good to be out of the hospital and back in the mainstream of camp life with some of my buddies whom I had left behind when I had

Area in back corner of Dapecol where some POWs had gardens. Photo by Glenn Nordin.

gone to Lasang. I soon found out, though, that in that group of men who had gone to Lasang lay the majority of my friends and my unit, men with whom I had worked on one detail or another. We had been the strong ones, the work force, the regulars. I found that I missed them. I'm glad that I didn't know then that I would never see them again.

There was another advantage to being back in the barracks; I could now return to tending my long-neglected garden. It wasn't all that much, but it served a couple of useful purposes. It gave me something to do that helped take my mind off the hopelessness that was so evident all around me. In addition, it added a little to my diet. The little plot of ground that I had staked out as mine was only about 8' by 10' and supported only two or three plants of Chinese cabbage and a couple of hot pepper bushes, one red and one green. We never could figure out the thinking of the Japanese. They were so opposed to having us bring in any kind of food most of the time, but they encouraged us to have garden plots and they even allowed a few seeds to be sold at occasional commissary privileges. Another strange phenomenon was that there were cases of stealing in camp (as in the case of my missing T-shirt), but it seemed that a man's garden plot was inviolate.

So I went about my gardening. I had worked it up with a stick at first, and then I prepared it for planting by further breaking up the soil with my mess spoon. The Chinese cabbage provided me with a few somewhat sweet-tasting greens, and I used the peppers to make a hot sauce to pour on my rice for a little flavor. Somewhere I had found an old pop bottle, which I used for my hot sauce. It got pretty hot after it cured for a while; in fact it was almost rank, but it gave the rice a flavor all its own. It also helped me to forget about the worms in the rice. They were the same color as the rice except for a little black head at the tip. When they first started to show up in our rations, we picked them out and discarded them. When we realized how much we were throwing away of each meal and that these worms were the closest thing to protein in our diets, we just pretended that they weren't there. With the small amount of rice that we were getting by that time, we couldn't afford to throw anything away.

April 2, 1944—A new Japanese major came to take command. Four days after the new major arrived, the remains of one man who escaped and was shot by guards were brought in and buried. These were very likely the remains of navy officer Boone.

April 8, 1944—One box of Red Cross chow and one and one-half packages of Lucky Strike cigarettes were issued to each man in Dapecol. The committee had thought that everyone would be better served by spreading distribution of the Red Cross supplies out over a period of time rather than putting them out all at once. This system helped to prevent the men from gorging themselves, thus depriving themselves of the maximum benefit to be obtained from the food. The supplies had been securely locked in a warehouse during the interim.

Last Days at Dapecol

It wasn't that I was letting myself go. I was keeping myself as clean as I was able to under the circumstances and with the facilities available. It's just that there was another infestation of pubic lice. About the time I discovered that I was infected, I began to hear of others who were going on sick call for blue ointment, so I decided to go right away in case there was a run on it. To my dismay, I got the same verdict I had received a couple of years earlier at Camp Casising. "Sorry, too much pubic hair. It would take more than we can spare." Whereupon, I explained my experience with the distillate the last time I was afflicted and showed the doctor the scars of the resultant burns. He understood and sympathized with me, but the verdict was still the same. Then we struck a deal. He promised that if I would somehow rid myself of that hair, he would let me have some blue ointment.

Since Easter was coming up, I had planned on getting a haircut for the occasion anyway, so a plan began formulating in my mind. When the barber had finished cutting all the hair off my head, I prevailed on him to let me borrow his hand-operated clippers for a little while. So I found a spot in back of the barracks that was semiprivate, and went to work. I struggled and scrunched and did about everything but stand on my head before I realized that it wasn't going to be that easy after all. About that time I spied Bill Lowe, an easygoing and accommodating sort of fellow, so I thought, "Why not ask him?" After all, hadn't I shared cigarettes with him when tobacco was short at the plantation on Mt. Apo, even if it was only one-sixth of a cigarette at a time? In my desperation I thought, "Sure, he owes me one."

After I explained my predicament to him, he said, "Sure, no problem, but we've got to find a spot where I can get underneath you." There happened to be an old drainage ditch that was several feet deep and quite narrow in another part of the compound, so I straddled that ditch, and Bill went to work with that hand clipper—ever so carefully. Finally, after a few minutes of carefully working the angles, he stuck his head out from under the canopy of my crotch and looking up at me, he said, in all seriousness, "You know, Nordin, only a buddy would do this." It's funny now, and we have laughed about it on many occasions since, but at that time it was a serious situation and was treated as such. He had given his full attention to the task, except for that one moment of realization that it was beyond the ordinary.

When the task was completed, I took the clippers down to the mess hall, dipped my canteen cup into the cauldron of scalding hot water, and used that water to thoroughly clean the clippers before returning them to the barber. Then I went to the doctor and got the blue ointment treatment. Now I was truly ready for Easter.

April 9, 1944—Easter Sunday. I attended sunrise services and took communion in the evening. This was the least auspicious Easter service I have ever attended in my entire life, but at the same time, the most meaningful.

More than a hundred men began gathering in the predawn darkness at a designated area between the barracks and the latrines. The scene looked almost eerie in the partial light given off by security lights in the distance. The service had been announced as an ecumenical one, so there were buddies gathering there with whom I had not worshipped before. For several minutes, you could hear the men, many of whom were lame, crippled, or sick as they shuffled into place. Some were able to sit on the grass, which was damp with dew, or on their haunches. Others stood. As it began to get light, you could put faces on the forms. Some had shirts and slacks or shorts. Some were clad in a G-string and a jacket. Some just in a G-string. Some had shoes; some were barefoot or wore clogs. But all were there because they wanted to be. They had spiritual needs that had to be met. They wanted and needed to hear again the Christian message of hope.

As the sun began to crowd out the darkness of the camp, we could see a makeshift altar and several chaplains. The service began with the singing of some familiar gospel songs and Easter hymns. I don't recall now who preached or what specific text or texts were used. That is relatively unimportant. What I do recall is that the message of hope and promise which we received that Easter morning left us with a warm feeling inside, a feeling we had not experienced in a long, long time. As the benediction was pronounced and the group dispersed, there were smiles, handshakes, "Happy Easter" greetings, and a light in men's eyes that had been absent for months. It was a truly memorable occasion.

That evening we gathered again for a short communion service. The Japanese had relented and had allowed a group of chaplains a little wine, which was much watered-down in order to make it go around. For the communion, they used a few particles of burned rice from the kitchen. I understand some groups or denominations had communion occasionally, but Easter of 1944 was the only time I was able to avail myself of that sacrament in the entire time I was a prisoner of war. It had been a joyous Easter.

April 17, 1944—Went to duty. Moved to Barracks #9. After a couple of days on some of the easier details, I was sent out to Mactan again. But this was not too disagreeable, as it was harvest time and the paddies were drained. Cutting the rice stalks by hand with sickles was back-breaking work. So was carrying it away with large baskets slung from poles between two men. It

The railroad to Mactan, an area of jungle and rice paddies. Photo by Glenn Nordin.

seemed good to be walking on dry ground at Mactan, however. The one big danger was snakes. There would be a couple every day that caused a few moments of excitement as the guys went after them with their sickles. Whenever that happened, there would be a snake on someone's quan fire that night. Harvesting at Mactan was always a complete operation, as they had their own threshing machine.

Except for the hard work, going out to Mactan on the little narrow-gauge railroad was interesting, especially in the early morning. As the train moved through the jungle, we could see the various creatures springing to life at the dawn of a new day. Colorful wild chickens would take off and fly for a quarter of a mile or more sometimes. Whereas domestic chickens can usually only fly to their roosts, their jungle counterparts can fly significant distances. There were many other colorful and noisy birds interrupting the silence as we moved along. And of course, the antics of the ever-present monkeys were always fun to observe—mothers clutching their young as the steel monster approached and the male glowering down at us as he stood guard. On the ground, and sometimes on the trunks of trees, we would occasionally see large iguanas. The largest one I ever saw measured close to three feet from nose to tip of tail. (Lots of good meat there.) Mornings on the way to Mactan would remind me of the fresh early spring mornings on the farm back in

Wisconsin, as creation seemed to come to life anew, only in the jungle it was even more interesting and refreshing.

Just as days in the jungle often have a spectacular beginning, so also do the evenings. As soon as the benediction of the day is over, with the last direct rays of the setting sun fading into the brief twilight that is characteristic of the tropics, the night life begins with the quiet yet pervasive phenomenon of fruit bats.

Without warning, the sky will suddenly be filled with them—giant bats with wingspans up to three feet and more quietly winging their way to their feeding area in some other area of the jungle. They would fly at an altitude of no more than fifty or sixty feet. There would be hundreds of them, so many that they seemed to fill the whole sky. It was impossible to see either the beginning or the end of the flight. How long they remained at their feeding grounds or when they returned to their nesting area, I do not know. I did not make a study of their habits, but as I recall, there were certain seasons when we would see them every night. I do know though, that during the nearly three years I was in the tropics, it was only in the jungle area of southern Mindanao that I witnessed this unusual phenomenon.

April 23, 1944—Odds and ends of Red Cross chow raffled. The items raffled off were from broken boxes or any items for which distribution had not come out evenly, items such as extra cans of food, miscellaneous toilet articles, and chewing gum. Attention was given to the relative value of the article in arranging the raffle. It amounted to about as fair a way as possible to handle the situation.

May 20, 1944—Major Harrison went jurmantado and took a guard's gun away in the scuffle. It happened on the rope-making detail in the forenoon. Even though this detail worked in a large shed just inside the compound and next to the main gate, we didn't learn much of the particulars until after the detail was released late in the afternoon. We knew there was a lot of commotion and screaming, followed by a bunch of other guards dashing in with bayonets fixed. Major Harrison had suddenly grabbed the lone soldier guarding the detail and began beating him on the head with an iron pipe. Then he grabbed the guard's gun in an attempt to shoot him, but the hammer of the gun just clicked. He had been guarding with an empty gun. When that went awry, the major dashed into the barracks.

When help arrived to aid the stricken guard, one of the first things the Japanese did was to beat the detail leader (their usual pattern). The next several hours were spent beating the detail leader and questioning the rest of the detail privately, one by one. By midafternoon, the Japanese were convinced that Major Harrison had acted solely on his own. The detail was then released to the compound.

Major Harrison was put in the guard house, which was close enough to the compound that we could hear his screams as he was being beaten and tortured. The further progress of his fate and those close to him is documented in the notes I wrote on May 23.

The "X" marks the spot where a POW was shot at for getting too close to the fence behind the latrine. Photo by Glenn Nordin.

May 22, 1944—The Japanese guard in the guard tower took a shot at Private Grossman for being too close to the fence. On this particular occasion, there were about six or seven of us out for an afternoon stroll. We were walking between the back of the latrines and the fence on the back side of the compound. Earlier we had discovered that an edible weed grew in places back there, so we were looking for some afternoon lunch, as it were. Suddenly a shot rang out. Grossman had spied a plant rather close to the fence, and without remembering that we were not supposed to get closer than one meter from the fence, he tried to get it. The Japanese were good enforcers of the rules. It was also further evidence of how jumpy they had become in the wake of the escape of the fence detail and Major Harrison's sudden burst of violence.

May 23, 1944—Lt. Col. Olson (our camp commander) and other men close to Major Harrison were put in the guardhouse. Whether it be a detail leader or a camp commander, according to the Japanese way of thinking, the person in authority must share in the responsibility, and often the punishment as well, for any infraction of the rules committed by persons under him. For that reason, it was not surprising that Col. Olson was taken into custody and punished for a crime he did not commit. Probably because Major Harrison's actions were so bizarre and because he ran back into the barracks after trying to kill the guard, the Japanese continued to suspect collusion on the part of those around him. At any rate, we couldn't help but feel sorry for those innocent men who had to suffer for what seemed to be just a foolish act.

May 24, 1944—Dysentery smear. Up until this time, I had been making entries in the diary I had begun in 1942 at Camp Casising. Because of the paper shortage, the entries had grown further and further apart until finally there was no more paper to be had. I continued to have an inner desire to keep some kind of record, so I devised a little notebook using cigarette packs and liners in lieu of regular paper.

The second diary differs from the first in several ways. In the first diary, I began by making daily entries until I realized that it was not feasible because of the lack of paper. When the entries were less than daily, I endeavored for a long time to make them at regular intervals, at least for as long as was practicable. In the second diary, entries were made primarily as I was able to, depending on time available, circumstances, and opportunity. Another big difference between the two was that in the first diary, I had not only recorded some of the things that went on in camp that it was best that the Japanese did not know, but also our thoughts and impressions of them and their actions. This type of comment was too incriminating to take further chances on, so such comments do not appear in the abbreviated diary. It was written in such a manner, however, that I was able to hide some of these things between the lines.

Finally, I should explain that because of extenuating circumstances, the diary may not be well composed in places, and sentence structure and grammar may leave a lot to be desired. It is, nevertheless, a diary of an unusual experience.

May 28, 1944

Paper is so scarce around here that I couldn't get any more to put in my regular diary, which has necessitated my making this notebook of empty cigarette packs. In fact, paper is so scarce that we have been using toilet paper for cigarette papers for months. About once each two months, the Nips issue enough coarse cigarette paper for two cigarettes. This has been an eventful week. Monday a Nip on compound guard took a shot at Blackie Grossman for gathering kang kong back of #3 latrine. (Tuesday. The Nips took all of Major Harrison's stuff to their headquarters.) He is gone now, they say to Davao. They also put Lt. Col. Olson, C.O., and Major Harrison's barracks leader, bay leader, and detail leader in the guardhouse. Friday all available men in camp were turned out to weed a camote field. We finished in the A.M.—Saturday A.M. I was on a detail getting squash and unloading it in Bodega #2. Very few details go out in the P.M. anymore. No one but special duty men work more than one-half day at a time and then only about two times a week. Lt. Col. Stubbs is camp commander in Olson's place, and he has adopted system whereby the e.m. (enlisted men) furnish all the men for detail until two hundred men have been used and then the officers do likewise. I finished reading *Gone with the Wind* last week. Before that I read *Mother* by Pearl S. Buck. [There had been a small library at Dapecol for the Filipino prisoners, and some books were added by the Americans.] For some time the rate of malaria cases has been very low. It seems that various forms of paralysis and insanity prevail now. Our chow has been drastically reduced since Major Harrison went jurmantado. An average day's menu is 1) rice, salt, or sometimes sugar. 2) rice, tea, and salt. 3) cassava and squash pudding. Sometimes we get a little kang kong or telinium soup, or a little fish. And of course, whatever we get is in small quantity. [Although the cooks used the same containers as before in giving out the rice, by now they were extremely loosely packed.] Re: salt. Though taken away after the first escape, it was restored periodically after a year or so. What little food we can raise in our gardens comes in mighty handy nowadays. Don't know where the rumors come from these days, since we are so isolated, but rumor is that Pelau fell and that there has been some kind of air activity on Luzon. Our activity around here decreased a little! Dear God, how I wish I were a free American again!

June 4, 1944 (Sunday)

The officers who were held responsible for Major Harrison's misdemeanor were released from the guard house last Sunday P.M. Major Harrison was taken to Davao shortly after the incident. About four days ago, the Nips told us that he died of his wounds. Last Thursday a survey was held of all men who were on the list that were inspected for dysentery, in other words, those not on the hospital or bioki (sick) list were surveyed. My name, along with some others was taken off because of my recent dysentery case. However, another survey was held today of those of us who had been taken off. I was put back on the list of well or working men. Everything indicates were are all leaving soon. I think we will be separated from the sick and the officers, except for what few officers we have in charge. Lt. Yukki told Sgt. Roeske the other day we would go to a higher elevation, and that there were asphalt roads there. I have a hunch it will be Japan or that vicinity. I worked Wednesday P.M. and Thursday A.M. gathering gabi. The Nips are stripping the fields. Chow has been very poor and skimpy, but there has been a little improvement the last couple of days. We got fish once and carabao once last week. There is carabao in the kitchen now. Some of the boys killed a dog Memorial Night and cooked him up the next day, so we had dog meat for several meals. It's a cross between mutton and pork. It's surprising what a person will do when he's hungry. Right after evening roll call, Blackie Harrison, our bay leader, hurriedly got the eight in our bay together. He was unusually excited as he said, "We're going to knock off a dog tonight. Meet me in the bay in five minutes. I've got it all planned—I've already got the dog!" When we met, sure enough the dog was already tied to a post underneath the barracks, and alongside it was the big rock he was going to use to kill it. Not only that, he had already borrowed a quan stove and a couple of knives fashioned from hacksaw blades. Then came the assignment of duties—someone to carry water, another to see that we had charcoal brought from the kitchen in a mess kit periodically, one to take the entrails to the latrine, guards for the front and rear of the barracks to alert everyone when the Japanese guards approached on their rounds. I was assigned to watch the back of the barracks. Then of course, there were the technicians. One guy to pump the bellows of the quan stove, and the main guy—the butcher/cook. Blackie took charge of that. Shortly after lights out, we two guards gave the all-clear sign, and the crew went to work. Blackie did a perfect job with the rock. There wasn't one sound from the dog. We knew that by starting when we did, we would have at least thirty minutes before any Japanese guards came around. Then by the time he came around again, there would have been time to finish butchering and get the entrails out to the latrine. It all worked perfectly—water and charcoal were supplied as needed, and in the thirty-inch space under the barracks, the main crew was hard at work. One time after the guard had passed my station, I went to the scene of action to observe and to relieve the guy pumping the bellows for a few minutes. It was a clandestine scene I will never forget. By about 3:00 A.M. or so, we got the word that it was ready for sampling. We spent the next thirty or forty minutes feasting ourselves before grabbing about three hours of sleep. To our knowledge, not a person other than those who participated knew until afterward what had transpired in the shadows under the middle of the barracks that night....

Stoudt smuggled in some gabi and camotes the other day, so one way or another, we've gotten by pretty well this week. They have started giving out garbage to a barracks at a time, so the men can pick out whatever is edible in it. Our barracks got it yesterday. Our bay (nine men) got enough out of our share for one gallon of cooked cassava. Things are coming to a pretty pass. On top of that, there is no more tobacco in the PX and a lot of men are completely out. We drew our last month's pay yesterday. I drew fifteen centavos (7½ cents). We wrote cards home Friday and signed them Saturday. I told my folks to send food if they had a chance. Rumors: the Balkan situation is tense. Turkey and Bulgaria are on the verge of going in with the allies. The allies bombed islands in the Marshall and Gilbert group. Allied front in China extends into Indochina.

Just as cigarettes seem to curb your appetite, so too did they help ease the pangs of hunger, which was a major factor at that time. Any smoker or ex-smoker also knows that there is a certain amount of pleasure or satisfaction obtained from smoking, health factors notwithstanding. Happily, it's been forty years since I kicked the habit, but at that time and under those circumstances tobacco was important to me for the reasons just mentioned, and since I was a light smoker, the surplus over what I used gave me food-purchasing power.

What happened next at Dapecol is difficult to describe. When we were told at evening roll call that we must be ready bright and early the next morning to leave Dapecol for good, it was as if a completely new mood—almost a holiday mood—swept over the camp. It had been our home for so long, and we had changed so much, that there was a certain nostalgia, not caught in the diary account, that seemed to pervade at first. Then when we finally realized that we were getting out of that suffocating jungle complex and that we were more or less free to make the most of all that remained, we turned to the task at hand with reckless abandon. Camp fires for cooking purposes, quan stoves for the same purpose went all night. Our barracks leader had a big dog that he had been saving because she was pregnant; he had hoped to increase the dog population, but now she had to go. One excessively hungry man retrieved a couple of those unborn pups from the latrine, cleaned them up, butchered them, and then cooked them. Any plant around that could be cooked was pulled and cooked. I have rarely seen such release as happened that night.

June 5, 1944 (Monday)

We were notified at evening tenko that the entire camp was leaving: one group was to leave by 3:00 A.M. and the other one-half of the camp was to leave by 7:30 A.M. I was in the first group. That night, everyone was busy packing; cooking up everything in the gardens and camotes, cassava, and squash that would be left over in the kitchen. Some fellows killed dogs, cats, day-old puppies, and cooked them up. So everyone got good and full before they left.

The Japanese also turned over some mail to be distributed before we left. Those of us who did not receive mail at that time were assured there would be a major distribution of mail and personal packages when we arrived in Manila. Feeling quite confident that I would then receive the backlog of mail I should have received over the last two years or more, I lost myself in the euphoria of the evening. After all, I could wait a little longer.

Hell Ships

Be still and know that I am God.
—Psalms 46:10

Few things have been more aptly named than the infamous hell ships that transported thousands of prisoners to their watery graves and a few hundred of us, who survived the terrible ordeal, to even worse prison camps in the Japanese home islands, Formosa, Korea, or Manchuria. There we were forced to do slave labor with the most meager of rations, endure beatings, and often suffer torture.

The ships themselves were hardly fit for human cargo. Over a thousand of us were jammed in one hold of the ship. In order to accommodate that many men, they had built tiers out of lumber, but they were so close together that one could not sit up straight. Neither did we have room to stretch out full-length when lying down. Those who did not get a spot on a wooden tier had to lie on the steel deck. There were a few "benjo seats" built over the side of the open top deck of the ship. But we could only use those when the Japanese allowed us on deck; the rest of the time we had to use five-gallon buckets placed near the bulkheads of the hold. Of course, for that many men, they were woefully inadequate, especially with so much diarrhea among the men. In rough weather, they would slosh over, so after a while the deck was covered with feces. To add to the misery, too often for a half day or more at a time, the lights were not on, so men would stumble, fall, or step on someone as they tried to get to the latrine can. Many times they did not get there in time. Because of submarine activity, we usually only traveled during daylight hours, staying quite close to shore and dropping anchor in some cove or little harbor during the night. Since there would be no breeze when we lay at anchor, the heat and stench would be almost unbearable at times. As time went on, patience wore thin, tempers often flared, some went insane, and others died. When a man began yelling and screaming in his madness, it became incumbent on those next to him to silence him, no matter if it meant knocking him out. Otherwise, we were all in danger of being sprayed with gunfire or having a grenade dropped into the hold by the guards. Almost all of those who died were buried at sea. We had no ordained or commissioned officer chaplain, so a brief service or a few prayers would be said, oftentimes by an enlisted man. I recall one instance when several men prevailed on me to take charge of a service because the same man had been volunteering time after time. When we had divided the dead man's clothes and other effects among the most needy, we hoisted the body, wrapped in one of his blankets, up to the topside. There we found a piece of steel for ballast and wrapped it in with the body as tightly as we could. Then with two men holding the body, we moved over to the rail where I was going to quote a verse or two of scripture and say a prayer before we threw him over the side. Just as I was about to begin, the man who had been volunteering so many times stepped from behind a winch and took over. Since the guards had been kind enough to allow us to have a brief service, it was no time for argument, so I just let him take over, as I stood there in amazement. Since we weren't always aware of people dying, especially if it happened in another part of the hold or in the night, I do not know how many died on that voyage, but I do know that we did try to give them a decent burial.

These are some of the things I thought it best not to mention in my diary should the Japanese find it, but they are so clearly etched in my mind that I doubt I will ever forget them. As someone else once commented about the hell ships, "Instead of a place, hell seemed more like a condition."

June 6, 1944 (Tuesday)

At 1:30 A.M. we had a big meal of soft rice, salt, squash with carabao in it, sorghum, B-1 (rice polishing). After that, we got a full mess kit of rice and salt for noon lunch. Toward morning we were taken out of the gate and loaded in trucks (thirty men to a truck). They certainly didn't take any chances, as we were forced to remove our shoes and socks, and then we were blindfolded and then tied one to another with ropes which were tied to the sides of the truck, and then we were forced to sit down or kneel and keep absolutely quiet. What a rugged trip that was! After we got out of the jungle, we were allowed to stand up. By looking out the corner of our eyes, some of us were able to see guards all along the road. [Could the note that Pease and Brown left for us that was recovered by the Japanese have had anything to do with these elaborate precautions?] At Banawan, we loaded a few barges, ate our lunch, got on the barges, and were then loaded on a boat. It was a small freighter, and the whole camp was put in the forward holds, bag and baggage included. It was as bad as the proverbial slave ships. Included were the sick, the paralytics, and the insane. Water was limited, many men had diarrhea, and there were few toilets. We were terribly crowded, it was hot as hell, and we got two meals of rice and squash and camote soup with a little pork in it per day, so it was a rugged trip. [The soup we were given was made with the vines only, not the camotes themselves, which resemble sweet potatoes. It is a bitter soup.]

June 8, 1944 (Thursday)

We were issued our fourth and last box of Red-Cross chow and given orders to eat it while we were on the boat because they wouldn't transport it for us, so everyone ate heartily. While lying in the harbor, we were given the opportunity to swim twice. While in Davao, we saw a Nip bomber crack up and explode when landing. Diarrhea kept getting worse. I was lucky to get a spot near a porthole. [Being near a porthole offered two advantages. I was up on the wooden tier rather than on the steel deck. And it was nice to have some light and be able to see out.]

June 12, 1944 (Monday)

Left Davao about 4:30 A.M. Beautiful trip going out Davao Gulf. We entered the Celebes Sea. Our convoy consisted of four merchant men and three sub chasers. Stayed close to land and had an escort constantly. The southern part of Mindanao is rugged and extremely wild. Anchored overnight in Sarangani Bay.

June 13, 1944 (Tuesday)

Crossed the Moro Gulf. Catobato Valley was beautiful. Anchored in Catobato Bay near Parang (one of the invasion points) overnight.

June 14, 1944 (Wednesday)

Entered Basilan Straits and arrived at Zamboanga toward evening. It is a beautiful little city. Weather hot, water short, and diarrhea bad aboard ship. Stayed here overnight.

June 15, 1944 (Thursday)

About 12:30 A.M., we were suddenly awakened by lots of shooting. It was found that Col. McGee went over the side and very likely was aided by Moros in bancas in his escape. Everyone was forced to stay below decks. It was hot, crowded, and tension was high, making it a veritable nightmare. Left Zamboanga about 8:30 A.M. We were allowed on deck during the day, but had to stay away from the rail. Still traveling close to land. About 9:00 P.M. we were awakened by shooting from our boat and the one behind us. It sounded like a young war. It was learned that Lt. Wills had gone overboard. During one burst of gunfire we heard him scream. We were about five miles from land, so it is doubtful that he made it. Another hectic night below decks with excited guards.

After the war, we learned that Col. McGee had made arrangements to have an officer friend throw McGee's barracks bag over one side of the ship. As it hit the water, Japanese guards began shooting at it, figuring the splash was caused by someone jumping off the ship. While the ensuing melee was occurring, McGee jumped unnoticed from the other side. He was able to get safely to shore and through the Japanese garrison, and he eventually became a leader in the guerrilla organization. Three months later, when survivors of the ill-fated Lasang detail reached land after their hell ship was torpedoed and sunk off the western coast of Mindanao, it was Col. McGee who rounded them up and arranged for a submarine to bring them secretly to Australia and safety. Similarly, many years later, we learned that Lt. Wills made it safely to shore, and he too spent the rest of the war fighting the Japanese with the guerrillas. Interestingly, he had been the librarian at Dapecol, and it was to him I had returned *Gone With the Wind* only days before we had left Dapecol.

Xxxx xx, xxxx

Left Mindanao, crossed some open water and skirted along Panay and then Cebu. We were allowed above decks to get chow and go to the latrine. Arrived at Cebu City in the evening. Quite a different arrival than that of two-and-a-half years before. Have seen lots of ships in every harbor and several convoys—all escorted by air and naval craft.

June 17, 1944 (Saturday)

We were taken off the ship and put in Fort San Pedro (former USAFFE headquarters). All except the sick had to stay on the ground. We were here four days and nights. It rained two of the nights, making it very miserable. As a result a bad cold epidemic started. Working details went out the last three days to unload and load boats. Our baggage was transferred to a large freighter, formerly a German boat. Working men were given three meals a day and a chance to take a bath.

About fifteen or twenty of us were able to find a spot on a large rock pile where we could bed down. It was very uncomfortable, but at least it was dry. Merrill Forsythe and I had been sharing our Red Cross food. First we would split a can of his corned beef, and the next day it would be one of mine. We were down to one four-ounce can of butter, which I had hidden among the rocks before going out on detail. When I went to retrieve it for supper that night, it was gone. Someone had found the hiding place and had stolen it. We were devastated over this loss of four ounces of butter.

Several items about the next phase of our trip stand out very clearly in my mind. First of all, this second ship had not been converted for carrying prisoners with tiers and other installations. It appeared to have been pressed into service on short notice, so we were forced to bunk down in whatever nook or cranny we could find. I happened to end up on a ledge next to a man named Fox. I had known him at Dapecol, but our acquaintance up to that point had been mostly casual. By the time we reached Manila, we had learned to know each other very well, and a mutual respect had developed between us. Fox was a Jew, devout in his faith, and he knew I was more than a nominal Christian. During long hours of serious conversation, I learned more about the Diaspora (the scattering of the Jews), their ancient struggle as a people without a homeland, and their frequent persecution. I was particularly impressed with his knowledge of his own forbears and their wanderings through the centuries, plus the strong conviction of his faith. Of course, we talked of the Messiah and our respective interpretations regarding who He is. Fox respected my beliefs and even hinted that if he became as convinced on that point as I was, then he too would espouse Christianity. Our conversations made our Judeo-Christian heritage more relevant to me. One thing we did agree on was that if the world could live according to the principles of our respective faiths, we wouldn't be where we found ourselves at that point in time.

Late one afternoon, as Fox and I were engaged in conversation, we heard a terrible commotion just below us. Then we saw a couple of men struggling as they were assisting a third man up the ladder to get some air because he was terribly ill with dysentery and the heat in the hold was stifling. He was practically naked, as he was unable to care for himself properly. Even as they were trying to assist him up the ladder, excreta leaked from his body. Then our eyes met, and I saw it was Lt. Wedin of Minneapolis, Minnesota. When he recognized me, his eyes gave a look as if to say, "Please help me—I'm so sick," but all he could do was moan. He and I had become acquainted at Dapecol, and since we lived only about eighty miles apart, we often talked about things back home. For one thing, I had learned that he lived practically next door to an aunt of mine. They finally did get him up on deck, but he died before morning. Since we were nearing Manila, our ranking officers prevailed upon the Japanese to agree to take him ashore and bury him at Bilibid Prison. A problem arose, however, when for some reason the ship dropped anchor outside the harbor. As the hours passed with the corpse out in the hot sun, it began to get ripe pretty fast. Finally, though, we did pull into the pier, and the second leg of our journey was over. Coincidentally, after the war was over and I was visiting my aunt in Minneapolis, she said, "How good it is to see you come back safely from prison camp. Just the other day I was talking over the backyard fence with neighbor lady, and she told me that she had just been notified that her son, Lt. Wedin, had died on a prison ship."

The Japanese lined us up in a column of fours and marched us from the pier through the streets of Manila. What a spectacle. What a ragged, motley, dirty bunch of men we were. So completely opposite to the young, virile men in clean, neatly pressed uniforms and spit-shined shoes they had seen two-and-a-half years ago. As we dragged along in loose formation, we could only wonder what the Filipinos thought of us now. We had lost their war and look at us now. Then we heard the answer. They were not allowed to speak to us, but all of a sudden from an upstairs window came the words of a song that was popular in the 1940s. Some brave soul was playing the record "There's a Great Day Coming Mañana" (tomorrow). What a day-brightener!

The greetings as we marched in the gate at Bilibid Prison were indicative of our condition and what was uppermost on our minds. Many of the men who had come to Dapecol from Cabantuan were meeting old friends again whom they had not seen since they were split up two years earlier. Instead of greeting them by name and asking how they were, the question from the men coming in was Invariably, "Hi, how's the chow?" And the answer was just as invariable: "Lousy."

Not too long after our arrival at Bilibid, we had to spread all of our personal gear and personal belongings out on the ground for the dreaded shakedown inspection. Early on, however, a friend of mine (who was almost as concerned as I was about my big diary) told me he knew of an officer in Bilibid who had completed the manuscript for a book but was concerned about it being discovered also. At any rate, this friend, Frank (Shavey) Peoples, said if he could have my diary right then, he and a guy he knew could keep it from inspection, so I gave it to him. It worked. After the inspection, we found a large bamboo tube, put the diary and the book manuscript in the tube, and wrapped it very well with a piece of canvas shelter half that was left over from someone who had died. Then "Shavey" went to the kitchen and heated some paraffin wax and sealed it all up. Then we went way under the center of the main prison building and buried it. We figured that the wooden tube covered with canvas and sealed with wax would keep it dry, even if a tidal wave should flood the area. Since the floor of the prison was solid concrete two feet thick and about thirty inches off the ground, the tube would survive any bombing that might ensue in the retaking of the Philippines. "Shavey" had found some paper, so we made three maps or diagrams of exactly where it was buried. The officer, "Shavey," and I each kept a copy of the map, with our three names and addresses on it. The agreement was that whoever got back to Manila first, if we survived, should retrieve the package and return the contents to the rightful owners. It was a relief not to have to worry about that diary during the inspection.

It was probably the next day that we had our first mail call. This turned out to be personal packages only. A lot of the men received at least one package. Some received several. If they contained food, it was usually spoiled, but at least it was something from home. It was hard to believe I didn't receive any. But as I told some of the men, "Wait till tomorrow when they give out the letters—that's when I'll show all of you up." I was trying to keep a stiff upper lip, but I was quite blue that night as the others were going through their treasures. Some of the men offered me tastes of their spoiled candy, raisins, or other goodies, but I was too depressed to want to share in their food.

Mail call began at 1:00 P.M. the next day. With that many men, it took quite a while to go through the alphabet—"Maxwell, Minotti, Moore, Nelson, Nolan," then I was hearing "Robinson, Roeske." I thought, "Hey, wait a minute. You've gone past the N's." In disbelief, I went up to the orderly, and we went through the few remaining letters one by one. Nothing. What had happened, I wondered. Had everyone deserted me? Had some terrible calamity struck all of them? But that couldn't be—they lived in different places. I reasoned it was just too much to fathom. Not only that, I felt so terribly alone. To my knowledge, I was the only one who had received neither a package nor a letter. That night, as I lay there on the cruelly hard concrete floor alone with my thoughts, I was the most depressed I have ever been. Various thoughts of wonderment would not leave me. It had been so long—had they all given up hope? My family? Fay? Maybe—I supposed I couldn't blame her. But oh, how I hoped not. How long I lay there in the dark trying to come to terms with my disappointment, I do not know. I do know, however, that if I could have cried, it would have brought some release. But I guess I was too sad to cry. Furthermore, by this time, we had become too hard, too callous to be able to release our pent-up emotions in a natural way.

Thirty-three years later, in 1977, Fay and I were in a group who returned to the Philippines as part of a "reunion for peace" program. I wanted to revisit Bilibid and the scene of my sorrow. So four of us rented a car and driver. First we visited Santo Tomas University, where Fay's second cousin had been interned as a civilian prisoner of the Japanese. She had been a missionary teacher in the Philippines before the war. And then, there it was—the same heavy gate, the same five-meter-high and one-meter-thick concrete and stone walls, the same drain gutter leading away from the compound, and sure enough, there was the same cell block, #17, that had been my home for a week. What nostalgia it all brought back to me. The building was still being used, this time as a prison for juveniles.

June 21, 1944

We were loaded on the ex–German boat. Everyone had to stay below, and we were not allowed to smoke. They said it would be only a seventy-two hour trip, but it took longer. One day we were given only one meal as punishment for having matches. At Cebu, they told us to dispose of them. However, they suspected we hadn't obeyed, so they pulled a shakedown inspection aboard ship and found some. Diarrhea still bad. Always a long line for the latrine. Still only two meals a day of rice and squash and camote soup with a little pork in it per day.

June 24, 1944 (Monday)

Lt. Wedin died early in the A.M. from diarrhea and weakened condition. The Nips finally decided we needed improved conditions or there would be more deaths, as everyone was growing weaker by the day, so our boat was docked and we went ashore and were marched to Bilibid Prison, which is now a POW hospital run by U.S. Navy personnel. It sure seemed good to get a bath and stretch out. We got three meals a day, but they were small. The soup was very good-tasting. Lt. Wedin was buried here. Our baggage was inspected on arrival. My service record and write-up on the Vasayan-Mindanao campaign were taken. I got my service record back later. While in Bilibid, most of the men received their personal packages and letters from home. I didn't score, which was quite a disappointment. We were issued cigarettes once and could buy one hand of tobacco for 3.50 pesos. We also got one coconut and a canteen cup of peanuts for 9.40 pesos. The men were put in three groups. The sickest remained in Bilibid, officers and men in poor health went to Cabantuan, and the rest of us were slated for Japan. A group of well men came in from Cabantuan to join us. Rumors were rampant, indicating an early end to the war. We were issued Japanese uniforms and underwear.

We didn't know it then, but by far the worst leg of our journey lay ahead of us. The ship, *Canadian Inventor*, was an ailing and miserable old tug. This time I drew a berth on the steel deck, which became more than messy before we reached our destination. Because the ship was either tied up at the pier or anchored out in the roadstead for almost two weeks, with no movement of air in the hot sun of the tropics, the hold was just like an oven. It was inhuman, but the Japanese forced us to remain below decks almost all of the time. About the only liquid we received was half a canteen cup of tea twice a day. On rare occasions, we could catch a few drops of condensation as they dripped off a steam pipe, if a guard wasn't watching the few times we were allowed topside. Most of the days we spent in the dark, except twice a day when they turned on the lights to feed us our meager rations.

When we finally got going, we began to think most of our troubles were over. But we had just nicely got out into the China Sea, considered by many to be among the roughest bodies of water in the world, when a full-blown typhoon hit us. With only a thousand men or fewer for cargo, we were just like a chip on the water in a windstorm as we tossed and rolled at every whim of the vicious wind and an angry sea. Given the ship's light weight, coupled with boiler trouble that greatly reduced the power capacity of the old ship, it is small wonder that before we got headed straight again, we had been washed almost to the China coast. It is not difficult to imagine how the five gallon buckets used for latrine purposes fared. The mess and the stench almost defy description. The incidence of men losing it all and screaming in the darkness of that hell hole was increasing now.

It seems that there is often some redeeming factor in almost all difficult situations. For us at that particular place and time, it was found in one R. D. (or Ray) Russell, who had come aboard at Manila, I believe. He was a tall, husky Texan who knew a lot of songs and could sing well and spin yarns by the hour. When weather and other conditions permitted, he did just that by the hour. He did an outstanding job of keeping morale from sinking out of sight on that voyage. But of course, when days turn into weeks and weeks turn into months, even the best of them run dry. Then it was up to each individual to hold on to what sanity he had. I recall praying by the hour to a God who was right down there in the hold with me. And if I wasn't praying, I just lay there quietly, telling myself, "Hang on, you can make it, you've got to make it, but you've got to hang on. Just one more hour, one more minute."

July 2, 1944 (Sunday)

At 10:00 A.M., we ate our last meal at Bilibid and were loaded on a ship for Japan. Back to two meals per day. Rice in the A.M. and rice with a few vegetables in it in the P.M. The water shortage was more acute than ever. On this boat, we had a little more room, but not enough to stretch out.

July 4, 1944 (Tuesday)

Left Manila. Everyone had to go below while passing Corregidor.

July 5, 1944 (Wednesday)

Had boiler trouble during the night, so left our convoy and returned to Manila.

July 16, 1944 (Sunday)

Have been lying in the harbor almost two weeks. Chow and water situation very acute. Weather hot as hell, making conditions almost beyond human endurance. Today we saw a Japanese freighter loaded with gasoline blow up and burn. It also burned another ship alongside. About 10:00 A.M., we pulled into the pier and had our boiler repaired. Left Manila again about noon in convoy. While in Manila, we were allowed on deck only in groups of fifty to eighty to smoke. Had to go below again while passing Corregidor. Mighty glad to be on our way again.

July 23, 1944 (Sunday)

Arrived at the port of Takao, Formosa (Taiwan). Most of our voyage across the China Sea was in a terrific storm, making the trip worse than ever on top of the already worse conditions. Most of us got wet from rain and waves washing over the deck and leaking down into the hold, so another cold epidemic broke out. Diarrhea somewhat reduced. I had been feeling out-of-sorts ever since I got diarrhea from the coconuts from Bilibid. Started feeling better by the time we arrived in Takao. Chow still the same—plain rice in the A.M. and rice with a very few camotes and squash steamed in with it in the P.M. Shaboti told us that, until we get away from P.I. and could draw rations some other place, he could do nothing to improve our chow. A couple of days before arriving at port, our money was exchanged for Japanese yen at the rate of one peso for one yen and one centavo for one sen. Had more boiler trouble about the second or third day out of Manila, so our convoy pulled away and left us to limp in by ourselves. By this time, the Americans had dubbed it the mati-mati-maru. Mati means slow or wait, and we had done plenty of waiting or slow moving. The boat from Cebu to Manila was dubbed *Singoto Maru* because of the work we did loading it in Cebu. (Singoto means work.) And the boat from Davao to Cebu was dubbed the *Benjo Maru* because of the diarrhea. (Benjo means latrine or toilet.) After we got out to sea, we were allowed on deck most of the daylight hours. By the time we arrived in Takao, we could feel a change in climate, which seemed a welcome relief (to some) after almost three years in the tropics. However, Formosa is a semi-tropical island. The port of Takao was not very large, but it was extremely busy. Here we took on a huge cargo of salt. Up to this time, we had been practically empty, making it toss and roll all the more in the storm across the China Sea. We also got to buy commissary products in the way of ketchup, fruit (canned), bananas, onions, garlic, all of which was very welcome. The bananas caused another outbreak of diarrhea, of which I was a victim. I took a sulfanilamide [*sic*] course before I got it slowed down. More rations were brought aboard for the rest of the trip. We got rice in the A.M. and rice with a few camotes and squash and some pork in it in the P.M. Toward the last, we would get fish instead of pork once in a while. Our trip took so long, that by the time we got to Japan, the pork was practically all spoiled, and even the fish cakes were bad. The pork would have to be sorted, cleaned, washed, and boiled before it was put in the chow, and still we ate a lot of rank pork. We also got B-1 paste made out of fish meal a few times before we got to Japan. Lying around began to get on our nerves, because conditions aboard ship were so bad that we were anxious to get to our destination. In every harbor we came to, we saw ships coming in with big holes in their sides, evidently from torpedoes, and also a few stripped hulls. The only time on the trip from Davao to Japan we weren't in sight of islands most of the time was crossing the China Sea.

August 4, 1944 (Friday)

Left Takao in convoy and traveled with Air and Navy patrol.

Two things happened at Takao, Formosa, that are worthy of note.

On the pier to which we were tied up while taking on a cargo of salt was a row of fresh-water spigots. The Japanese assented to our pleas to take baths and fill our canteens at these spigots, but we could only go in groups of twenty. With the number of guards available, that was a reasonable arrangement. Several groups had already gone down, and I was in the next group to go, when suddenly the whole thing was halted and it never did resume. How I had looked forward to a bath and a full canteen of water! It had been over a month since I had had either at Bilibid.

The other significant thing that happened at Takao was that we took on a cargo of bulk salt. This made the ship more stable, and since we were in submarine-infested waters, we thought that a torpedo would not penetrate very far once it hit that salt. We were happy, too, that we could surmount the bulkhead separating us from the salt, so those of us on the filthy steel deck could climb up there and find a clean place to bunk for the night. This proved not to work out so well, however. It felt good at first, but the movement of the ship caused us to settle into such a form-fitting mold that by morning we felt as though we were encased in concrete. Every curvature or indentation had been filled in, so now we ached all over. I did stick it out for quite a while though.

At first, the salt proved to be another boon also. We brought some with us every morning for seasoning our rice, but that got ruined also. When men should have gone to the latrine in the night, they just went in the salt a little ways from their bunk. Salt, being the great conductor that it is, it wasn't long before we couldn't use it on our rice. And in time, the entire hold got so contaminated that even the smell was prohibitive. In the end, the whole affair had turned out to be one giant act of sabotage.

August 5, 1944 (Saturday)

Had more boiler trouble during the night so pulled into another port in northern Taiwan, a fairly busy place. Here we got more commissary in the way of ketchup, salt, and toilet paper. It seems rather ironic for prisoners being transported by their captors to have to buy their own toilet paper and salt, especially being on a ship whose cargo was salt. Another cold epidemic broke out due to a bad rain while in this port.

August 17, 1944 (Thursday)

Left Formosa in convoy. Had a nice trip under the circumstances. Weather good, crossed a little open water, but in sight of islands most of the time. Big dealing ran wild on board this ship. Instigated mostly by the men from Cabantuan. We were sorry we had picked them up in Manila.

Our chagrin regarding big dealing was that it often led to disagreements and fights, especially in close quarters, and we didn't need any more trouble than we already had. Also not mentioned in the diary but worthy of note was the fact that from Formosa on we had a lot more sub-chasers escorting us, coming out to meet us, or dashing out on patrol. On one instance north of Okinawa, we were attacked by submarines, and as the sub-chasers dropped their depth charges, the noise and vibration from their explosions made it seem as if the sides and bottom of the old tub were going to collapse completely.

August 19, 1944 (Saturday)

Arrived at some fairly large port in Japan's southern islands. More repairs had to be made on the boiler. Climate and landscape becoming more and more like that of the temperate zone.

August 20, 1944 (Sunday)

Arrived at a beautiful cove in a strait of a small island. Dad's birthday, so I shaved, cleaned up as best I could, prayed and thought especially of him. Blades and toilet material running low, so it was to be my last shave until I arrived at my destination. Chow still the same. Pork getting bad.

August 21, 1944 (Monday)

Back to same place we left August 19. Had to have boiler repaired again. Morale dropped 50%.

August 22, 1944 (Tuesday)

Pulled out again. It seemed as if we would never arrive at our destination. Pulled in at another little cove for the night.

August 23, 1944 (Wednesday)

Sailed out in the A.M. but toward noon went back to the same place we left that morning. The Japanese said it was in order to miss a typhoon, but the Chinese crew members said it was to avoid a bombing attack. Every so often at this stage of the trip we were run below decks, especially while passing a place of military importance.

August 24, 1944 (Thursday)

Pulled out from Naha, Okinawa, again. Weather fine ever since Takao.

August 25, 1944 (Friday)

Col. Weeks from Cabantuan took sick during the night and died in the early A.M. Cause of death listed as beriberi and malnutrition. He was buried at sea. Hanson acted as chaplain.

August 27, 1944 (Sunday)

Arrived at the fairly-large port of Nagasaki in the southern islands. More boiler trouble. Lots of activity. Beautiful volcanic mountains.

August 29, 1944 (Tuesday)

Traveled only a few hours and pulled into a small cove to repair our boilers again and our anchors. Our convoy waited for us this time.

August 30, 1944 (Wednesday)

Sailed again. Passed many beautiful islands. Weather nice. Pork really bad.

September 1, 1944 (Friday)

Had about our third stool specimen for dysentery taken aboard ship at night. Arrived at Moji, Japan.

At long last the horrible voyage was about to end. We only had one more night to spend in the hold of that ship which should have been scrapped long before. Except for a few days in Cebu, where we slept on a rock pile, and about a week in Manila, where we slept on concrete, our home had been in the bowels of three different hell ships since June 6—an entire summer. Except for a few fortunate men at Takao, we had not even had an opportunity to bathe in all that time, except at Cebu and Manila. We rarely had enough water to drink, let alone bathe. Our bodies and our clothes were positively filthy. Men had died. Men had gone crazy. Some had almost given up all hope. They would have been the next to die. But those who did not succumb in one way or another had grown stronger within. What may have appeared as quiet determination was actually fierceness. Sadly, even that would eventually break in many cases as the months wore on. After all, there is nothing without its limits.

In summation, there had been a number of hell ships where there was greater loss of life and greater suffering, but in what research I have done on this subject, none had exceeded our length of time in hell.

Japan:
Land of the Rising Sun

For I the Lord thy God will hold thy right hand, saying unto thee, Fear not; I will help thee.
—Isaiah 41:13

We had to remove our clothes before leaving the ship, as we were marched through a delousing spray. Even though our quarters for that first night on Japanese soil were in a stable, they seemed quite luxurious to us after living on board those ships. The stable had been occupied by horses before we moved in, so even though the remnants of their excreta were to be found here and there, at least this type could be moved merely by rolling it away. Quite unlike the slime on the decks of the prison ship. And there was so much room. And so much light during daylight hours. And such a nice breeze of clean air seemed to move through the building. We almost felt liberated.

September 2, 1944 (Saturday)

Had chow at 6:00 A.M. and got an extra partial ration to keep for lunch. Got off the boat at about 9:30 A.M. and marched about three blocks and were put in stables. That night we got a pretty good ration of rice, and a nice variety of pickled vegetables, and seaweed, and the first taste of Irish potatoes in years. Good cold fresh water was really a treat.

Moji is at the extreme northern tip of the island of Kyushu, separated from Honshu, Japan's largest island, by about three miles of water. The railroad crosses from Kyushu to Honshu via an underwater tunnel. Not aware of this, we entered the tunnel with the train windows open. As the smoke, soot, and cinders bounced off the walls of the tunnel and swept in upon us in the breeze from the fast-moving train, we nearly suffocated. It didn't bother the Japanese guards, as they were in the car ahead of us with the windows closed. Later we complained to them and asked them to notify us ahead of time as we approached more tunnels. Sometimes they did, sometimes they didn't. Consequently, we were far from clean when we reached our destination. Other than that and the crowded conditions for two days and a long night, it was a nice trip.

September 3, 1944 (Sunday)

Got up early and boarded a passenger train at 5:23 A.M. We rode six men to a double seat. It was very crowded, but much better than we

154

Japan

expected after our past treatment and mode of travel as prisoners of war. The countryside and small villages of Japan are really beautiful, and well-kept. Saw no end of rice paddies or fields. Trains are about the only mode of transportation, and there are lots of them. The extent and efficiency of their railroads was amazing. Traveled close to the sea in a northerly direction most of the time. Got another meal similar to the one of the night before with a little fried fish at about 11:00 A.M. Another meal at night was barley in the rice and a little boiled beef with the viands. Passed through Kobe about 11:00 P.M. It is a very large city.

September 4, 1944 (Monday)

Labor Day! Arrived at our destination. A large manufacturing area close to Osaka and 250 miles south of Tokyo. Had another meal before getting off the train. The plant we are at seems mostly a sulfuric acid and copper plant. Everything was taken from us except one undershirt, one pair of undershorts, one pair of shoes and socks, one washcloth, one towel, and a few personal articles. We have been given about two weeks of Japanese drill, speech, calisthenics, etc. So far we have received two bars of soap and one set of clothing. We can draw shaving and sewing equipment. During one recent recruit training, the boys were pushed around and beat up a lot by a Japanese sergeant whom we dubbed Herman. (Sometimes we called him Herman the German because of his militaristic style. Other times we called him Herman the Vermin, for obvious reasons.) An interpreter came down from Osaka and improved conditions somewhat. We have been eating 55 grams of rice and barley and good vegetable soup every day with occasional fish soup. We have had three cigarettes issued to date (September 12). NCOs get twenty cigarettes per issue and privates get ten.

The men who had come from the Philippines in our particular ship were sent to various camps in Japan. The largest contingent, between four and five hundred of us, was sent to a large copper smelter at Yokkaichi, near Nagoya, which was one of the largest industrial areas in Japan. It was a large factory with its own internal narrow-gauge railroad system. To help carry the fumes from the sulfuric acid and the smelting process into the atmosphere, it had either the tallest or the second-tallest chimney in the Orient—300 meters tall (between 990 and 1,000 feet). It was an amazing structure with a base in excess of 50 feet in diameter. Some coal, but mostly coke, was used to fire the blast furnaces.

The prison compound was enclosed with a solid-board fence about twelve feet high, so once inside the camp, all we could see were the inside walls of the solid fences. In the middle of the area was the barracks, with an aisle down the middle with sleeping bays on either side. These were double-decked, of wood construction, with a thin straw tatami covering them. Attached ladders gave access to the upper deck. In the center of each room was an open-pit fireplace. They were very inefficient and provided no escape for the smoke. Attached to one end of the building was the latrine and a bathhouse with an 8' by 10' square tub with a heating element in it. Next to that were two or three cold-water showers. In going to the latrine, we had to pass a guard station, and just opposite that was the American camp commander's office. The kitchen, dispensary, and guardhouse with a couple of cells made up the other buildings of the complex. About four inches of loose black volcanic sand covered the surface of the entire area, inside and out. The buildings and the fence were all painted black inside and out. It was about as cheerless as it can get.

A very conscious effort was made to let us know that we were now in Japan and that from now on, it was all going to be done their way. For the first couple of weeks, we were given Japanese recruit drill. We would now march to and from our work to Japanese commands and do the goose-step in the proper way and at the proper time. Herman, our instructor, was a hard, impatient taskmaster and a big man, adept at jujitsu. If you didn't get it right, he would approach you, storm at you, and flip you right over his shoulder. Most of our training was done on the beach. He was especially fond of flipping his victim out into the bay.

At the same time, they informed us that since we were in Japan, from now on only Japanese would be spoken. No more interpreters. So we had to learn the Japanese language. In order to accomplish this, each day a group of Japanese words, with their English equivalents, would be posted on the bulletin board. They would furnish no instructions. So each bay or room selected a person to get the words off the board. The forenoon was spent learning Japanese drill, and in the afternoon we studied and practiced the language. Then at evening roll call, the guards would do language quiz. If you failed a word, you got beaten. You not only had to know the word, you had to pronounce it properly. I was chosen to represent our room. What a terrible assignment! Every night there were beatings up and down the aisle. I've even seen them throw fairly large men right through the wall and into the center aisle. Also from then on, each room had to conduct tenko (roll call) in Japanese, giving an account of each category such as sick, kitchen, or guardhouse.

The next step in our indoctrination was the assignment of a number to each of us. This was to be worn on our caps and our outer garment at all times, as well as on a wooden dog-tag suspended from our necks. From now on, we were a number, not a name. (As time wore on, detail leaders or foremen would call us by name, but only in the confines of the detail. In the factory at large, we were only numbers.)

At first our food was rather tasty, but that did not last long. It was also in very short supply. In Dapecol we had got up to 600 grams of rice a day, but we were now down to 55 grams, and that was mixed with barley, which is hard to digest and is of inferior taste. The standard meal in Japan was rice and pickled daikon (white radish) three times a day. About every six weeks a motorcycle with a sidecar attached came into camp with some horse bones and dog bones in a thirty-gallon barrel. The cooks would boil them three different times in order to get all the marrow cooked into the broth. Any other food items mentioned were given to us occasionally and were a bonus. At least our rice ration was increased once we began working.

September 17, 1944 (Sunday)

Yesterday a few of us went over to the factory to try out for our jobs. I put in for road and railroad maintenance (kosaku nikko). They had six of us carry a couple of rails and drive some spikes. In our weakened condition, it was too much for us. (We were in horrible condition when we arrived, but the rest had done us good. Everyone is underweight, and beriberi and

Pocket notebook, New Testament, cap with prisoner number, and diary made out of cigarette packs.

sores are very prevalent.) We started on a ration of 700 grams a day last night for workers. It seems like a very good ration. There were about two hundred Dutch (also Javanese) and English prisoners when we arrived, so a lot of story swapping has been going on. They passed us up at Takao. They arrived here three weeks before us and are already working. They came from Thailand. There are now about six hundred men in camp. A lot of Americans left us in Moji (for other camps.)

The sores referred to were skin ulcers, some of which became quite huge and hard to cure. They were the result of improper diet and not being able to keep ourselves clean. The story swapping was about our respective military campaigns, prison camps, and always food, of course. We learned that before going to Thailand, this group of men had been part of the slave labor gang that built a railroad bridge over the Kwai River in Burma. This took on added significance to us some years later when that detail was made famous by the book and the movie *The Bridge Over the River Kwai*. While we got along very well with these men and made friends with many of them, a sort of tempest in a teapot arose regarding who was going to be commanding officer inside the camp once we arrived. Our ranking man was Lt. Col. Earl Stubbs. Their ranking man was a rather impressive-appearing extrovert from the Dutch army, but he was only a warrant officer. Since he was already camp commander and had developed a rapport with the Japanese officials, he

Prison camp at Yokkaichi, Japan. (Note prisoners on beach gathering parachutes. The initials PW were painted on the barracks after the war ended to indicate where Allied pilots should drop food for the POWs.)

thought he should continue in that capacity. He was really quite adamant, but in the end Col. Stubbs prevailed.

Personnel, rules, and regulations in Japan were markedly different in several ways than they had been in the Philippines. Quite noticeable to us was the greatly reduced number of interpreters available. In order to get along, we had to learn the language. In Japan, we had to really march—not walk— to work, and this was done according to commands given in Japanese, by Japanese military guards. Even in the case of one or two small details with prisoners in charge, the commands were still given in Japanese. Shintoism being the national religion, the Japanese had dutifully erected numerous Shinto shrines throughout the area. At each of these shrines, we had to do the goose-step in lockstep before we got to the shrine, halt and face the shrine, bow for prayer, face away again, and continue the goose-step for another fifteen paces beyond the shrine. (We prayed for more food and later for bombs and bullets to hasten the end of the war.) Once at the work site, we were turned over to the Japanese foreman or honcho. The military guards would stay in the area, but to enforce discipline, they had what we called "stick guards," men with a heavy stick or club about the length of an ordinary cane. A lot of punishment was meted out in this manner. It was much more cruel than the beatings and slappings we had received in the Philippines. A case in point: whenever a prisoner had to go to the bathroom, or benjo, he had to ask the stick guard for permission to go. One day we noticed a man being severely flogged not far from us. Later we learned that this Englishman had diarrhea and had wanted to ask the guard for permission to go to the benjo, but the guard was passing the time of day visiting with another guard. Not wanting or daring to interrupt the conversation, the Englishman decided to go anyway in an attempt to avoid an accident. By the time he emerged from the toilet, the guard was back at his post. Noticing this man coming from the toilet and realizing he had gone without obtaining permission, the guard clubbed him to death right then and there. This was not an isolated incident. I have seen cases where men were beaten so mercilessly that they have gotten down on their knees and begged to be killed—anything but to continue in their misery, but the guards would not oblige them. They only beat them more.

There were a couple of other forms of punishment or torture that were quite distasteful. One was to give a man a bucket of rocks in each hand and force him to keep running around the barracks in the loose sand, followed by a guard with a fixed bayonet jabbing him in the butt if he slowed down. When the guard tired, a relay guard would spell him off, but the prisoner had to keep on running. When he passed out, he would be revived, put on his feet, and forced to run some more. This would keep on until he was completely exhausted. Then he would be put in the guardhouse. Another form of torture which was employed the next spring and summer was to lean a ladder on the south side of the barracks, hang the prisoner by his wrists and ankles on the underside of the ladder, facing the hot sun. Then they would tie a bucket of rocks or water and hang it from his neck, just so it wouldn't quite cut off his windpipe entirely. If he passed out, he was revived, but he always had to remain hanging there until all of the details had returned in the evening from work. The Japanese hoped this would provide an object lesson for the rest of us. The real sad part is that these war crimes were committed against the prisoners for little or no provocation.

I did not record such cruelties in my diary because I was afraid that it might fall into Japanese hands. And that is exactly what happened.

One of my bouts with dysentery suddenly turned from diarrhea to severe retching and spasms of my entire insides. When some of my buddies came in from work, they found me lying on my tatami, barely conscious and retching fiercely. The only thing I remember is Bob Dennis saying, "No, by God, we're not taking him out feet-first. He's coming back. Turn him around!" Most of the next few days are a blank to me, except a blur now and then. I recall some Japanese stopping by for a minute with a corpsman, but then moving on. They were talking in low voices, so I could not hear what they said. Some days later, two Japanese came by again—one was an interpreter. They laid my diary and service record in front of me and wanted an explanation. I was flabbergasted that they had gone through my belongings in the barracks while I was in the dispensary and was frightened when I saw what they had. I explained that my service record was a document kept up by my commanding officer, not me, but that these records were given out to us when capture was imminent. Then the interpreter shook the diary in my face. "You could die," he said. I tried to look calm, said nothing, and steadily looked him in the eye. Inside I was all butterflies. Then he said, "Maybe you die. We see." Then they left, taking the documents with them. A few days later, the service record was left with the corpsman, and he delivered it to me. I never heard another word about the diary until several weeks later, when I received word from the front office to report there. Col. Stubbs, in handing me the diary, said the Japanese told him they would let it go this time but said he should advise me it could be a serious offense. Then he said to me, "You were pretty lucky this time." My decision to write so that the real message was between the lines had been vindicated.

As is always the case, there are good among the bad. We who were on the railroad repair detail (kosaku niko) were particularly fortunate. Our head honcho, Ikuta-San, was a hard man, but he was a fair and decent man. He was a former soldier who had been wounded in China. Having been a soldier who had seen action, he seemed to have an affinity for us and our plight, but he didn't show it until he really got to know us. He expected a day's work out of us, but he rewarded us for it in ways that seemed insignificant, yet were meaningful to us. For instance, he was quite generous with yasume (break or rest) time, and if we got wet on the job, he would bring us into the shack where an old oka-san (lady) kept a good fire going in a big heating stove. In this way, we were dry and warm before going into a cold barracks. This came to be very important as the winter wore on and as pneumonia became one of the killers. And he always seemed not to notice if we were trying to smuggle something into camp. After he got to know us better, he liked to joke with us and would sometimes call us by name. His first assistant was a very taciturn, stocky little man named Sato-San. Third in command was a jovial, not too ambitious, somewhat older man named Shinogi-San. In addition to us prisoners, the detail included two Koreans who were slave laborers. They had a difficult lot. They received poverty pay for their work, had poor living conditions, and were considered to be even below us. Our American honcho was good-natured, easygoing Robert Yaeger, who because of his angular face, long thin chin with a sparse, light-colored goatee, was aptly nicknamed "Goat." Since he was our honcho, Ikuta-San needed to know his name. So he told him his name was Yaeger. Ikuta-San could hardly contain himself as he repeated, "Yagi, yagi." We learned later than in Japan the word *yagi* means goat.

October 27, 1944 (Friday)

In this entry I will try to make a brief resume of the highlights of the last six months. On the night of September 17, a typhoon blew up, causing a tidal wave which flooded our camp, and did some damage, so the next day all Americans were busy cleaning up the place and building a sort of sea wall out of sand. I came down with diarrhea and a sick stomach on the 17th. On the 19th we were taken to our respective places of employment at the factory, given instructions, etc. On the 20th (my birthday) we started work. Our detail (railroad repair) shoveled sand most of the day, filling in some tracks washed back on the beach as the tidal wave receded. I got seconds on rice, which was the only thing that went toward making my birthday a happy one. (It was my third birthday as a prisoner.) The Japanese civilians under whom we work are very good to us, and treat us with consideration. In most cases, the details are treated quite well. Our cigarette issues in camp don't quite amount to enough to keep us going, so occasionally a Japanese foreman or guard will pass out a few cigarettes, or give us some synthetic tobacco to smoke in special little pipes.

Various experiments have been tried in regard to our working hours. This system, used now, is 5:30 A.M. first call and breakfast. 7:00 A.M. tenko with work call following immediately. 11:00 stop work and arrive in camp about 11:20. 12:30 work call. 4:00 P.M. stop work and arrive in camp about 4:20 to 5:30. Supper. 8:00 tenko. 9:00 lights out. We get two days off a month. Our food consists of rice and barley mixed most of the time (sometimes only rice) and vegetable soup. The variety of vegetables ranges from seaweed, peppers, radishes, etc., to eggplants, a few carrots, and sweet potatoes. Once or twice we have had bean soup, which was very good. Occasionally we get some fish, meat bones (horse and dog), and a little meat, which improves the soup very much. About once a week we get a slice of bread or a sort of biscuit and cookie combination with a little sugar over the top. We have tea all three meals. Just recently we have received a few commissary privileges. We have been able to buy a few spices such as curry powder, pepper, powdered horseradish, powdered mustard, fish powder, popcorn, and fish once. I hope the privileges continue, because it is a great help. (Not many calories, but it improves the taste.) I drew one yen, twenty sen for the work I did in September (about twenty-four cents). I was on quarters the 29th and 30th with diarrhea and also October 4, 5, 6, 7. October 8 was to be a day of rest, but another typhoon hit the night of the 7th, which was worse than the one before. The tidal wave caused the water to get almost hip-deep in camp. It came up on the lower level. (We had to move all of the 110-pound sacks of rice twice—first from the kitchen to the lower level. Then, as the water kept rising, we had to lift them up over the side to the top tier. It was terribly hard work. A lot of our food got wet, and much damage was done around the camp. It caved in all the fence next to the sea and one-half of the latrine. Several men were hit by flying glass and other floating debris. Private Wood had a toe cut completely off and another partially severed when he stepped through the glass of a floating door in the dark. He won't be able to work for several months. We spent all day of the 8th cleaning up and putting the camp back in order. Diarrhea was running strong about this time, with many men on quarters, and many working who were really too sick to work. I weighed 125 pounds on arrival and about three weeks later had gone down to 116 pounds. I had diarrhea twenty-one days. Part of the time I could hardly eat anything, and what with pick and shovel work, tamping, etc., I'm sure that I went down. I'm back up to 124 pounds again now. The Japanese are quite anxious and concerned about our health. (After all, they need slave labor!) So far we have received three diarrhea and dysentery shots and two tetanus shots. We have been issued overcoats, flannel shirts, cotton long-underwear pants, lined jackets and trousers (all of poor quality, as were the blankets that replaced the Army blankets they took from us). In our run-down condition, we have suffered from the cold more than normal. Since our arrival we have been able to write one letter of one hundred words, and one card home.

That one-hundred word letter was the only instance in over three years in which we were allowed to write more than ten words. It did not arrive in Siren, Wisconsin, until October 1945, one year later. In fact, even a year or two later, mail that either my folks or I should have received years earlier would arrive. Evidently it was discovered by the Army of Occupation and sent on, which may explain why I failed to receive mail earlier.

October 27, 1944 (continued)

The Japanese have also said it may not be possible to get Red Cross by Christmas. A very few letters and telegrams have come in. D. D. Jensen got a letter. October 18 I came down with sick stomach and diarrhea again, so I am on quarters. October 20 afternoon I vomited profusely, became violently ill suddenly, so was brought to the hospital on a stretcher by Vance, Dennis, Brubaker, and Peery, who had gone to the doctor to report my case. Never have I appreciated the value of good friends so much as this. I was pretty sick for several days, but gradually began to feel better and regain my appetite. At present my diarrhea is improved, but am still very weak and coming down with beriberi, which seems to follow diarrhea cases oftentimes. I noticed that my eyes are becoming weaker. My vision is still pretty good, but it seems that my eyes have to work harder to produce that vision, so they become tired very easily. We have a few books in camp, and two decks of cards per room (forty men) for pastime in our idle hours. However, sick men are not allowed to read, play cards, or smoke. Likewise, they do not draw cigarettes except for killing flies. (They get one cigarette for every one hundred flies turned in.) Four razor blades are issued to each room (the morning of our day off), and collected in the evening. (Later, as they became more worn, they only issued two at a time. The razors themselves were in the custody of the bay leader. Shaving became very uncomfortable.) We have been issued toilet paper twice since our arrival. Each room has a sewing kit at its disposal. We have cold showers and a tank of hot water to bathe in. It is a community bath, so after the ore-handlers bathe, it is pretty filthy, but it is a great asset. At present, it is out of order, however. October 22 was another rest day. There was a shakedown inspection, followed by a program gotten up by the men in camp. We have a few musical instruments at our disposal. I was too sick to go over to see the program. Diarrhea patients get lugao, or pap as the Dutch call it, to eat. It has the vegetables in it, but no peppers, as they are hard on the stomach. Vance, Bailey, and Dennis have been on quarters this past week with diarrhea. Also McCabe and Brubaker have been troubled with it on and off. Time seems to go pretty fast for us in the camp. We are hoping and praying though, that the war will soon end so that we can all go back to our respective friends and families.

By late October, we became aware of the fact that the mainland of Japan was being bombed quite heavily. Within another month, they were hitting the Nagoya area regularly, and as time went on, the raids became a daily occurrence and the target area became larger. Toward spring we realized that America had a new weapon—the B-29—because the Japanese kept saying, "B-ni ju ku dami" (B-29 no good). Now we could understand why they flew so high and carried such huge bomb loads. Obviously, I made little mention of the air raids in my diary. Similarly, I did not mention how we were obtaining some of our food. There were a lot of rats in camp, so one day the Japanese brought a cat to camp because they said they were afraid the rats would spread disease. But since starvation was a greater threat than disease spread by rats, the first thing the men did was get rid of the cat. We had managed to smuggle in materials for fashioning a box trap, complete with a door that tripped when the rat reached the bait. The night I used it, I begrudged giving up enough rice for bait, but I was successful in catching the rat, which I in turn stewed up over our little open fireplace. I can say without reservation that it was the poorest food I have ever eaten. I did not mind passing the trap on to the next man in line for it. The incident does illustrate, however, to what lengths a starving person will go. By now, we were past the hunger pangs stage and past the stage of deluding ourselves with fancy recipes. Starvation is a far different matter than hunger. It becomes a matter of knowing within yourself that your system is drawing from within its very reserves just to keep itself alive—a consciousness that slowly but surely you are losing ground. Whatever it takes for sustenance becomes acutely important.

Compounding this condition was the almost incessant diarrhea, which increased the drain on our systems.

November 12, 1944 (Sunday)

Today is a holiday for one-half the details. The other will be off tomorrow. Ours is usually off on Sunday instead of Monday, as is the case today. Some boys in the next bay have borrowed a few musical instruments from the Japanese and have an old-time hillbilly orchestra in full swing this P.M. It seems good to hear even old-time music and the boys in a merry, carefree mood. There are American, Dutch, and English, all playing together. Today they started organizing a harmonica band also. This A.M. we had an exchange of library books in the bays. (Seventeen books for forty men.) A few of the books are pretty good. I came back to duty last night. I feel pretty good now, and am glad of it. They tried everything on me, including enemas of potassium permanganate, and doses of paregoric [*sic*], but the turning point that finally stopped my diarrhea and fixed my stomach up was sulfadiazine. Thank God for sulfa drugs! They are wonderful. In a place like this they are veritable lifesavers. Diarrhea has diminished to a minimum in camp right now, but colds, pleurisy, and chest ailments are rising (including several cases of suspected TB) due to being cold all the time, working in run-down condition. If we could just be back in shape, it wouldn't be so bad. We also need certain food in larger quantities, and heated quarters. Yesterday an American dentist came to our camp to stay. He has been in Japan two years and says we are undergoing the same sicknesses, etc., that all prisoners have after arrival here. He doesn't have much equipment. We have been told we may get Red Cross before Christmas, so everyone is living in hopes it will materialize. We have received a few sweet potatoes and some real meat in the mess, but it is put out in very small quantities. Tonight each man will get a slice of bread made out of rice flour and sweet potatoes. One night last week, each man got one cookie at .04 apiece. It was very good, if we could only get enough of things like that to do some good! November 3 was a very rainy day, so most details didn't work. The Japanese observed the Emperor's birthday also, and allowed us a handful of some sort of roasted soybeans, so I observed Mother's Day by eating roasted beans. I was glad to get something special for the occasion, no matter how meager it might be. I pray to God that I may celebrate the occasion in grand style with her next year. [In a way, that prayer was answered. I arrived in Siren the day before her birthday that next year.]

The new interpreter has been allowing men to write letters for broadcast to U.S. The main requirement is that we plead for peace. [Most, if not all of us, refused to do this. We wanted peace, but we refused to be used as propaganda tools. We thought that the military and government knew more about how to pursue this matter than we did. We also believed it was up to the Japanese to ask for peace, not us.]

Occasionally we can buy a few cigarettes through the commissary. As soon as we get paid for last month, we may be able to buy some spices, seasonings, and fish powder. We have some mesau (a concentrate of some kind) in our soup quite a lot lately. It flavors it and adds a little richness. Once in a while they put out a little dab of it to the men. It reminds me of primost. We also get tiki tiki issued to us. It is ground up rice polishings and contains vitamin B-1. Lately there have been several air raid practices. About a week ago the alarm sounded, and judging from various things that took place, we might be led to think there was a raid somewhere near. However, we have no way of knowing. Our water heater still has not been fixed, so all we can get is cold baths. Sometimes certain details get to take hot baths over at the factory. I am on the reserve list for worker's rations of lugao. In the meantime, I am taking another man's place for a few days while he is on quarters. [That way, I received worker's rations of the easy-to-digest lugao, and he, being on quarters, had to revert to the smaller sick ration.]

I'm afraid dry rice might upset me again. Lugao is easier to digest and it is usually always hot, whereas dry rice is always cold. We now have a tailor shop and cobbler shop in camp.

November 26, 1944 (Sunday)

Today is a holiday. Some of the details are working, but they will have tomorrow off. I did a little laundry this A.M. and shaved. About twenty minutes after I hung my laundry out, I discovered my cotton long johns had been stolen off the line, so now I must get along without them, which is not a very pleasant prospect at this time of year. There has been quite a lot of stealing in camp, especially clothes. My impression of humanity is still the same—that a thief is about the lowest thing that walks. I have worked every day since I came back to duty. Most of the time I feel pretty good, but every few days something will upset me and I will have sick stomach and diarrhea for a day or two. However, instead of staying sick now, my stomach will level off again, so I am getting better. We have had beef broth a couple of times, which usually gives me a little trouble. Our rations have been cut drastically for the last ten days. We get no barley now to help the volume. There have been some beans and sweet potatoes to go with the rice, but it does not give nearly the volume. The men are really getting weak because of it. We have had fish once and real meat twice in the last two-and-a-half weeks. We still get tiki tiki (rice polishings) every few days. There have been several commissary issues of curry powder, fish powder, and missabi (horseradish). I am about out of funds now. Cigarette issues have been few and far between, so smoking is pretty scarce now. I used the last of my P.I. dobie tobacco about five days ago. We were weighed today. I now weigh 54 kilos (118 pounds). There have been several air raids—alarms lately—usually around noon. One day we had a practice on picking up for a quick move if necessary. Yesterday A.M. we heard the Red Cross would be here in a day or two, and when we came in from work this P.M., some details were already bringing it in from trucks. Then we all fell in to bring in the remainder (in the rain). There are 495 large cartons. Everyone is happy as can be over the prospect of Red Cross again. Last night a committee was formed of one man from each of the eight bays, and Lt. Col. Stubbs is chairman, making a total of nine. I am the representative from group eight. Blankenship is also on the committee, so we have at least two of last year's men on it. Orders from Osaka are that 50% will be held back for emergency, 5% will be held for special medical purposes, and we will receive the other 45%. We don't know when we will get it, but we are living in hopes of getting some by Thanksgiving. We are also living in hopes of getting clothing, medical supplies, and personal packages later on. The cold epidemic seems to have been somewhat checked here in camp. The average normal temperature is about five or six degrees centigrade. Diarrhea is down to a minimum now. Vance has been in the hospital about a week, but is due to be discharged any day. Our bay has been on guard the last three nights.

Probably the most devastating blow to hit the factory during the entire war occurred on December 7, 1944 (Pearl Harbor anniversary date on this side of the International Date Line), when a very strong earthquake struck. Understandably, news of the quake and attendant damage was not broadcast because the Japanese did not want the world to know of the damage to their war effort. Years later, however, we learned it was one of the biggest earthquakes they had experienced since the killer quake struck Tokyo in 1921. Some of the damage to the factory never did get completely repaired, especially the damage to the concrete in the area of the blast furnaces. Less than half of them ever got back in production. Railroad tracks resembled pieces of cooked spaghetti strewn about, locomotives lay on their sides, sulfuric acid mains had broken, and acid had erupted like geysers all over the ground and flowed at will. Some of the men received burns from the acid, and it damaged some men's clothing. We were fortunate to be with Ikuta-San because he was familiar with the layout of the factory, and led us away from the danger spots. My shoes did get acid burns, however, especially one of them, which deteriorated to the point that I had to tie it together with rags. Keeping it tied helped some in keeping the snow out. (Until that time, Yaeger had had an understanding with me that if I died first, he would get my shoes.)

By now, cold weather was becoming a serious factor to contend with, so we usually slept with our clothes on. Japanese blankets left a lot to be desired. The only way we could keep warm was to double up; sleeping thus gave us twice as many blankets. Even then we had to sleep head to toe in order to avoid the gap caused by two sets of shoulders side by side. It was a difficult winter, and by spring, more men had died from causes related to the cold and dampness than from malnutrition.

December 15, 1944 (Friday)

Today is a holiday for everyone in camp. We were supposed to have December 10 and 11 (one-half of the men each day), but on December 7, a terrific earthquake occurred at 1:35 P.M. I was tamping ties on the railroad. When it first started, I thought that I was about to faint, because I was sort of weaving around, but soon I realized what it was. Buildings began creaking and wobbling. The earth was moving in waves and swells, like the surface of a lake on a windy day. Then the chimney was weaving back and forth as 200 feet of the tallest chimney in the Orient began toppling to the ground. Right after that, we had to run to another area because underground acid pipes were breaking all over, and acid was shooting up and running all over the ground. As soon as order could be established, the POW's were moved to a very windy and cold grade just outside of camp, and a checkup was made. No one was killed, and only three or four men suffered minor injuries. It was anything short of a miracle, and only proved further that a very benevolent God is guiding the destinies of this group of men. Our camp was pretty well shaken up, with broken beams, etc., but not as bad as the factory. The concrete bases of the iron cooking cauldrons were cracked, but to our surprise, we didn't miss a single meal as a result of the quake. The Japanese brought a few meals in. However, we have been short on water, because all the water mains are broken. For a few days, most of our meals were gumbo (vegetables cooked in the rice). Now our chow is almost back to normal. They have water pretty close to camp, so it is not far to carry it. Most of us get our canteens filled on detail, and we get one-half cup of tea at most of our meals. However, there has been no opportunity to wash, so everyone is mighty dirty. It was a rough-looking crew, but today Frank Saunders, an Englishman, has been shaving men for cigarettes, so most of us look a little better.

Things in general at the factory are far from being on an even keel. Most of us are either working on railroads or various pipelines. Details are so large that there is no system to anything. Our detail has been enlarged by twenty men from Siran Sanka (ore detail), two of whom are permanently attached. Besides that, we have a lot of temporary men from other details every day. Dalton has beriberi, Corson and Fandry have TB, and Yaeger has bronchitis. Batson and I are the only original RR men left. The weather has been very cold and windy for the most part, so there are lots of colds, bronchitis, and some pneumonia. It is getting harder than ever to get on quarters, especially since we got a new medical corporal. We also have a new camp commander and a new quartermaster. The old one is in the local guardhouse. We are allowed to have fires until evening tenko, but our charcoal is so limited that the only time we have them is for the evening meals, so we can heat our food and have at least one warm meal a day. We had a fire all day today, and hope to have one all day Christmas. It does take a little of the chill out of the barracks, but for the most part, we suffer from cold 24 hours a day. Dennis and I sleep together, which helps toward keeping warm. On December 12, my sister Hazel's birthday, we had fish soup for breakfast, and horse-meat soup for supper, so although it wasn't like a birthday party meal, it was a little extra anyhow. For a while we got rice and part millet. Now we are getting mostly barley, so the volume of our chow is pretty fair. We get horse bones once in a while, and our soup is mostly radishes, peckaye, turnips, and seaweed, etc. We are supposed to get December 25 off. The factory is supposed to give us a small package, and we are supposed to get part of our Red Cross, so we are all sweating out the next ten days. We also hope to get letters and personal packages pretty soon. Today we got a biscuit at 4:00 P.M. and tea; also a commissary comprised of curry powder and two cigarettes. Our cigarette issue comes on the 5th and 20th now (100 cigarettes for non-commissioned officers and 70 for privates per month.) Today we had to list all valuable articles. Larsen got run over by an ore car last week, so he is in the hospital with bad feet and ankles. There have been several pretty bad earthquakes at night since the 7th, and several long air raid alerts, that of the 13th being the longest. I am reading *Damion the Leper*. I am feeling so well now that I volunteered off lugao, but meat broth still bothers me.

Sometime in late November, several of us began talking about how we missed having a chaplain in our midst to conduct some sort of worship service. As our conversation on the subject developed, we decided that there was no reason that should stop us from at least getting together for devotions of some type, at least once in a while, so Kenneth Olson from Menomonie, Wisconsin, Jim Seabrand, and I began getting together in the bathhouse for devotions occasionally. Later on, we would spread the word to others who might want to join us. It got to the point that sometimes there would be ten or fifteen of us gathered for scripture, prayer, and discussion. At that time, we moved our location to the latrine, to avoid arousing suspicion among the guards. We had two Bibles.

At Christmastime, we received some Red Cross food. Since we had a halfway decent fire in each room, I used my Red Cross food to try to make my Christmas meals resemble what they would have been at home with my mother's cooking. The Red Cross food really was a lifesaver because we were gradually losing ground on the subsistence diet of our daily rations. There evidently was a measure of wisdom in the Japanese decision to only put this food out a little at a time. If we received too much in one issue, there was a tendency to gorge ourselves and lose the full potential benefit. By spreading it out, there was that little extra later on to pick us up when we really needed it the most.

As food became scarce between Red Cross issues, several different phenomena developed. Men would begin borrowing ahead. A man might be particularly hungry at noon, so he would make a deal with another man. "I'll give you three-quarters of a bowl of rice tonight for half a bowl this noon." Often, when pay-up time came, the man that owed might hedge or try to get by with a light portion or refuse entirely, begging for more time. Too often, this led to trouble which would end in serious fights. Scroggins, the man who had earned a bowl of rice by knocking a guard in the rice paddy, got in several such fights. In one encounter, he broke a hand. This still did not deter him. He later broke the other hand. Consequently, he was unable to perform any work after that and as a result drew light (sick) rations for the duration. Other men had the smoking habit so strongly that they would sell their food for cigarettes. Then they would go to another bay and try to borrow a portion of rice for some time in the future. In all cases, most of the borrowers got so far in debt that there was no hope of them ever getting caught up. Before the war ended, the situation got so serious that some sort of system had to be devised to protect both the borrowers and potential lenders. The health of the borrowers was being jeopardized by both beatings and starvation. Potential lenders might not be aware of the credit status of the borrower or might not want to refuse a friend, but they needed protection against making a bad loan.

Under the new camp-wide system, a victim could file a grievance against a poor-pay person with the camp commander. A notice would be posted on the bulletin board that all other people to whom this man owed rice should report the information to the front office. When all the information was in, the commanding officer would conduct a hearing which the defendant and plaintiffs were ordered to attend. The defendant was entitled to be represented by counsel of his choice. The hearing board consisted of the bay leaders in camp, chaired by the camp commander. Both sides had an opportunity to present their arguments. Then the court of bay leaders would make a determination based on all of the information presented as to whether the defendant would be able to make restitution without jeopardizing his health. If it was thought that he could do so, a repayment plan was worked out. If it was thought that he could not, the court would declare him bankrupt, in which case he was declared free and clear of his obligations. If he was declared bankrupt, however, his name was posted on the board, and from that day on, no one in camp was allowed to lend him rice. Being blacklisted gave him another chance, but protected others from acquiring a bad debt. The system really worked quite well and saved some lives, I'm quite sure. There were a couple of cases, one a smoker, that had gone too far before their cases were brought to court. They did not survive.

That winter in Japan brought another hardship; undernourished men had to work in that cold, damp climate and come home to a cold barracks.

A lot of colds developed into pneumonia, which became a serious matter because in their run-down condition, many men could not fight it off. Sometimes they would die in as little as two days after coming down with pneumonia. Some of those cases are still vivid in my memory.

There was the case of Ernest (Ernie) Meyers, a fine young man who had interrupted his studies at Stanford to go into the army. He worked on the same detail as Bob Dennis. He became wet out on the job, caught cold, and went to the hospital with pneumonia. Two days later we were astounded to learn that he was dead. And then there was Tim Hardy, formerly a big, husky man from the South. He and I worked side by side a lot doing pick and shovel work. He began having chest trouble in January. The doctors diagnosed it as possible TB. February was cold, wet, and windy, and Hardy used to wonder how long he could continue. Finally, he heard that by March the weather was supposed to be better, so he would ask me several times a day if I thought that was true. Then it got to the point that he believed that if we could just make it till March 1, we would have it made. He died March 1. And there is the case of Dalton. One day at Dapecol, I saw Dalton in back of the barracks looking quite dejected, so I asked what was wrong. He had just found out that he had pellagra. Later in Japan he used to say, "Well, this pellagra hasn't gotten me completely down yet. Maybe if I can live to get out of here, they can cure me back in the States." He died in March or April.

In Japan the bodies of all the deceased had to be turned over to the Japanese for cremation, after which the remains were brought to our camp commander in a box approximately 12" by 14" by 4". These boxes were stored against the back wall of his office. The Japanese also provided their version of the cause of death. Invariably it was, "Heart stopped." That absolved them of any responsibility such as malnutrition, exposure, or other conditions indicating irresponsibility on their part.

These situations made us all acutely aware of the importance of keeping dry and warm if at all possible. I'm sure there would have been more deaths on our detail that winter if it were not for Ikuta-San's concern and his efforts to send us into camp warm and dry. Dennis was not that fortunate. One day when I came off detail, Larsen met me and informed me that Dennis had a terrible cold. It had come on suddenly in the night, leaving him unable to go to work. Knowing that Dennis had lung trouble anyway, I gathered up several canteens, filled them with hot water at the kitchen, and brought them to Dennis' bunk, where I packed them around his body, especially his chest and back. I kept refilling them as they cooled until lights out. In the morning I did the same thing bright and early. Then I asked Larsen, who was on camp duty and around camp during the day, to put hot water in the canteens while I was on detail. In the evening I would spell Larsen off. We kept this up for a number of days until Dennis was out of danger. Fortunately it paid off.

The line between life and death is very thin sometimes. An incident that occurred during one of my stays in the hospital brought this to my attention very graphically. The man alongside me was too sick and weak to feed himself, so a buddy would come in at mealtime, cradle the patient's head in one arm, and feed him a little rice at a time with his other hand. On this particular morning, the patient said, "Good morning," took a few bites of food, and then simply expired in the man's arms. He had just simply used up every ounce of reserve, and his body was unable to function any longer.

January 14, 1945 (Sunday)

Things have been so upset, and there is no time for anything but work lately, so I have neglected my diary. We got one box of Red Cross Christmas Eve. A few of the boxes were inspected by the Japanese Military Police. Dennis and I split his coffee, and we traded mine off for a can of meat pate. Christmas Eve I made a regular rice groat (mush) out of rice, milk, sugar, cinnamon, and butter over it. (Just like home.) Christmas morning Dennis and I had stewed raisins, sugar, and milk on our rice. For noon I made a bread pudding out of two biscuits I had saved, raisins, butter, sugar, tangerine peel, and prune pit meats. I got so full I couldn't eat it all. After breakfast, I had a toasted jam sandwich, and in the forenoon I had a toasted cheese sandwich. We had extra meat and biscuits in the mess for Christmas. At night we had a sweet potato turnover. Christmas Eve I had read the Christmas story (from Luke) to Dennis. I intended to go to church, but it was so much delayed because they waited for the Japanese C.O., so I had to give it up for a later date. In the afternoon, there was an outside program which we all had to attend, so we all got a freeze job out of that. Just before noon, we all had to fall out for a speech by the new C.O. (our old C.O. and Q.M. have been relieved). At New Year's Eve, we got off one hour early in the P.M. I really enjoyed that box of Red Cross more than any other, because I am feeling better than I have in the past three years, and I did a lot of fancy quanning-up. I did not spare the larder. I made two delicious chocolate puddings, one chocolate milk drink so thick that I had to eat it with a spoon, one salmon loaf, one bread pudding, two sweet potato pies, one meal of meat pate gravy on rice groat, toasted cheese, jam and Spam sandwiches, fried luncheon meat, butter, cheese, jam, salt, etc., on burned rice. It was wonderful while it lasted. We are all hoping to get another box today, but I have my doubts. Corporal McGinty died of beriberi and malnutrition on December 17, 1944. Private Hoffman almost died about Christmas, but he got his Red Cross box a few days early (as did nine others of the sickest men), and when we got ours, we contributed food that he could eat. He is still living, but now that it is gone, he is slipping fast. A lot of the men have really snapped out of it since the Red Cross came, so I only hope we get enough to do some good. December 21, just two weeks after the earthquake, we got water in camp again, so things are back to normal. We have an electric heating unit in our bathtub, so we have hot baths, but the barracks are cold, and there are so many to bathe that the water and the tub cools off quickly, so most of us are hesitant about taking a bath. It is hard to keep from catching a cold, which is what everyone has and can't get rid of. Chest colds are increasing rapidly. However, we did get a lot of sulfa drugs in the Red Cross, so that helps a lot. The Japanese check our numbers as we bathe now. Everyone has to take at least two baths a week. I got a haircut just before Christmas, which will have to last the winter, because it is too cold to get another. The temperature here doesn't get much below freezing, but the air is so damp and the wind so bad that a person suffers a great deal from it. We had snow several times so far. It just barely covers the ground and lasts a day or so. Our detail is getting back to normal now. We've had men from various details helping us since the quake, but we are almost caught up now. Our work is very miserable this time of year, but they try to get us by a fire at break time, and we quit early enough to get warmed before going in. We have a fire in the barracks, but all it does is take the chill off the air, and it gives us a chance to heat our chow. Our schedule has changed though, so we don't get much of a chance to quan at morning and noon meals. I have been able to get hold of some extra salt, curry powder, and chow lately in exchange for cigarettes. My appetite is larger than it has been for years. Our chow consists of rice, barley, and millet or a combination of the three, and mostly radish and turnips with a few meat bones now and then, and a very few greens at this time of year. Sometimes we get part of our ration in flour, and then we have biscuits from that.

Air raids are becoming more frequent all the time, averaging about two per day. None in the immediate vicinity as yet, though. Earthquake tremors are still occurring frequently, with another fairly hard one at 4:00 A.M.

Americans are starting shift work tomorrow on certain details, so we had yesterday off for the purpose of realignment of camp according to details. I am now in 7-B at the opposite end of the barracks and am on top instead of bottom, so I lost by the deal. Besides that, I was made bay leader, which is an awful headache. Dennis is in 6-B, so he and I got split up. I am sleeping with Kleeman now. Everything is all upset today, so it turned out to be a yasume day. I did some patching of clothes and got my shoes temporarily repaired, besides working on rosters, etc. Day before yesterday, each man was issued one pair of light gloves, and one pair of socks. Also, there were a few small towels, of which I was able to get one. Most men's shoes are in deplorable condition, with a lot of them wearing canvas shoes, and few or no socks. Several telegrams came in yesterday. Corporal Bailey got one from his folks. Baca is in the hospital with pneumonia. Webb was in for a few days with a bad stomach. Batson, Yaeger, and I are the only ones left in the original railroad detail. (There were eighteen to start with.)

The winter of 1945 was the most difficult time of our entire prisoner-of-war experience. Food continued to be woefully inadequate, both in quality and quantity. The cold, miserable weather took a heavy toll. Our barracks were always cold. We had two uniforms and had to wear both of them in order to keep warm. My shoes finally gave out completely, so I got a pair of used Japanese military canvas shoes with the extra compartment for the big toe, but they were ill-fitting and badly worn. Men were beginning to give up, and if they did so, in a couple of days, they would be dead. A man named Driver in our own bay didn't budge for morning roll call. He had done some barber work, and the last time he had cut my hair, he had told me he was about at the end of his rope. A Corporal Brown, whom I had known in Tanku-lan, simply wore out and died. The stack of boxes containing ashes in the commanding officer's office was getting bigger. If we had not gotten a small portion of Red Cross food now and then, it would have been even worse.

As conditions grew worse, we grew more adept at smuggling and fending for ourselves in general. If we got near a garbage can, we would go through that. Salt was often a problem, so we devised little sacks that hung in our crotches inside of our clothes. These sacks worked pretty well for helping us elude the guards when they shook us down at the gate. And they were just the right size for carrying in chemical salt, a fine substance that seemed to be a by-product of the copper-smelting process. When we saw small deposits of it here and there in the factory grounds, we scooped it up and slipped it into the pouches slung in our crotches. It had a salty taste and didn't seem to hurt us, so we used it to give our food some flavor. Another little trick we used for smuggling was to tie the bottoms of our inner uniform tight to our leg at the bottom. When we let the outer pant leg hang loose, the tied inner leg was quite inconspicuous. This gave us a perfect hiding place for larger objects. We were always short of fuel, so if we were anywhere in the area of the blast furnaces, we would try to grab a few pieces of coke now and then. With its rough and irregular shape, it would usually scratch our legs pretty badly, but it made good fuel. On one occasion, I happened to see a broken piece of plank close to two inches thick. It was about five inches wide, and two feet long, so I hurriedly shoved it down inside my inner pants and went about my work. By misfortune though, there was a protruding knot that bit into the inside of my knee with every move I made. Worse yet, I discovered later that the plank and especially the knot was soaked with acid. The real test came when we approached a shrine and I had to begin goose-stepping. On every one of those high strides, that knot just gnawed deeper and deeper into my knee. Somehow I made it through, however, and even moved just right to fool the guards during shakedown. I was really pleased with myself and thought that I had done a number on the Japanese. But I soon learned that I hadn't been so clever after all. That acid soaked sore began to fester, and after a while, I had one sore, stiff knee. I kept on working as long as I was able. I didn't want to tell anyone if Ikuta-San should find out I was unable to work as the result of smuggling, he would keep a closer watch on me in the future to see that I didn't try to smuggle anything else. Worse yet, I didn't dare go on sick call because if the Japanese doctor, who kept a pretty close tab on people who were sick to prevent abuses, saw my case and learned the circumstances, I would really be in trouble. Finally the sore got really bad and began to change colors, so I sneaked over to the dispensary and got ahold of a Dutch medic whom I had gotten to know quite well during previous stays. He recognized my dilemma, but was not supposed to issue any medicine to take out. I knew him well enough to know that when he got to Java, having some American money would really be a big plus for him. I had one five dollar bill that I had been saving just for the day we got back with American troops so I wouldn't be broke. To get the medicine I desperately needed, I made a deal with the medic—five dollars for one sulfa pill. He told me to mash part of it each day and put it right in the sore. It mixed with the matter and stayed pretty well. That one pill was large enough to make several applications. In just a couple of days, the sore began to improve, and eventually it healed completely. That one pill may have saved my leg, or even my life.

On the job, we tried to hold back as much as we could—anything to keep from aiding their war effort. We even tried to sabotage it whenever we could. We soon found out that the best way to accomplish that was to gain their confidence, so we worked on that first, mostly by talking and even joking once in a while, not by trying to impress them with hard work.

The first few months on the railroad repair detail, the Japanese did all the technical work such as determining grade, setting the pitch of tracks on turns, and gauging the distance between the rails. The prisoners did all the heavy work—carrying steel rails and ties, pick and shovel work, tamping ties, and later on driving the spikes into the ties (under supervision at first). After a few months of gaining their confidence, and especially when our detail became larger because of the extra work required to repair the railroads after the earthquake and later the bombings, our harried foreman would entrust some of the technical work to us. We performed very well at first, and they were pleased. Then as the ground became disturbed and uneven from the bombings, we purposely gauged one track a little too wide, and sure enough, when we came to work the next morning, there was a locomotive lying on its side. The Japanese blamed the accident on the ground not being solid enough, so that it was more difficult to tamp the ties in properly. Having gotten by with that one, we didn't try anything else for a while. Later on, when a project came along that called for laying some track along the top of a bank near the water's edge, we saw another opportunity. This time, we took advantage of a curve. In putting track down on a curve, the outside rail is laid a certain degree higher than the inside one, depending upon the sharpness of the curve. We made it almost the proper height, but again we gauged it a little wide at a strategic point, so just as the locomotive reached the peak of the grade, which was also where the track had to curve, the outside wheels of the seaside track fell inside the rails, and the locomotive rolled down the bank and into the bay. It was still there when the war ended.

In another area of the factory, an American had been operating a huge crane that propelled itself on tracks along a pier for many months. He was an exceptionally good operator and had performed faithfully and well. Then one hot day in the early summer of 1945, the guards were inside a huge warehouse quite a distance back from the pier having tea and a smoke. I understand the bunkers or the end of the pier had been loosened. At any rate, when no one was around, this navy man put the crane in gear and headed it out to sea, climbed down, and watched it go over the end of the pier and into the bay. It too was still lying there when the war ended. No one had seen it go, and when he came walking up to the warehouse and explained that somehow it had slipped in gear and got away, the Japanese were so glad to see he had not gone with it that they offered him cigarettes.

The following information regarded air raids from *Japan at War—World War II* (Time-Life Books, 1980, p. 66) corroborates allusions to air raids in my diary and also provides information I did not know at the time. March 10, 1945—more than 250 B-29s loosed some 2,000 tons of incendiary bombs on Tokyo. Following the first success, the B-29s obliterated great areas of Nagoya, Osaka, Kobe, and other industrial centers. March 18, 1945—Nagoya was the target, and this time American naval aircraft from a carrier joined 300 B-29s in the attack. The onslaught left three square miles in ashes and sent thousands of refugees fleeing into the countryside. Many others made make-shift shelters in their damaged homes. Some patched together shacks in the rubble, and some simply survived as best they could in the open. Four hundred planes hit seven different targets on May 10, 14, and 17, and another 500 took part in each of two massive raids that left one-quarter of Nagoya in ashes (p. 167). The U.S. Air Force was trying to knock out Japan's industry with precision bombing. The Mitsubishi aircraft plant in Nagoya was a frequent target (p. 160).

Life was becoming more tenuous than ever. In addition to the ever-present specter of starvation, we were now becoming more endangered from bombing day by day. In addition to those harsh realities, we were now beginning our fourth year as prisoners. Freedom and normal living had long since seemed like only a dream. We had to stop and think about what it must be like. And although we never doubted that America would win the war, it had become very difficult for us to comprehend any other way of life than what we had been forced to endure for so long.

In early April, I was brought back to reality for a little while when I received two International Red Cross cards—one from Fay and one from my sister Luella. Although each of them was only allowed ten words, at least it was a message from home. I was still worried about my parents, especially my dad, since I had had that dream about him being near death several years before. Those two cards were the only mail I received in all that time. I must have read them fifty times.

May 13, 1945 (Sunday, Mother's Day)

God bless her and grant that we may be reunited by next year!
This is the first time I have had a chance to write for a long time, so it will only be a brief resume of the past few months. It has been so cold and

FORM 227
JUNE 194.

From: MISS LUELLA NORDIN
SIREN
WISCONSIN

NOVEMBER, 1944
(DATE)

(FULL NAME AND ADDRESS)

Dear: CARL,

WERE TO AUNT ELLA'S FOR THANKSGIVING YESTERDAY.

JUST GOT YOUR NEW ADDRESS. KENNY GOING UP TO

ESTHER'S DEER HUNTING, TOMORROW.

LOVE,
LUELLA

Messages must be not more than 24 words. Type or hand print in block capitals.

FORM 2277
JUNE 1944

From: FAY M. LEWIS
SIREN
WISCONSIN

NOVEMBER 23, 1944
(DATE)

(FULL NAME AND ADDRESS)

Dear: CARL

HAPPY TO GET WORD FROM YOU AGAIN. HOPE

YOU'VE HEARD FROM US. PRAYING ALWAYS THAT

YOU'RE WELL. MARY, FRAN, ALL SEND GREETINGS.
MUCH LOVE,

FAY

Messages must be not more than 24 words. Type or hand print in block capitals.

These two International Red Cross postcards from Fay and my sister Luella are the only mail I received in almost four years. They arrived on April 4, 1945.

miserable on yasume days that I haven't felt like writing. Then too, we have had Red Cross almost every rest day due to the fact that the Japanese finally came around to putting it out by one-quarter boxes, so I would spend most of the day quanning, as did everyone else. That small amount made just a good day's eating and quanning. We got the last of it two weeks ago today. We still have fire privilege at mealtime, so we still heat our chow and try to make it a little more inviting than it was when it came from the galley. All winter we got rice or barley and dried pickled radish soup with mesau in it, with fish or meat bone in it on rare occasions. Now we are starting to get vegetable greens such as carrot trimmings, young onions, etc. Once in a while we get seaweed, bamboo shoots, etc. Our ration has been cut, so now we are continually hungry. We have received small issues of salt and curry powder in the last few months, but not enough. Now that the war is cutting off supplies, we can hardly get anything through the commissary, so we stand very short on spices. Some chemical salt has been smuggled in from the factory. It is very poor stuff, but it answers the purposes after a fashion.

We get no cigarettes through the commissary, and the Japanese don't issue them regularly as they used to, so there is a tobacco problem. What with the American cigarettes in the Red Cross and being a light smoker, I never ran out—yet. (I would have today, but we are supposed to get some tonight. Something always seems to come up at the last moment to save the day.) Some of the men are selling their chow for cigarettes, and others are selling their cigarettes for chow, of which the latter are the wiser, because chow is what will bring us home. I have bought some chow, curry powder, salt, soap, etc., with a few of my cigarettes, but have tried to keep from running out completely, because to be without tobacco in this place is hell. It is the only pleasure we have left. Life has become more dull than ever it seems, due to the routine, constant work, and always getting the bad end of the breaks. It seems that an effort is being made to make things as bad and hard for us as possible. However, according to all indications, even the Japanese are suffering quite a lot from the war in the way of food, tobacco, fuel, etc.

By 1945, we saw very few trucks in operation, and the ones that were running were powered by gas converted from burning rice straw in a contraption set in the bed of the truck just behind the cab. I only saw one car during that last year, and it had that same type of a mechanism situated in the trunk. Vehicles powered with this crude contraption had little power or speed, especially in cold weather. It was not unusual to see eight or ten men pushing on a truck to assist it in climbing even a slight grade. Their fuel shortage was acute.

Xxxx xx, xxxx

During the winter we would have several air raids a day, and some were pretty close. Now we don't have as many raids right here, and they are smaller, which indicates that the bulk of the action is elsewhere. As near as we can figure out, the war in Europe is over, and possibly close to over in this theater of war. We are all hoping to be free sometime this year. We have heard that Roosevelt died April 13 (the Japanese were only too happy to tell us) and that Truman is the new President. Also heard that Hitler is dead. We lost fifteen men this winter. [The figure of fifteen men lost covered only part of the winter. I let that number stand, as it would not look too bad in the event that my diary would fall into Japanese hands again. I do not have the exact figures of how many more died; the figure also does not account for those killed later during air raids.] One was beaten to death for nothing, one was killed in a factory train accident, one fell down an elevator shaft, others died from pneumonia, beriberi, starvation, etc. Hardy and Dalton died in March. Whittlemore, Cameron, and Nichols have been added to our detail. Dennis was pretty sick a couple of months ago, so he has been on light duty until last week. I have been on light duty six and a half days since last November. Otherwise I have felt good except for a few colds and diarrhea. I did have a siege of boils on my neck for a couple of months, which was pretty aggravating. Rumor has it we are moving from here soon. Everyone is hoping it will be a general concentration camp, which will be an indication that the war will soon be over.

After the war, I learned that Vernon Johnson from Grantsburg, Wisconsin, sixteen miles from Siren, had been in another prison camp near Nagoya. They spent their entire time carving a huge cave out of the side of a mountain. Its main purpose was to have been a gathering place for all prisoners of war in the area in the event of an invasion. Once inside, we were to be completely sealed in and then executed. They had no intention of turning us over to the invaders. The sudden change in events caused by the atomic bomb foiled their plans and saved our lives.

Xxxx xx, xxxx

I got a card from Fay and one from Luella on April 4. They were dated November 4, 1944. It is the first word I received since before the war, except for a telegram from Fay in December 1941, so I was really thrilled. No mention of Dad or Mother.

May 27, 1945 (Sunday)

Just have time for a short entry before tenko. Today has been a good yasume day. Nice weather, and I had most of my chores done up, so I have taken it easy. The weather has been cold, rainy, and miserable almost continually the last couple of days. It is almost a known fact that we are moving, but there are conflicting rumors as to when, where, or what we will be doing in the new camp. We are pretty sure that we will be moved in groups, rather than in a single group. Work lately has been fairly easy. I have been having a lot of trouble the last week with diarrhea, due to the fact that our grain diet has been mostly barley, but I finally got slowed up by some medicine that the doctor gave me for amebic dysentery. We haven't been given many vegetables lately, but we have gotten fish quite often the last couple of weeks. Tobacco is very scarce now. All American and Nip cigarettes have been issued out, so there are only a few that filter in from the factory. I have been doing up my spring laundry in my spare moments this past week. It's a heck of a life. A couple of nights ago, I had Ketner down to eat with me on my bunk, and we had our first bull session since leaving Dapecol. Tonight I had Dennis over. Time for tenko.

Rumors had been part of our life for over three years now. Sometimes they seemed, and were, preposterous. Other times they seemed, and turned out to be, logical. In either case, they gave us something to talk about and took our minds off our miserable existences, at least for a while. One rumor that seemed to persist more stubbornly than others was the one that kept going the rounds in the spring and early summer of 1945, the rumor that we might soon be moving. Coupled with that was often an admonition that it might be a sudden move, that we should be ready at all times to move on a moment's notice. Although we didn't have a lot of gear left by this time, we did try to keep it orderly, so we could get it together in a hurry. I still had my field pack and by now was pretty adept at packing that in an orderly manner, although it was a little more difficult with the bulky Japanese blankets.

Not only the blankets, but all of the Japanese-issue clothing was very inferior in quality. For that reason, it seemed that we were forever patching and fixing our clothes. Rumors of moving made it even more incumbent on us to have our clothes in the best condition we possibly could. As far as clothing was concerned, one of our biggest problems was with shoes. It helped that Paul Brubaker had been able to smuggle in canvas, rubber belting, handmade knives, and an awl over the months, which he, in turn, used to make a moccasin toe, rubber-soled loafer type of shoe. They were rather stiff at first, but after they got walked in, they were tolerable and were much better than nothing. We had to make do with what we had. The cleverness of the smuggling activities and the ingenuity displayed in camp were sometimes amazing.

June 7, 1945

Today has been a rainy, stormy day, so they didn't send us out this A.M. At noon they told us this would be our yasume day instead of Sunday. It kind of screwed us up, because we spent all forenoon in readiness to go out on a moment's notice, but even so, I made arrangements to have pockets put in my Japanese-issue pants. I did part of it myself. Besides that, I made a mess kit pouch, and sewed on some buttons, made a new salt shaker, and read some of *The Celebrity* (which by the way takes place around Lake Superior, seemingly close to Duluth). On June 1, two groups of 150 in each group left here for some place northwest of here. Dennis, Bailey, Baca, Webb, and Peery out of our outfit left, so there are only five of us left here, namely Vance, Larsen, McCabe, Hicks, and me. Corson, Yaeger, and Fandry from the railroad detail left.

It is rumored that we will leave soon, probably in two groups also. I believe I would just as soon stay here, because we have more room now, and our soup has been slightly better. As long as I am a POW, I don't expect to have any better quarters, food, bath facilities, water, or detail bosses (honchos) than I have here. The only move I would welcome would be a general concentration of POW's, which would indicate peace in the near future. Some say this is the beginning of it. At any rate, I am getting my gear ready and clothes ready in case we do move soon. It is just a year ago today since we left Dapecol. We have only twenty men to the bay now instead of forty. I am still bay leader of 7-B. I got on tiki tiki last week for my beriberi. My kidneys get me up three or four times a night (caused by all the fluid from beriberi.) Now that we are on straight rice, my stomach is feeling better.

Some of the boys have gotten ahold of canvas and rubber and are making themselves sandals, as there are very few leather shoes left. Most of us have been wearing ill-fitting, poorly constructed cloth and rubber shoes for a long time. Everybody is busy getting addresses of all their friends in case we are split up. Lately we are getting fish more often than we used to, which pleases me. I never eat fish now, but I think of how much fish I am going to eat when I get home. Yesterday we were issued curry powder and mesau from the kitchen. We have a new camp commander now because the other one left with the other groups. This one believes in beatings and strafings [slappings] because he says punishment by putting men in the guard house isn't sufficient, so men caught bringing in salt [chemical], wire, nails, and other contraband have been severely beaten. We get shook down every time we come in camp. Among other things, they seem to be looking for Jap newspapers, indicating there must be something going on they don't want to take any chance on our finding out.

June 10, 1945 (Sunday)

We gained a day on the Japanese! Some of the details, including Kosaku Ika and Kosaku Nikko (our detail) got a day off, in spite of the threat that we would work today because we had Thursday off on account of rain. For once we were lucky. Also yesterday there were two raids in which the short blast blew, so we didn't go to work until after 11:00 A.M. Air raids are becoming more frequent in our area during the last few days. Some say we are to move in the next few days. Others say we will stay here.

Today has been a beautiful June day. I have been busy patching clothes, doing laundry, shaving, and even did a little reading. Private Sherman has started conducting Protestant church services (in place of just devotions), so I am planning on attending them at 7:30 P.M. Our vegetables have been cut in half of what they were right after the camp split up. We get a few dried anchovies now and then. (About three kilograms for three hundred men.) The tobacco situation is bad. There is a rumor of a small issue of monkey hair (synthetic tobacco) in a day or so. How I wish this would all end soon so we could go home!

As the summer season approached, the air raids became larger and more intense. Not only that, it turned out that by now a lot of the activity was concentrated on our immediate area. One day the first bombs began dropping at noon. After an hour or so, the all-clear sounded, but we had barely begun our normal routine when another raid of a couple of hours' duration took place. This on-again, off-again routine continued until 2:00 A.M., a time span of fourteen hours during which we were seldom free of air raids. By now the B-29s were meeting less and less resistance. Once it became dark, they would come over in single file about a minute apart and drop their loads. During raids on our factory, the Japanese would sometimes bring us out on the beach in order to minimize the danger. One night during the single-file portion of the bombing run, we could tell that they were getting dangerously close. Then I heard this freight train noise coming right at me, so I buried my face in the sand. Suddenly I heard a fast, swishing sound and felt a breeze by my right ear. At the same instant, sand splashed up on my forehead and in my hair. I reached into the hole that had been dug and burned my hand as I pulled out a jagged piece of shrapnel about five-and-a-half inches long and about two inches wide. If that had landed two inches to the left, it would have taken the right side of my head off.

That same night, a couple of fellows had left the beach, gone into the Japanese headquarters, and stolen some rice balls and saki which the Japanese were about to enjoy when the last raid began. We didn't get into our barracks until about 2:30 that night because of the raid. At 3:00 A.M. we were all awakened and brought outside to be inspected for evidence of the stealing. By the time the shakedown and the subsequent lecture were over, it was 4:00 A.M.

A few nights later we witnessed our first incendiary raid from the latrine windows, as they firebombed the Japanese military airfield less than a mile away. The more incendiary raids we saw, the bigger they became.

On another occasion, our camp commander was notified that there was an American airman at the gate. When Capt. Thompson was brought outside the gate, there was a dead American lying there who had tried to parachute to safety. There was a rumor that he had been beheaded. Although we heard later that Japanese civilians were doing this to downed airmen, I cannot say with certainty that that was the case in this instance. I do know, however, that Capt. Thompson took whatever personal items the man had and his shoes into camp. His remains were cremated and brought back to camp a couple of days later.

Even though we were in more danger now since the air raid war had intensified, we were also happy about it. Happy that at least it was our bombs and bullets we were dodging, happy that America was bringing the war to Japan (not that we wished harm to the Japanese people, but we knew that's what it would take to end this war). And we were happy that the prospects for peace and a return to freedom were becoming brighter than they had been in years.

Along with that happiness came curiosity. We all wanted to see our planes. We wanted to see the stars on the wings, especially since low-flying navy shipboard fighters were now getting into the act.

So on one of our rest days, unbeknownst to me since I was asleep at the time, two men in our bay took it upon themselves to make that more possible. They had sawed two of the 2" by 2" window bars on a slant, so they could be lifted out, thereby making a hole large enough to stick one's head out and get a good look during a raid. (If an air raid such as a strafing raid occurred suddenly, making it impossible to get to the beach, our orders were to report to our respective bays for the duration of the raid. This was especially true for bay leaders.)

The next morning the Japanese tenko party had just left our bay and was proceeding to the dispensary when they happened to see sawdust as they passed our window. Then I guess they saw the saw marks, although they were pretty fine. They immediately returned and, confronting me, demanded an explanation. I had none because that was my first knowledge of the affair. The men in the bay were still in roll call formation—a U-shaped line reaching down one side of the bay across the end by the barred window and up the other side, and ending with me. Then the Japanese began a systematic beating of the group, each Japanese in the party using a different weapon, so to speak. One used the palm of his hand, one drew his saber and hit hard with the flat side, another used his leather garrison belt, another the butt of his rifle, and the last one punched with his clenched fist. Around and around they went, yelling and hitting. About every ten or fifteen minutes, they would stop, and the leader would demand an explanation of me. In each instance, I had none, so around and around they would go again, with each of us standing rigidly at attention. After an hour or two, the standing alone became very tiring. At about 9:30, the man using the garrison belt (by now he was hitting with the buckle end) knocked an upper front tooth out of Walsh, a man from the Fourth Marines. I hoped this incident would prompt them to stop the charade, but it didn't. Instead, one guard took Walsh to the dispensary, where they removed the remainder of the tooth, got the bleeding stopped, patched up his lip, and then returned him to his place in line for some more beating. It was now becoming quite severe. We were getting badly bruised and dizzy and were generally in pretty bad shape. Finally, at approximately 10:30 A.M., when they stopped briefly to question me again, and I repeated yet another time that I had no knowledge whatsoever about the details, I asked the number one guard for permission to speak to the group. The gist of what I said went something like this: "I don't know who did this, and I don't care, but it is becoming obvious they aren't going to stop this wholesale beating until they find out who did it. I'm not asking anyone to rat on anyone here, nor am I asking anyone to confess if they do not want to. Neither am I asking that you do it now. But I suggest you think about it during the next go-round, and when they stop the next time, I'll ask again. Then if you want to confess, fine. If you do not confess, that's fine, too. We'll just stand here and take it as long as they dish it out, and there will be no further questions asked by me."

With no answer forthcoming, the Japanese commenced again. At the next break, I turned to the men and asked if anyone had changed his mind. To my surprise, two men, Kleeman, my former bunkmate, and Nick Gallegos, did step forward. They were immediately taken to the guardhouse for further punishment. I had hoped that it was over, but it was not.

With that confession over, and the culprits taken away, the guards wanted to know where the saw was. Again I did not know, and again the Japanese resumed their beating. Each time they stopped, my answer was the same—I truthfully did not know. It was after 11:30 when I put forth a similar proposition, this time regarding the saw or any knowledge of it. When the guards stopped for a few moments the next time, and I turned to the group, who should come forward but Fitzjohn. He was the person who had been beaten so unmercifully at Dapecol for trying to smuggle rice into camp in his clogs. (I really felt bad for him.) Then, of course, they asked him to produce the saw. Sadly, he was unable to find it. He had lifted the tatami and the boards of the sleeping deck and thrown it down in the loose sand. He climbed down there and tried to find it, but to no avail, whereupon he too was taken to the guardhouse. It still wasn't over for us. The guards were angry that the saw had not been produced, so they lined us up again for some more of the same treatment, hoping they could punish us into bringing forth the saw. Finally the 12:00 noon whistle blew, and realizing that they had lost half a day of work out of us already, they decided to cease and desist. We had been beaten almost steadily for over four hours. We were a horrible-looking group of men, but we had stood up to the Japanese and taken whatever they handed out. I was proud of my men. No one had pleaded for mercy or clemency, and no one complained afterward. The three men who had been taken to the guardhouse suffered terribly. As was customary, they always received their worst beatings whenever details went by as a sort of object lesson. Fitzjohn, who had been beaten deaf in one ear at Dapecol, lost the hearing in his other ear at Japan. As for me, I received a reminder on the last go-round that remained with me for a number of years. The last guard had been using his fists. As I stood there at rigid attention on that last pass, he came up from the bottom with a mighty upper cut and caught me squarely under the chin. The blow was so powerful that it lifted me several inches off the ground. I had to bow and say "arigato" (thank you). With certain movements, my lower jaw bothered me for years. I had literally taken it on the chin. More important, I had not succumbed.

June 27, 1945 (Wednesday)

Last Sunday was supposed to be yasume day, but due to having some time off the previous week because of air raids, it was a work day. They did say, however, that we would get the regular yasume days this month.

The night of June 17 there was a big air raid over Yokkaichi, consisting mostly of incendiary bombs. The morning of the 18th there was another raid in which the fertilizer department of this factory was hit, so we didn't work at all that day. Since then, air raids have been more frequent and severe than ever before in this area. Last night there was another large raid of about three hours in duration in which this factory and the one across the bay were hit. I don't know the extent of the damage yet. We spent most of the night on the beach, and after the raid, we were shook down because POW's had stolen some rice balls from the Japanese officers during the raid. (Saki had been stolen also, so in addition to the shakedown, they went up and down the line smelling our breath.) Yesterday there was a big raid (600 planes) between here and Nagoya. We have reason to believe that some Yanks were brought in last night who had parachuted down when their planes were destroyed in a raid last week. Yesterday we got weighed. I've lost eleven pounds this month, so I only weigh 108 pounds now. I can sure tell it, too. In fact, I got so weak, and my legs became so near giving out, that I had to get off heavy duty beginning last Sunday, June 24. Up until today, light duty has been working quite regularly, but it's better than heavy duty, because hours are shorter, and you work slower. We have to get coal for the kitchen, help clean up the barracks, work in small garden plots they are preparing around camp, etc. Lately we have been getting some beans (in lieu of rice) and some dried fish, so there has been a welcome variety in our diet, but the last couple of days there have been no fish issued. It seems that we can never have anything good (at least for long). For instance, our vegetable ration was good for several weeks, until Yok-kaichi got bombed, but now there are hardly any vegetables at all. We get dried seaweed, and pickled radishes, but not much of it.

Rumor has it we will move to a general concentration camp area at Toyama soon. We hope so!

No lights and no water today. Time for evening chow. Had Brubaker make me a pair of shoes out of canvas and rubber soles. My Japanese shoes are shot, and we can't get any more.

Deaths in camp let up for awhile after the first fifteen that had occurred in camp. We hoped that after the cold and pneumonia season was over that there might not be anymore. But that was not to be. Life had become more tenuous than ever, and it was as if we were living by sheer willpower. But there comes a time when even that is next to impossible. It was becoming more and more common for men to finally give up, and when they did that, they would likely last only a few days until finally there was not sufficient willpower remaining to cause the body to function any longer, and they were gone. Sometimes a friend could snap you out of it for a time, but of course even an extra push could only last so long.

Having a friend do that to me is the only thing that saved me, in my opinion. Initially I had not thought in terms of giving up per se, but I had begun to realize that I could never make it to another Christmas. Reality told me that. At the rate I was losing ground, I knew within myself that six months would be the outer limit of my ability to go on. I knew within myself also that if the war didn't end soon, I would never see Fay or my family. The thought made me sad, of course, but not the kind of wrenching sadness a well, strong person might experience. Emotions were no longer sharp; they were dull.

Then one day, without realizing that I had verbalized it, I said to my bunkmate, Merrill Forsythe, as I came off detail, "Merrill, I don't think I can possibly go out that gate to work another single day. I think I've had it." Then he started in on me. He bawled me out to a fare-thee-well, bringing in Fay, my family, the guy that used to have such high resolve and just generally putting me down till that one strong emotion we all have buried in us began to evolve. The longer he kept on, the more angry I became, to the point that my resolve right then was, "OK, I'll show you. I will go out tomorrow," which

I did. I really tried hard. I did not want to give in, especially to Forsythe. But the human body can only do so much, so the same thing happened again, with the same identical results. So I kept going a while longer. Men continued to die, however, up until the last night in camp.

Of course all of us were heartened by the increased and massive air activity, again corroborated by the account in *World War II: Japan at War* (by the editors of Time-Life Books): "The largest coordinated air attack on Japan— 2,000 aircraft in all—came on the 10th of July 1945. More than 500 planes bombed five cities; Wakayama and Sakai near Osaka, the oil refineries in Yokkaichi near Nagoya, Gifu in the mountains behind Nagoya, and Sendai to the north of Tokyo. One thousand planes from aircraft carriers pounded airfields around Tokyo, 300 hit airfields in Kyushu, and the rest struck Osaka and Nagoya" (p. 168). "By the end of July, nearly 500,000 Japanese had been killed in air attacks. Another 13,000,000 had been displaced from their homes" (p. 169). (© 1980 Time-Life Books Inc.)

July 8, 1945 (Sunday)

Today has been a yasume day, much to our surprise. I was off eight days on camp light duty, on account of general weakness, caused from beriberi and malnutrition. Last week, seven of us from Kosaku Ika and Kosaku Nikko [detail names] worked several days for Mr. Kiro [an interpreter] on an air-raid shelter, for which we received a little extra chow which came in mighty handy. The last day we didn't have enough shovels to go around, so three at a time took turns resting inside the shelter. I was one of the men resting when a guard caught us, so we had to stand at attention and go through a general hazing in front of the guardhouse for forty-five minutes.

There is not much doing at the factory except cleaning up and building air-raid shelters. A few departments are doing a little producing. There seems to be a greater feeling of ill-will toward us among the Japanese, and food is getting more scarce, and there is no tobacco, so things must be tighter. There have been no air raids lately, but every day one or two planes come over for observation purposes, most likely. Gallegos and Fitzjohn got out of the guardhouse today. They were in a little over a week for sawing off the bars in the window of our bay. We all got beat up before they confessed who did it, and where the saw blade was hidden.

Lately all we get to eat is one-half bowl of rice and one-half bowl of barley for breakfast and lunch; half a bowl of rice, some thin radishes [daikon] and some seaweed soup for supper. It's getting rough. The Japanese have greatly reduced the quota of men allowed for light duty. All in all, the squeeze is on, so I think that we may move soon, that there is a naval battle south of here, and that there will be an invasion soon. We have zigzag trenches on the beach for our use now. I have most of my clothes in pretty good shape now, as a result of spending most of my spare time mending. Quite often we get to go swimming in the ocean in the evening lately. How I wish it were Silver Lake!

July 23, 1945 (Sunday)

Today should have been a yasume day, but we got Friday P.M. and Saturday A.M. off on account of rain, so we had to work today. Work at the factory is pretty much at a standstill since the last raid (July 9). Most of the work is cleaning up, building air-raid shelters, and generally puttering around. Part of our detail has been digging a well and also digging an underground rice shelter. The rest have been cleaning up at the sawmill or building an air-raid shelter between the factory and the village. So far there have been fifty-two air raids this month. The last few days there have been fighter planes over several times. Hardly a night goes by that there is not an alert, and usually we have to go out to the trenches for a couple of hours. It is starting to tell, too. Everyone is getting thinner, more irritable, and all tired out, including the Japanese. On top of all that, we are horribly afflicted by fleas, so much that we can't sleep or rest well at any time. I hope this comes to an end soon. There are certain things that indicate it might, such as no incentive to get the factory producing, a more resigned attitude among the civilians to all appearances, and a more disgruntled attitude toward us prisoners. They use every little excuse possible to beat up on us and mistreat us. There is less food and tobacco for both the civilians and us, and a general arming and drilling of the civilians.

I am just getting over another case of diarrhea, so I am pretty weak and very thin. Vance has been on light duty for a long time now, and the other day he was told he might have TB. Lord, I hope not! I have had about five drags of tobacco in the last two weeks. Tonight I got two drags of monkey hair from Al Nichols, and it made me dizzy. It really doesn't bother me to go without tobacco now, but I certainly do enjoy it when I do get it. Now and then, I smoke a little dry tea in my pipe just for the heck of it. There is still a little nicotine left in my pipe which I get out of it by smoking tea in it. [The pipe referred to has a long stem and a very small bowl for smoking synthetic tobacco, a nicotine-treated, shredded wood product dubbed monkey hair. The bowl only held enough monkey hair for two or three drags.]

Lights just went out temporarily, so I must quit now. [We were without lights or running water July 9 through 19.] We still get one-half bowl of rice and one-half bowl of beans for breakfast and lunch, and one bowl of rice and a little dried fish soup for supper. Now and then we get a little piece of pickled radish [daikon] for supper.

I am eternally grateful for what Forsythe did to get me going. It worked for a while, but then I seemed to be losing out again. Everybody was. That was why it was so hard to get on light duty. Everybody needed every break they could get. Not only lack of proper nourishment, but now lack of sleep was compounding the situation.

It was difficult to tell which was the worse. It was bad enough to be rustled out of our bunk several times a night to go out to the beach for an hour or two, but almost worse were the fleas. They were everywhere. On rest days, if we sat on our sleeping platforms, we could actually see them jump out of the sand. Once they got in the straw tatami, they were there for the night, waiting for a human body to lunch on. If we stood in formation, they jumped out of the sand onto our clothing, eventually working their way to our bodies. The same thing happened at work. Lice, bedbugs, and the like are bad enough, but we were slowly going crazy from the fleas. It was no wonder we were so tired and weak and were losing weight. The last time I got weighed, I was down to 49 kilos or 107.8 pounds.

It finally got down to two basic things that we desired. Number one, get away from the fleas, and number two, more rice. We had long since learned that if one has to get along on just one food, rice is by far the best single staple food there is. In our starvation mode, it was rice that we craved. We finally got to the point that our ultimate idea or conception of wealth would be to own 100 kilograms (220 pounds) of dry rice.

Being a bay leader and serving on a number of bankruptcy juries had put me in closer touch with Capt. Thompson, our American camp commander. I tried to keep my rosters up to date, keep stealing and fighting down, and maintain a reasonable respect for discipline in our bay. I think that he appreciated it and respected me for it. Despite that feeling of mutual respect, I never asked for or expected any special favors from him. I was getting to the point, however, where I realized I needed some kind of improvement in my lot if I was going to stand any chance of making it.

There was one particular detail in camp that seemed to be the answer. It was called the Jap kitchen detail. It was a rather large kitchen situated about in the center of the factory area that prepared and served meals for the upper level of Japanese civilians working in the factory. The menial labor in the kitchen was performed by a detail of prisoners. For working there, the prisoners received all the rice they wanted at noon and in the evening before going back to camp at night. In addition, when they returned to camp at night, they could bring a full mess kit of rice with them to the barracks, plus they could fill their canteen cups with burned rice scraped off the sides of the iron kettles. And then, as frosting on the cake, they were allowed to go through the garbage cans unmolested. This detail usually consisted of one Englishman, one Dutchman, and two Americans, since Americans represented the majority in camp.

After the last weighing gave a rather graphic picture of my deterioration, I went to Capt. Thompson and explained my predicament. I told him I was not asking for special treatment in wanting to be put on light duty— everybody needed that. But I asked that I might be considered for the Jap kitchen detail, not to replace anyone presently on it, but to be put on the list. (They rotated every ten days or so.)

When I eventually did get on the detail, I made the most of it. Since the Dutch mess kits hold about three times what an American mess kit does, the first thing I did was to exchange mess kits with a Dutchman for the duration of my time on the detail. This was done with an agreed-upon payment of rice. Since we continued to be eligible for rations at the camp mess, I designated my daily noon and evening rations to him. That way he received double rations for those meals.

Of course we really filled ourselves up over at the Jap kitchen, and when we came in at night, we each had a jam-packed mess kit and canteen cup full of rice. Sometimes I held some back for a bedtime snack. The rest I would loan out at the rate of half a mess kit per meal to be collected on certain days in the future. (When the war ended, I had a half mess kit of rice coming in for every meal far into October.) It had been years since I had had that much food.

Another of the advantages of that particular detail was that the work was not all that hard. And what we did do could be done pretty much at our own pace.

It almost ended in curtains for me on one occasion, however. We, along with the Japanese stick guard, were going over to the village to bring some rice back on a cart one nice sunshiny day. We were about halfway there when the American B-29 reconnaissance plane was making his daily trip. All of a sudden, we heard that awful freight train sound and could see a big 500-pounder plunging toward earth, almost directly at us. The rest of the detail ducked behind some protection. I was bringing up the rear, so I fell to the ground right where I was. The bomb hit with such force that it bounced me a couple of feet or more in the air, knocking the breath out of me when I landed. My first thought after gathering my wits about me was wonderment that I was still alive. When I looked around, I realized that I had been so close to the point of impact that all of the shrapnel and debris had flown in an arc right over me without touching me at all. Miracle of miracles! I realized it all the more as I gazed into an ugly bomb crater about twelve feet deep and fifteen feet in diameter. There was a navy tank farm nearby, and I guess the plane had one bomb just for that. When I walked over to where the others were, they were so surprised to see me that one Japanese gave me a taste of a boiled Irish potato he had been eating. Starved as I was for sweets, it tasted like candy. I received quite a welcome. They all thought for sure that I had been killed. I was getting kind of tired of close calls, but I was thankful that they were just that—close, and no more.

August 11, 1945 (Saturday)

Today I have had a holiday. A week ago I had the pleasant surprise of being put on the Japanese kitchen detail, so I get all I want to eat and more. It consists mostly of rice, but sometimes we get some noodles, mesau, pickled radishes, etc. I have been able to trade around and get some green vegetables from Don Jensen, who works in the Japanese kitchen here in camp. My surplus chow I loan out for the future and give some to my friends free. The work consists of breaking up firewood, carrying rice from the village, and other odd jobs. We have to keep going pretty steadily, but it isn't very difficult work. The other men on it are Choate (American),

Larry Larkom (English), and Allen Van Rlenedyk (Dutch). Most of the other details are cleaning up the factory after the air raids. A couple of the departments are doing a little producing, mostly acid and cobalt. The employers seem to have lost heart and interest in their work. In other words, the atmosphere is of a rather resigned nature. We have run out of beans in the camp, so now we get rice noodles, a little bean mash made into soup. Our rice ration has been cut to 640 grams per day. (It was 750 at one time.) I weigh 115 pounds now. I hope to pick up some weight if I can stay on this detail. Inside details were all changed the other day, so Tony McCabe got on one of the policing-up details. Vance is back to work, feeling pretty good. There is an epidemic of fever, sick stomach, and headaches going around. They think it is caused either by the fleas or the mosquitoes. I had it last week and felt really rugged. The fleas in camp are terrible. Some nights a person can hardly sleep at all, and under the circumstances, we have no way of getting rid of them. We are also greatly afflicted with body lice. My God, I'll be glad to live like a human being again, instead of like an animal. I have been troubled with diarrhea lately. On July 31, we got some tobacco (mostly hair), one pack for ten men. Today we got five cigarettes and one-third bar of soap per man.

Rumors are sounding good. It starts to look like this may be over soon—we hope so! We heard that Lt. Col. Stubbs' camp was bombed—twenty-seven men were wounded, mostly in the arms and legs. We have had several daylight raids by pursuit planes. On July 30, five men were wounded, and one was killed. An explosive bullet tore up his insides.

During daylight raids, we were all supposed to go to our bays, especially bay leaders if we happened to be in camp. As I dashed past this particular bay, I saw a big lanky Dutchman lying face-down in the middle of his bay—his back blown open and his kidneys lying on the ground beside him. In the next bay was a man shot right through the stomach.

Xxxx xx, xxxx

Sgt. Bailey of the Medical Corps lost both of his legs below the knees. It sure was a shame. He is getting along pretty well now. The other men suffered shrapnel wounds in various parts of the body. The other day, a recon plane dropped a bomb across the channel over by Yokkaichi and one in the naval yard close to the factory. I was over at the village after rice, so I was pretty close to it. In fact, I was so close that I saw the bomb falling, and the wave of detonated shrapnel flew all around us. I was lying flat on the ground because I couldn't get to a shelter. Very few men in the camp show any fear at all now. Personally, I seem to have lost all signs of any emotion. I can't understand what has come over me. I am of a much different temperament than I used to be.

Our air-raid shelters have been fixed up better with a roof over them since the raid of July 30. Rumor has it we are to get Red Cross soon. We still hold Protestant services about twice a week. I gave the sermon last Monday night. How I look forward to going to church with my family again. It is almost tenko time, so I must stop.

The Sun Sets on Japan

He makes wars cease to the end of the earth; he breaks the bow and shatters the spear; he burns the chariot with fire.
—Psalms 46:9

August 19, 1945
O happy day! All indications are that the war is over.

We always wondered just what the circumstances of the end would be like when it finally did come. Would there be death-dealing air raids, or since we were on the beach, would there be an extensive softening-up by massive shelling from the sea, followed by an invasion? Or would we be slaughtered first? I don't think anyone expected a general surrender—not by the Japanese. I suppose that is why when the end finally did come, it was difficult for us to believe what was happening. It came so easily and so quietly.

Undramatic as it was, my recollection of the final outcome is uncannily vivid, even though it occurred almost forty-nine years ago. I had just come off the Japanese kitchen detail and had gone back to my old job on Kosaku Nikko, the railroad detail. We had gone to work as usual in the forenoon of August 15 and had returned to camp at noon for lunch, just as any other day. As our detail was returning to work at 1:00 P.M., we were stopped at some superintendent's office. After a few moments of animated conversation between our guard and the factory official, the guard returned to camp, leaving us standing there in formation. In a few moments, he was back, spoke a few words to the official, then gave us an about-face and marched us back into camp with no explanation whatsoever. As soon as we broke formation to return to our respective bays, Blackie Grossman came over and said to us, "Did you hear the news? The war is over." Since not everything Blackie had told people in the past was above question, we passed it off as so much baloney, and some of the guys told him what they thought he was full of. "No, honest," he said, "I was working back of the guardhouse on camp duty, and the guards began jabbering all of a sudden. They didn't know I was back there, but they kept saying 'Sensor yame, sensor yame' (The war is over, the war is over.)"

It still did not seem possible. It had been so long in coming that it was not possible to conceive of the fact immediately that there was a different

190

type of life. And besides, nothing cataclysmic had occurred to signal that great a change. But then other details began returning, just as we had. And those that had been forming to go out were dismissed.

No details went out to work the next day, nor the day following. So we just lay around in camp in a sort of limbo, not hearing anything further, not knowing what to make of this strange situation. We were enjoying the rest, but we wanted to know what was up. Did they anticipate a giant air raid? Were they preparing for an invasion? Or was the war indeed over?

Finally, Capt. Thompson went to the Japanese commander and told him, "We have reason to believe that the war is over. And if it is over, we have a right to know it is over, and demand that you tell us. Also, if the war is over, this camp is no longer a Japanese prison camp. It is an American military installation. As such, no Japanese enters it without our permission. Furthermore, we demand a twenty-four-hour perimeter armed guard to protect us from your people. "To this the Japanese camp commander responded that he was going into the village (Yokkaichi or Nagoya?) that evening and he would know more when he returned.

August 17, 1945 (Friday)

On August 15, details went back to work at 1:00 P.M. as usual, but when we got over to the factory, all the employees were taking off for home, bag and baggage, so we were taken back into camp, and haven't been back to work since, nor have there been any air raids. Since it has come in from several sources (all unofficial) that we surrounded Tokyo, bombed, strafed, shelled, and finally took it over, and that now men are arriving at the peace terms. Most of the men in camp are taking it in stride. In a way they believe it, yet it has been so long, and we have been disappointed so many times, that it seems inconceivable that anything like that could happen to us. Then too, this bunch of men has become much harder than we realize and has lost practically all signs of emotion. Now we are all waiting for the official announcement and the first sign of the Yanks. The first day we heard about it, a couple of guys who had been quartermastering American and Nip cigarettes passed out several packages of them.

The entire Japanese kitchen detail was changed, so I went back to work on the railroad August 14. Work on that detail has been very easy lately. All we were doing was putting in our time by making a pretense of working.

Summer has finally come to Yokkaichi. We have had one shower in three weeks, so the weather is hot and dry.

When I came off the kitchen detail, I had a full belly, some mesau and vinegar, a pair of home-made canvas shoes paid for in food, and a little over twelve bowls of rice loaned out to be paid one-quarter bowl per meal each day, so I am eating well now.

The last couple of days I have had a bad case of diarrhea, passing a lot of blood and mucus. It seems to be getting a little better since they put me on sulfaguanidine. The medical corporal came down from Toyama the other day with news that Chief Williams had died of TB, and some Dutchman was killed in the mines. Also that they had gotten through the last big bombing raid OK.

The Nips are putting out some stuff they have been holding back in the commissary such as toothpaste, tea, etc. Also they are getting the payroll up to date, so there are lots of things indicating that our POW days are soon to be over. Lord, I hope so! Rumor has it that we are supposed to go to Tokyo in five days.

We have run out of noodles in the kitchen and have gotten some bean mash instead, thank goodness, so our ration is one-half bowl of rice and three-quarters bowl of beans, and seaweed soup for supper. What everyone is clamoring for now is more chow and some tobacco. For the first time in a couple of months, I am craving nicotine. How I hope we are soon taken over by the Yanks so we will get some of these things. Time will go slowly now until that time comes. Last night, a small group of us Protestants got together and held a service of mostly songs (patriotic and religious) and prayers of thanks.

I plan to swim in the ocean and take a shower now, so will bring this to a close, hoping to have good news soon.

In the meantime, we continued to mark time by resting between meals and speculating about the future. There was already a relaxed feeling because there was no tenko and no Japanese agenda for us. Capt. Thompson had also emphasized that the men wanted to swim in the ocean, and they demanded that privilege. (We were still bothered terribly by the fleas.) He also announced that because the Japanese were forbidden to enter our camp without permission, we in turn were not to mingle with the Japanese—military or civilian— without permission. On one occasion, however, Three-Finger Jack came to the gate and asked permission to enter. He wanted to talk. He had been a mean guard—always quick to shout at, belittle, and beat prisoners. Obviously he had a guilty conscience and wanted to clear it. The men near the gate let him in and ushered him into the barracks. I was not present at the time, but those who were said the conversation went something like this:

> JACK: You think I'm bad?
> POWs: Yes, we think you are bad.
> JACK: Will Americans find out?
> POWs: Yes, Americans will find out.
> JACK: You think Americans will punish me?
> POWs: Yes, Americans will punish you.
> JACK: You think I should commit hara-kiri?
> POWs: Good idea.

After that exchange, Jack left camp and was never seen again. (About forty years after the war, I learned from Barney Grill, a Fifth Air Base medic who testified on atrocities at the Japanese War Crimes Trials, that Three-Finger Jack had gone into hiding rather than commit suicide. Several years later he came out of hiding and lived in disgrace.)

On the third day after Capt. Thompson's ultimatum, the Japanese camp commander returned and told Capt. Thompson that there had been a cessation of hostilities, that he doubted the war would resume, and that details of a formal surrender were being worked out. He also brought a radio into camp so we could listen to the broadcast of the surrender in Tokyo Bay. The Japanese commanding officer had also ordered a large number of civilians to roll cigarettes to be distributed in camp, plus of course ordering extra food and new clothes. They even marched in two live hogs to be butchered. In addition, he arranged for some civilians to paint a huge PW in white on the roof of the camp. We learned later that this was to identify our camp for the purpose of making aerial food drops. (How we wished those markings would have been there to mark our camp during the air raids of the previous months.)

Some of us were out on the beach one day (before the PW sign was painted on the roof) when three navy fighter planes came over quite low. It appeared as though one was having trouble and was about to crash land on the beach, when all of a sudden the engine coughed and it continued on its way, but not before we discovered it had RAF markings on its wings.

The next day, to our amazement and glee, these same planes came over again and dropped dozens of bright yellow parachutes containing hundreds of loaves of bread, treats, magazines, and messages containing all kinds of information about the last several years. Probably most important of all was the news of the two megabombs. We knew nothing of them until that air drop. That explained to us why on those two days the Japanese had been glued to their radio sets. It also explained why they were contemplating surrender without the further ado of an invasion. The planes also identified themselves as coming from the British aircraft carrier HMS *Indefatigable* and informed us that they would pay daily visits until the B-29s took over with food drops.

Two days after the British discovered us, the first B-29s came over, and the sky seemed filled with parachutes, some red, some white, and some blue. Some of the larger loads were carried in two 55-gallon drums welded end to end and the remainder in single drums. Occasionally a chute would not open, and the load would plummet to the earth like a bullet and explode with a frightening force on impact. On one occasion, there were three or four Japanese civilians sitting around a small table having tea and hoping to gather up some food left on the ground. A chute carrying gallon containers of canned peaches came plummeting to earth and landed squarely in their midst. They never knew what hit them: killed by canned peaches.

With these multicolored parachutes, men of the three nations represented in that camp began making handmade flags of their respective countries. They were crude, but to us they were beautiful. On September 2, 1945, we hoisted them from poles set in the ground on the beach as we sang our respective national anthems. Four hours later, the surrender documents were signed aboard the U.S. battleship *Missouri* in Tokyo Bay. (The U.S. flag we made in camp is on display at the Pioneer Village Museum in Minden, Nebraska, Capt. Thompson's home state.)

Carl Nordin in front of flag made from parachutes used to drop food to prisoners in Japan. (The flag is on display at the Pioneer Village Museum in Minden, Nebraska.)

August 23, 1945 (Thursday)

We are still in the same camp patiently awaiting orders to move. On the 19th the Japanese CO returned from Nagoya and told us that there was an armistice while the peace terms were being drawn up, but that there was only one chance in a thousand that the war would be resumed. He said that he would get us more chow and tobacco, and that treatment would be more lenient. We have received an increase in rice and beans and dried fish, but as yet no fresh vegetables. Now we get a little more than 500 grams of rice and 300 grams of beans per man per day, plus dried fish, seaweed and radish soup with mesau in it, plus a little tea or coffee. On August 20, we were issued six Quince cigarettes per man, and today we are to get four more. They also brought in new clothes, so everyone is pretty well outfitted. We hold our own roll call, and the Nips leave us pretty much to ourselves within camp. We are also allowed to go on the beach swimming, so things indicate that, if peace hasn't been signed, it is, at least, very imminent. Also they let us sleep on the ground (out by the beach) at night. I have been doing so because it is much cooler, and the fleas are not nearly as bad.

The men are getting fairly well filled-up now. I have been taking in one-quarter bowl of rice per meal every day on what I had loaned out while on the Nip kitchen detail, so I have really been getting full. A lot of the men have been troubled with diarrhea and cramps, caused mostly by some roasted beans we got August 19 and 20 which were very difficult to digest, especially for our weak stomachs. I am still troubled with diarrhea, but it has improved immensely. In fact, I am standing this increase in chow and general diarrhea epidemic better than the average, much to my surprise. The doctor ordered three meals of lugao for the entire camp to straighten out our stomachs.

Everyone is in a good mood, naturally, but still there is not as much sentiment or emotion shown by this group of men as one might imagine after having waited so long for this. It's just that it seems impossible for something this good to happen to us.

We hear all kinds of rumors of leaving, getting on ships, going to Manila first, etc. We won't know for sure what our program will be till we actually experience it. We hope and rather expect to leave before the first of the month. Life is much easier—more pleasant than it has been for three-and-a-half years, but still we are anxious and impatient to get started on our journey home. For some reason, they are painting a big PW on the roof of our camp. It seems ironic that all through the war our camp was not marked, but now that it is over, they are going to mark it. It is another example of the Nip logic.

I am anxious to get where some other prisoners are, hoping to meet up with some of my old friends and to see how they are. All day of the 20th I thought of Dad, it being his birthday, hoping he is alive and well, realizing that my chances are very good of celebrating with him on his next birthday. God, it is going to be good to be home again. Time for chow now.

August 27, 1945 (Monday)

New things are happening every day now, so all I'll do is hit the high spots. We have been issued more new clothes—those we need. [It seems that the Japanese did not want the Americans to see how we actually had been clothed the last year.] Also, we have gotten some new shoes. [I did not receive new shoes, so I was liberated wearing my handmade canvas shoes.] We get as much food as we want now. The variety isn't so big, but the amount is more than we have had for three-and-a-half years. We do get a few eggplants, squash, potatoes, etc. Friday we got three apples per man. On August 23, we got one bottle of wine for every eight-and-two-thirds men. We have received a total of nine cigarettes for privates and sixteen cigarettes NCOs since August 15. That is one thing these people can't seem to get for us. They have certainly given us a lot of things in the last two weeks that we should have had before.

On August 24, the Nip CO entertained Capt. Thompson for dinner. He told him four important points. First, the war is over. Second, the peace treaty is to be signed August 31. [It was signed September 2.] Third, we should be leaving for home sometime after September 1st. Fourth, U.S. planes would drop food at the camp in the very near future. (So far we have not received any because the weather has been bad for several days.) [We learned later that a typhoon had struck Japan.]

Today we were visited by Swiss delegates from the International Red Cross. They told us lots of things, the most important being that two cities were destroyed by one bomb each, which was the determining factor in ending this war. Planes would drop Red Cross food before we leave, we would be among the first to leave due to our position (location), and that we would leave about September 1st as transports are already on the way over. The worst hospital cases will be taken out by ambulance planes. Roosevelt and Hitler are dead, Truman is president, Russia entered the war against Japan a short while ago, we are still recruiting men and building ships, baseball is the only sport they kept up during the war, and there will be a world-wide baseball jamboree next year; many countries have tried to send Red Cross in to us, but Japan would not allow it. We also heard that there are 3,160 American POW's left in Japan. It is astounding.

Today some U.S. pursuit planes flew over. Some of the men have been taking undue advantage of our increased liberty and have wandered off to the factory and village to deal clothes off for cigarettes. It is off-limits for us, so Capt. Thompson has had to punish them. Last night was the climax when McChane, Walsh, and Underwood were caught in the Korean barracks. They are now in the guardhouse and will have to stand trial when they are turned over to the proper authorities.

I have been doing a little reading and a little sewing, such as putting collars on collarless shirts, also sleeping a lot to pass the time away. Today I have a fever again. Last night, I was terribly sick to my stomach. I also forgot to mention that we received three live pigs in the last few days. Tobacco is the worst problem now. It seems too good to be true that all the trial and tribulation is over and that we will soon be going home.

The other day, some fellows broke into the Nip office and got a lot of the rogues' gallery pictures that were taken of us last fall. They will be the best testimony we could have of what this group of men has endured. I weighed 61 kilos, or 134 pounds, last night, so it shows what a little extra food and rest will do. A month ago I weighed 115 pounds. I'll be glad to get back in shape and be healthy and strong again. Thank God all this is over. The best days of our lives lie ahead.

There was a navy PBY plane that, along with the other planes, played a rather significant role in these last days. After first finding us, it flew by daily, leaving messages and making deliveries of items that we had requested by scratching our requests in huge letters in the sand. It made its last delivery of blood plasma to us the last day we were there. (Unfortunately, the man died the last night we were in Yokkaichi, but the PBY tried.) It also happened to pass by with its huge side door open just as we were raising our respective countries' flags on September 2. A navy photographer standing in the doorway of the plane was taking pictures. It should be noted also that in addition to being a bold statement of victory by once-vanquished men, the flag raising took place three hours before the instrument of surrender was signed aboard the battleship *Missouri* in Tokyo Bay.

Those flags made one more significant statement as we left that camp forever on the morning of September 4, 1945. Since our bay was at the end of the barracks, we were the first men out of the camp. Acting in as military

Top left: Japanese army photo of Carl Nordin, October 1944. This photo and the other "rogues' gallery" shots that follow were stolen from an office of the Japanese army in August 1945. Top right: Robert (Bob) Dennis, Japan, October 1944. Bottom left: Odell Hicks, Japan, October 1944. Bottom right: William (Bill) Lowe, Japan, October 1944.

Left: Dwight Shaw, Japan, October 1944. Right: Albert (Al) Nichols, Japan, October 1944.

a fashion as we could, we lined up in a column of fours. Being bay leader, I was stationed to the right of the front rank of the column, with a young lad named Medinah carrying the Stars and Stripes on my immediate right. I could not see, but I presume that the Dutch and English flags accompanied their respective contingents.

I was hardly prepared for the surprise that greeted me as we marched out the gate, for we had no more than cleared the gate than Ikuta-San and Sato-San stepped out of the civilians crowded along our path of march and walked up to me. Striding right along with me, they began handing me gifts—new chopsticks and a monkey hair pipe along with some monkey hair—saying "Sava-su" (gift, or I give). I wanted to stop and shake their hands or do something as a sort of kind acknowledgment, but I thought that it was incumbent on me to continue in the orderly and dignified departure we wanted to present to the world. I did, however, accept the gifts as graciously as I could under the circumstances and gave each of the men a friendly "arigato."

We continued in formation through the factory area to a waiting ferry tied up the pier. Since the front rank boarded first, we made our way to the front end immediately. I was amazed at the crowd of civilians who had gathered to see us off. And there in the very front of the group stood Sato-San and Ikuta-San looking intently at us. Then as the ferry began leaving the pier, Ikuta-San brought out a white handkerchief, began waving it, and with unabashed tears streaming down his cheeks kept repeating, "Sayonara, Nordin, sayonara, Nordin" (Farewell, Nordin, farewell, Nordin.) I was no longer "san yacko san ju yan" (#334). Finally, I was a name instead of a number. I was so moved by everything that had happened that I wanted to go down there and hug the men, especially Ikuta-San, and tell them that we were no longer enemies—now we were friends. A great sadness arose in me that a cruel war had placed such a great gulf between such nice people and us, a war that neither wanted. As the ferry pulled inexorably away, I was seized by a great longing to come back some day and fulfill my desire for reconciliation. And strangely, I always had a feeling way down deep that it might occur. Stranger still was the fact that after thirty-two years, it did occur.

As our trucks carried us from the ferry to the train depot, we were amazed by the destruction that was once Nagoya, a huge industrial complex. Whole sections of the city were utterly demolished, locomotives lay on their sides, and there was evidence of devastating fires. It's a wonder people could live through it all. The main railway depot had been damaged, but portions were still usable.

Our guards, now docile, stayed with us as we were escorted into a cavernous waiting room. The quietness and somber surroundings of this once-bustling hub evoked an eerie feeling. It seemed so unnatural. There was one lone passenger sitting by a window when we arrived—an American serviceman. He too was being liberated. He had been in another camp near Nagoya, but had been brought into the city quite recently to undergo an appendectomy and was to be liberated with us. It was from him that we heard the first of countless horror stories we would be hearing in the weeks ahead, stories of atrocities committed against our buddies, stories of the deaths of our buddies by the hundreds at a time.

The POW we met in the train depot had left the Philippines on the hell ship *Oryoku Maru*, which to hell ship survivors has become synonymous with atrocities at their worst. It was sunk by bombs, and survivors were transferred to another ship after being denied food and water for days. A second ship was torpedoed and sunk with great loss of life. They continued on to Japan in a third ship. He told of men being crazed from thirst, of saving urine and drinking it after it settled, of attacking and killing others for their blood. Of the 1,619 officers and men who embarked on the *Oryoku Maru*, fewer than 435 reached Moji, Japan, six weeks after leaving the Philippines, and many of them died soon after as a result of their weakened condition. We were appalled, but this was just the beginning.

The first Yank I saw as our train sped through the Japanese countryside was a middle-aged major with a huge blonde walrus mustache. Then we saw them—young strapping men that looked like giants to us puny POWs. I was close to the front of the lead car, so I got a real good firsthand look. I let out a yell—"Hey, you Yanks!" Immediately all you could hear up and down the cars as the train slowed to a stop was, "Yanks, Yanks, Yanks!"

As we dismounted out in the middle of the country, we were surrounded by these huge, healthy, well-dressed, well-equipped men. One after the other of them asked us—"Are there any mean ones here?" (speaking of the guards). "Got any you want us to take care of?" "Want any souvenirs?" "Rifles?" "Cheese knives?" (sabers). But all we wanted was out. Had we been stronger, more full of vim and vigor, there might have been some requests, but in the absence of that, we were lined up for a final roll call as prisoners of war. The guards were visibly nervous; some were actually frightened as they prepared to turn us over to the Americans. What a switch! We were informed that those who were well would be taken aboard various naval craft, and those of us who were not considered well or fit would be taken aboard the hospital ship USS *Rescue*. The ships were lying out to sea, a mile or two away. Then came the roll call, the exchange, and finally after three-and-a-half years as prisoners of war, somewhere along the east coast of Japan between Nagoya and Osaka, we became free Americans again. It was unbelievable; we could hardly comprehend it.

September 7, 1945 (Friday)

So much has happened since my last entry that I shall just enumerate the high spots. On August 29, sixteen dive bombers off HMS *Indefatigable* found our camp and dropped packages of food, cigarettes, etc., by parachute. Also papers and news sheets and a few notes from crew members were dropped. On the 30th, they came back again. On the 31st, our own B-29s found us and dropped great loads of chow, tobacco, and clothing. By this time, hardly any chow was eaten out of the mess. The B-29s came over a couple more times. On September 2, we had a flag-raising ceremony of three nations (England, U.S., and Holland) at 6:00 A.M. on the beach. Just as we were raising the flags, both U.S. and British planes came over and saw us. It was one of the most remarkable coincidences I have ever experienced. It was a year ago to the day since we had first landed in Japan (Moji). On the night of the 3rd, we received orders to move by 5:00 A.M., so in the morning of September 4, we left Yokkaichi exactly one year to the day after arriving there.

We went by train down the coast about four hours' ride. At 1:30, we saw our first free Yanks in almost four years. What a wonderful, thrilling sight! They were marines off the cruiser *San Juan*. Soon after getting off the train, we were taken to the U.S. Navy hospital ship *Rescue*. (Since we were so lousey, we had to remove our clothes on the platform at the top of the steps going up the side of the ship and throw everything but our personal belongings into the ocean.) There (inside) we were deloused, cleaned up, and given new clothes, diagnosed, classified, and fed supper of fried eggs, bread, butter, jelly, and chocolate sundaes. Some went out on APD boats that went right to Tokyo. Others, including myself, stayed aboard the *Rescue* for treatment. God, it's great to be free again!

Part III

A.D. (After Deliverance)

The Long Road Home

—Psalms 55:6

The five days and nights spent on the hospital ship *Rescue* were so completely different from anything we had known for four years that we almost had to pinch ourselves to realize it was all actually true. We felt so dressed up in our new clothes. Actually they were olive green marine fatigues, but to us they seemed fancy enough to go to a military ball. And the food; we just couldn't get over it. Since our first meal was rather impromptu, we were served eggs—three the first serving, and two for seconds, and the guys could go through the line as many times as they liked. But perhaps one of the most astounding things was the beds. Individual cots with mattresses, pillows, and clean white sheets and pillowcases. Before our conversation had become almost entirely food-oriented when we were prisoners, we used to talk of someday sleeping on mattresses and clean sheets—a nice clean soft bed. But on this score we got fooled. We had slept on one hard surface or another with only a blanket between it and our body for so long that when we got on these soft beds, we couldn't relax. To the great surprise of the medical personnel, many, if not most of the men, went up on deck, where they slept like babies. I was tempted to do so because it had been a long day, and I was tired, but I decided that sooner or later I would have to become accustomed to this new way of living, so I was determined to stick it out. Lights out was at 9:00 P.M. At 11:30, I was still wide awake. I just couldn't relax. At midnight, I got up and asked the nurse for a sleeping pill. At 1:00 A.M., I asked her for another. Finally at 3:00 A.M., I explained my predicament. I really did want to get accustomed to soft beds, so could she please give me another pill? The third sleeping pill did it, but I had to have two the next night, and one the next two nights before I could relax enough on those soft beds to drop off to sleep. But oh, the delicious feeling to wake up in the morning and find yourself enveloped in nice, clean, white sheets!

Several hours each forenoon and afternoon were spent in processing, later called debriefing, plus physical examinations and just doing everything to get us oriented to go back out into the world. On two occasions, I was called back to assist a couple of the panels. The lieutenant commander who had first interviewed me and then called me back for assistance told the panel, "You wouldn't believe this man's memory, his recall of dates, events, names, and places."

For identification, each man was given a large sign to attach to his clothing bearing the words, "Project J." This seemed to entitle us to priority on just about everything. Also during those five days, the reunions with men who had gone to Toyama or other camps when we had landed at Moji a year ago were beginning. I met up with Roeske, Baca, and Gonzalez from our outfit. Every day was a holiday.

As we steamed toward Yokohama, everyone kept looking for Mt. Fujiyama, the one symbol of beauty that Japan will always have, but we had mostly cloudy, foggy, and rainy weather. On Sunday morning, however, we had a church service on deck along with Holy Communion. It was a beautiful, meaningful service in every respect, and then just as the service ended, the clouds lifted, and there to our left, lo and behold, was Mt. Fujiyama in all its magnificent beauty. What a way it was to celebrate the close of a Communion service. It was almost as if God was revealing himself to us. What a way it was to reenter the real world.

On September 9, the *Rescue* tied up at a pier in Yokohama just opposite the hospital ship *Hope*. Later that day, the *Mercy* pulled in on the other side of the *Rescue*. All three ships were discharging liberated personnel for onward transport. The very ill remained on the ships until they reached the States. While waiting for our transportation to Atsugi Airfield, we were visited by a number of high-ranking officers. One of them happened to be Lt. General Eichelberger, who had served under General MacArthur in the southern islands and who less than two weeks before had been detailed to lead an advance team into Japan to secure the area and make the arrangements for a place for MacArthur to stay once the surrender was signed. In conversation with General Eichelberger, we learned a lot about the campaign in the south that had brought us to this day.

We couldn't help but marvel at the excellent job of organization that had been done at the Atsugi Airdrome. There was a steady stream of men coming and going, trucks and planes arriving and leaving. It is a large place, and it served the purpose well.

Not only were there various canteens, but there were also places where Project J men could send one free cablegram to next of kin. It was a noble try, but things were jammed up so badly that mine didn't arrive home for several weeks, leaving my family uninformed for longer than they should have been and thus causing undue concern about my status. While our group was just standing around waiting, a British naval officer sauntered over and, noticing the Project J, asked where we had been held in prison. When we replied, "Yokkaichi," his face really lit up, and he introduced himself as an officer from the HMS *Indefatigable*. Then he proceeded to tell us how happy those pilots were to find us and how they pleaded to go back the next day. He said they sort of adopted us as their charges. He went on to relate how they used up all the flour they had stored up in case they were involved in an invasion force. That flour made 1,300 loaves of bread, and they dropped it all on our camp.

Even though I signed off my diary with a "finis," I began keeping notes again after I found some paper. I later transcribed them and have added them to my original diary. I think the reader will gain a sharper perspective of the thrills I was experiencing when one realizes that at the time I went overseas, there was no such plane as a C-54 and probably not even a C-47. Passenger service via air was in its infancy. Those were still the days of the Ford tri-motor plane and other planes of a similar vintage and capability. The extent of my flying experience had been a couple of rides in a two-place, open-cockpit plane flown by barnstormers. Also of significance will be my accounts of seeing firsthand all the ships, planes, equipment, and men I saw on my journey home. For someone who had fought a war without enough equipment, guns, ammunition, or food to carry on a winning campaign, what we saw wherever we went was simply mind-boggling.

September 9, 1945 (Sunday)

Left USS *Rescue* at about 1:00 P.M. Had chow and was reprocessed on the pier. Went out to Atsugi Airport near Tokyo. Had more chow. Red Cross canteens at every place of detention where POWs can get tobacco, candy, gum, toilet articles, etc., free of charge. Everyone treats us wonderfully. All of us are in hog heaven. While at Atsugi, I had a chat with an officer from HMS *Indefatigable*. (It was planes from the British aircraft carrier that first discovered our camp and brought our first bread to us.) Upon seeing our fleet, air corps, and other military equipment, it is the most awe-inspiring, almost stupefying feeling one can imagine after having been out of existence for so long.

Boarded a C-54 and took off from Atsugi Airport at 8:15 P.M. A wonderful plane, it belongs to United Airlines and was flown by five civilians who were under contract to the army. It carries thirty passengers. Flying at 8,000 feet, it brings in airborne troops for the occupation of Japan. The first stop will be Okinawa, where we will change planes en route to Manila. What a thrill!

September 10, 1945 (Monday)

We arrived safely at Okinawa at 1:30 A.M. The departure has been slowed up because of bad weather, so we may be detained a couple of days. Right now we are in temporary quarters (tents, canvas cots, etc.) Right after arrival we were taken to a Red Cross canteen and given coffee, donuts, Coca-Cola, confections, etc. It is amazing how much equipment we see everywhere. Had Grape Nuts for breakfast, among other things. Saw Dennis today.

It was good to see Dennis again. The way things were when the group he was in left for Toyama almost three-and-a-half months earlier, we never knew if we would see one another again. Like the rest of us, he too had lost considerable weight during those last three months, but he was doing his best to gain it back. A slight man anyway, he told me that he had gone to 44 kilos or about 97 pounds while at Toyama.

Not only were we being reunited with buddies from whom we had been separated at some prior time, but I experienced an even stranger coincidence while on Okinawa. I had noticed that every day when I made my morning visit to the latrine, there would always be trucks passing just back of the latrine taking GIs in blue fatigue clothes out on work details. This one particular day, I was sure I caught a glimpse of Harold Olson, one of my cousins from Wisconsin, but in an instant he was gone. It was such a surprise because I had left home before the draft was ordered up, so my mental picture of people back home didn't envision friends, neighbors, or relatives in uniform. Moreover, the America that I had left was an America at peace. Shortly after that, we found out that a Japanese soldier had been holed up in a cave and had sneaked out and killed the lieutenant of the guard. Now I had something to identify the time with. So when I saw Harold three or four months later, sure enough, he had been sent to Okinawa after spending most of the war in the Aleutians, and sure enough, he had been stationed at that airfield, and sure enough, he had kept an eye out for me as they took that route to work every morning, and sure enough, he remembered the lieutenant of the guard being killed. (I can still see him turning his head the other way just as I saw him. We came that close to meeting face-to-face.)

The next leg of our journey made us a little nervous. We had an early breakfast, were loaded on trucks, and were taken to the airfield. We passed row upon row of planes. We had never seen so many planes in one place before in our lives. Word came down that we would ride in bombers to the Philippines. It was just getting to be daylight, so we could enjoy the fancy paintings on the sides of the planes and the clever names the crews had given to them. The one our group was assigned to turned out to be the cleverest one of all. It had a brightly painted picture of a voluptuous cowgirl astride a wildly bucking donkey, and off to the side was painted, "Wild Ass Ride!" We began to believe it was aptly named after some of the crew members began passing out parachutes. Then they gave us instructions on how to use a parachute in one easy lesson, explaining that many of us would have to ride in the bomb bays, which had been known to rattle open, necessitating use of a parachute.

The plane was a B-24 Liberator, with an interior that was not nearly as inviting in appearance as the exterior. One quick look and it was easy to see this had been a workhorse, with lots of hours and undoubtedly lots of history to its credit. It was bare-bones throughout, with only a few 2" by 8" planks strewn on the bomb bay gates or doors. There were wide, gaping spaces between the planks, which widened and narrowed as the whole assembly shuddered and jiggled back and forth in flight. The first men on the plane were moved back into every available space, while the rest of us stood on the planks in the bomb bays. Eventually a few crates were made available so we could take turns sitting down. But whether sitting or standing, the only scenery was what we could see through the cracks between the planks. (We were surprised at how much shipping we saw.) Never far from our thoughts were the parachute instructions we had received before boarding. After we had landed at Clark Field in the Philippines, we learned that the bomb bay doors of another plane in our flight had indeed opened. Several days later, we were eating our noon meal, when two men came in after the meal had begun. They had just been brought in from northern Luzon, where they had parachuted to earth. It was serious, but it was also comical to hear them tell it. First was the surprise of falling out, then they fumbled for the rip cord and wondered if they would find it in time. Then they pulled it and wondered if the chute would open. Then when it did open, they just hung there in space and wondered if they would ever get down. Then as they looked around and saw that they were close to land, but were actually over water, they wondered if they would land in the water or if they would drift toward land. They finally landed in a rice paddy, and the shrouds dragged them through the mud and water before they could be pulled in. The next thing they had to do was try to explain to the Filipino farmer, who could not understand English, what their predicament was. We heard, but I cannot confirm, that there were others who were not as fortunate.

September 13, 1945 (Thursday)

Left Okinawa at 7:00 A.M. aboard a B-24 bomber. Arrived at Clark Field, P.I., at 12:30 P.M. Boarded a C-47 a couple of hours later and flew to Nichols Field (twenty-minute flight). From there we went to the 29th Replacement Center close to Manila.

September 14, 1945 (Friday)

Took a physical exam, got a telegram from Dad about 9:00 P.M. Oh happy day!

September 15, 1945 (Saturday)

Interviews, war and prison history, and general processing. Got some letters from Fay, Luella, Anna, and Dad. Found out all I've wondered about for four years. Now I'm really happy! Meeting old friends every day. Also finding out that many old friends are dead due to fiendish Jap atrocities.

I learned later that my family had been given an address to write to their next of kin, just in case he should be alive. (The War Department did not yet know my status, whether dead or alive. All they knew was that if I was alive, I would be coming through that replacement center.)

Although the letters seemed to have a sort of vague, not-knowing-for-sure tone to them, it was wonderful to be receiving mail so recently written.

The telegram from Dad was especially meaningful to me, as I had worried so about his health. Besides, he had always been more than a father to me; he had been my best friend. And the letters from family members were precious to me. But most important of all were the letters from Fay, naturally. I had so hoped she would still be there when I returned. And now it appeared that my wishes and my prayers were being granted. But there was something about me or within me that was a little strange. I was happy and all that, but it didn't all seem real. I don't know if it was that there had been such a sudden change that I couldn't quite absorb it all or if it was the inability to experience deep emotion that had become part of our psyches that seemed to separate me from true and complete reality. Anyway, that's the way it was until one day as I was in the midst of reading the eight letters I had received that day, all of a sudden, it was as if something had broken within me. I suddenly became warm and vibrant and tingly all over. I absolutely involuntarily jumped up on my cot and began shouting to my tentmates, "Hey, I'm going home. The war is over. I'm going home." Odell Hicks was sitting on his cot reading his mail at the same time. When I exploded, he said, "What's the matter with you, Nordin? Have you gone nuts?" "No," I said. "It's all over, I'm going home!" And from that very moment, I was completely human again. The same thing happened to Odell Hicks the next day. It wasn't unusual to see a man suddenly stop eating in the mess hall, jump up, and holler, "Hey, I'm going home" or "The war is over" or some such utterance of release, and suddenly it seemed as if their countenances changed and became more relaxed. It was a wonderful feeling.

There were reunions every day. One day I met and talked with Lt. Parks. He had been first sergeant of the Fifth Air Base Headquarters Squadron when we went overseas. He had received a field commission, and at Dapecol he was barracks leader of Barracks Nine when I lived there. I learned from Parks that he, Lt. Ricks, my commanding officer, and Corporal Bowden of our outfit had been on the *Oryoku Maru*. Parks had seen Bowden the night before he was killed by a thirst-crazed man. It seemed so hard to believe—Bowden, a quiet, studious man, whose desk had only been about six feet from mine when I worked in the property office at Fort Douglas. He had had to remain behind at Fort McKinley when our outfit was transferred to Mindanao in 1941. He needed some type of eye care and was supposed to come down and rejoin us later. But the early advent of the war had precluded that, so he remained on Luzon until he began that ill-fated trip to Japan on the *Oryoku Maru*. Another man from our outfit who had had to stay behind at Fort McKinley was Pvt. East who had remained because of an appendicitis attack. He survived the war and prison camp and was reunited with us there in Manila.

Little by little, snippets of information came in about the fates of other prisoners, many of them former buddies. It didn't sound good for the Lasang detail, but it had been a year since their ship was sunk, and the few survivors of that tragedy had long since gone home. Tom Earl and Mike Minotti of our outfit had been sent to Cabantuan from Bilibid Prison at the same time we went to Japan, but all indications were that they did not survive. (Odell contacted Tom Earl's mother after the war. He had not survived.) All indications are that Minotti did not survive either. Of the thirty-eight enlisted men in our detachment who left Fort Douglas, Utah, in 1941, nineteen are known dead—a loss of fifty percent. If Valdez, whom we had to leave in Hawaii, did not survive, the percentage increases a little.

The accounts of tragedies and horror stories kept pouring in. I met my first survivor of the Palawan Massacre one afternoon while having coffee at the Red Cross canteen. He told how the Japanese built a long pit in the sand, with barbed-wire entanglements around it. Feigning a presumed air raid, the Japanese marched 150 Americans into the air-raid shelter. They dumped drums of gasoline on them and set them on fire. The few that were able to get out before catching on fire were bayoneted or shot as they tried to get through the barbed-wire entanglements. It was learned later that eleven men did get through, many of them seriously wounded, and swam across a bay to safety. He was one of the few survivors. In later years, we learned that thousands of men had died on hell ships or in the water after the ships had been torpedoed and sunk. One of them was my very good friend Jug Imlay.

There were cases on the other side as well. One comes to mind. While we were at the 29th Replacement Center, I talked with a man who had been part of a group that was split off from us at Moji. He told of one man who had worked in the kitchen in Japan, so he was in pretty good shape at war's end. He had been a pretty big and rugged man to begin with. When the war ended, he went to the Japanese camp commander and told him, "You have mistreated and killed some of my friends. You have used weapons to kill them. Now I am going to kill you, but I will use no weapons. I will use my own two hands and beat you to death." And this man who witnessed it said that's exactly what he did. I was sorry to hear that. He very likely had good cause to be angry and resentful, but in doing what he did, he lowered himself to the same level as the man he killed. Once he had taken that man's life, what really had he gained?

Since the 20th was my birthday, Dennis and I decided to go into Manila and have a look-see. After all, I had spent my last three birthdays in prison camp and had come within sixteen days of spending my fourth there. What a disappointment trip that turned out to be; Manila was in ruins. The once-beautiful city that had been aptly called the Pearl of the Orient was nothing but a mass of rubble. The beautiful government buildings, churches, and boulevards were in complete disarray and strewn with rubble. About the only vehicle that could get around was the versatile jeep. A small shop here and there had put up makeshift hovels out of debris and scrap iron and was valiantly trying to get back in business. But since there was nothing to do, no place to go, and even if there had been, there was no way to get there and nothing to see but sickening ruins, we caught the first ride available back to the 29th Replacement Center.

Not long after arriving in Manila, we were informed that General MacArthur had advanced each liberated person one grade in rank, which made me a sergeant. I was, however, one of eight men who had been recommended for promotion from corporal to sergeant in April of 1942. But that early in the war, promotions had to be made through Washington. The names of those to be advanced were posted on the company bulletin board and then radioed from Mindanao to General MacArthur's headquarters, which in turn communicated with Washington, D.C., via cable. In April of 1942, however, all communications with Washington regarding the surrender of Bataan had a priority status, so communications regarding our promotions were put on the back burner. That promotion would have made me a sergeant from 1942 to 1945, and then with the one grade advance upon being liberated, I should have been a staff sergeant from the time of liberation until the time of my discharge (or until my next promotion, had I stayed in the service).

When Bob Dennis and I returned from Manila that Thursday the 20th, we were informed that those of us who had been denied that promotion because of unusual circumstances of the surrender could receive a field promotion right at the replacement center, making it retroactive to April 1942. All a person had to do was present a true copy of the promotion list, signed by one's commanding officer, to the personnel office right there at the replacement center, and it would be all taken care of. Lt. Ricks had come in from liberation in Korea, and although Tom Earl, our company clerk, was apparently dead, Glen Leroy Bailey had done the actual typing of the order in 1942 and recalled the original wording perfectly. By midafternoon of the next day, a copy of the original letter had been prepared by Bailey and signed by then-Captain Ricks. With it in hand, I proceeded to the personnel section of the replacement center, arriving there just at 4:00 P.M. Since it was now peacetime and this was the tropics, they had already adjusted to the relaxed schedule of former days and were just closing up for the weekend, so they asked me to come back Monday A.M., when my request would be duly processed. So I thought, "That's fair enough" and went back to my area, thinking it was only a matter of a two-day wait to secure my proper promotion. But it didn't turn out to be that easy.

Two days later, on Sunday afternoon, I checked the area bulletin board for the latest announcements, and there to my surprise were sailing orders for me for the next day, Monday A.M. On checking with the OIC (officer in charge) to see if I would have time to go to personnel before muster for sailing in the morning, I was informed that there would not be sufficient time. When I told him the reason, he told me it could be handled just as well in the States. He said I could just contact the air force liaison officer at my first stop in America, and it could be initiated through him. Not knowing any better and not wanting to delay my departure for home, I decided to pursue that course. It proved to be a costly mistake.

September 24, 1945 (Monday)

Boarded USS *Admiral Gray* (Coast Guard transport) at 10:30 A.M. Weighed anchor and left Manila Bay at 4:30 P.M. Passed Corregidor and sailed out of Manila Bay about 6:30 P.M.—almost four years after entering it. We were told that this ship would make a direct run to San Francisco and would be due at that port on the morning of October 9. She makes about 22 knots per hour. The passenger personnel consists largely of liberated POWs and a few high-point men going home. It's a nice new ship, and we expect and hope to have a good crossing.

While riding in the back of a big six-by-six GI truck on the way to the pier, I struck up casual conversations with two officers standing near me, finding we shared a common destination—Wisconsin. One was going to La Crosse and the other one to Ashland. But then I noticed a third officer who was very quiet and who seemed in need of a show of friendship. In striking up a conversation, I found out that his plane had been shot down out in the Pacific somewhere. Several of the crew members were killed, but he and one or two others had managed to get in a life raft. Low on food and water, they suffered greatly, especially because they were adrift for 46 or 47 days, longer than any other known persons, including Eddie Rickenbacker, and still they survived. Then, to compound this officer's problem, he was picked up at sea by a Japanese submarine which took him to Japan, where he was put in solitary confinement and treated horribly (the others had died). Then, to my consternation, I learned who he was—Zemperini, the great runner who had broken records and won medals for the United States in the 1936 Olympic Games at Berlin. He has distinguished himself greatly since the war by developing a camp and a training camp in the Sierra Nevada Mountains, where he works with problem youth. He has become a very committed Christian and proceeds from that perspective. It was a chance, but interesting, meeting.

Naturally, there was a bit of nostalgia as we left Manila and the Philippines. It had been a long four years since we had first arrived here. We were strong and healthy then, well-fed and well-clothed. Many were not much more than young boys then, but no matter what their age and condition at that time, all were leaving as seasoned men, accustomed to starvation, privation, sickness, ill-treatment, loneliness, and death. We had come with high resolve, but with insufficient numbers or materiel. Now wherever we went, we saw an abundance of men and machines, materiel, and the wherewithal to launch the largest offensive the world has ever known. We had seen the masts of Spanish ships sunk and lying on the bottom of Manila Bay after the

Spanish-American War. Now there were far more remains of both American and Japanese ships destroyed in this last cataclysmic confrontation. We had been with the losing side when we were fighting and had been with the losing side when we were interned, but now we were finally with the winning side. We had come over as free men, but had lost even our freedom, the most basic of human conditions. Having lost it, we had come to realize as few others can how intensely precious it is. And now having regained it, we were learning to appreciate it more than ever before. And it must be said that we had come to love these islands and beautiful people who inhabit them, but now it was time to go home.

September 27, 1945 (Thursday)

Passed close to the U.S. naval base in the Caroline Islands (Ulithi Atoll within twenty miles) in the mid-afternoon. Could see the whole setup quite clearly. Also passed about 450 miles north of Guam. Coming over in '41, we touched on the north end of Guam, stopped there about five hours. Fine weather and a pleasant voyage so far. Bought a supply of candy, cigarettes, etc., from the ship's store.

Snickers had always been one of my favorite candy bars, so after we got into international waters and the ship's store opened, I got in line and bought a couple of Snickers bars. Of course, they were gone long before I got down to my bunk, so I thought I'd go back and get a couple more. I soon changed my mind though because by the time I got back there, the line had extended more than halfway around that big ship. So since they only served two meals a day on the transport, I decided to go to my bunk and take a nap while waiting for the 4:00 P.M. meal.

There had been so much going on during the last couple of months that I had never really enjoyed the luxury of a good quiet nap, so I removed my shoes and stretched out on my hammock rack. Later on when I awoke and started to put my shoes on, I realized just how bad my beriberi was. My feet had swelled so much that there was no way I could get my shoes on for the remainder of the day. I had not realized the seriousness or degree of beriberi before because it had been a long time since I had had shoes with a laced, seven-inch top. I had put these new ones on in the morning and had left them on all day. So from that point on, I either left them on all day, or if I did remove them during the day, I just left them off.

I suppose my diet didn't help matters either. When I went to the ship's store the next day, I asked if I could buy Snickers by the box, and I was told there was no problem with that, so for the next several days I bought two twenty-four-bar cartons each day and consumed them. It is no wonder that by the time I got back to Wisconsin a month or more later, I weighed the most I ever had, although it was a puffy weight due to the beriberi and the diet.

October 2, 1945 (Tuesday)

Today is Tuesday, October 2, and so was yesterday because we crossed the International Date Line at 2:00 A.M. yesterday. So now we're back where we stared four years ago—that is to say we are in the same day as the U.S.A. again. Menus are exactly the same both days, because both days were Tuesday, October 2. We have met and passed a number of boats. This evening an object was sighted floating in the water, so the ship circled it and discharged a number of five-inch shells at it, thinking it might be a floating mine, I guess, but it didn't explode and nothing happened, so we resumed our course. It was probably just some floating wreckage. We had commissary privileges again today. We have movies every night. I attended open-air church services on deck Sunday.

October 3, 1945 (Wednesday)

Final entry. At suppertime today we were told that our course had been changed, and that we would call at Victoria, British Columbia, first, where the Canadians would disembark, and we would then proceed to Seattle where the Limeys and Yanks would get off. No reason was given. In a way, I would have liked to have come back through the Golden Gate, but then I've never seen the Pacific Northwest, so what the heck! We had a variety show after supper tonight put on by the passengers and crew members. It was really good. We've had fine sailing so far. The last couple of days the boat has rocked and rolled, more than the first few days due to a rolling sea, but it is not bad; we can notice the weather becoming cooler. A jacket feels good on deck now.

"Now hear this, we are entering the strait of Juan de Fuca. On the left is the Dominion of Canada, and on your right is the United States of America." A cheer went up as the men crowded along the rails. It wasn't the Golden Gate, but it was America. As I gazed at the land on either side, my first impression was how thick the forests seemed to be on either side and how dark the trees were. And they looked so different from forests in the tropics or the trees in Japan. I was also struck by so much uninhabited land and the vastness of those two countries. What a testimony it was to peace-and-freedom-loving peoples that we share the longest unguarded border in the world. I couldn't help but feel a sense of security begin to envelop me, which I had not known for four years. It was beginning to feel like home.

Our first port of call was Victoria, B.C., where we discharged the Canadians, but their homecoming was dampened because one of the men had become very ill, so the ship had radioed ahead for doctors and an ambulance to be on hand at the pier. Of course the parents were there also. I shall never forget the sadness of the occasion when they learned he had died in the night. I stood by the rail and watched as his dead body was laid in the waiting ambulance while the band played taps.

Our arrival at Seattle was definitely low-key and anything but glamorous. It had been over a month since the official surrender and six weeks since there had been any military action, so the hype which had once accompanied returning servicemen was pretty much gone, at least at the Seattle point of debarkation. A handful of people were on the pier. A small band played two or three desultory numbers as men started down the gangplank, only to be told to go back up on the ship because we had to spend another night aboard because there were no trucks available to take us away until the next day. There was also somewhat of a repeat of what had happened at Victoria. As far as I know, there were only two men in our group who had family members waiting at the pier. They were Coy Driscoll and Sgt. Balcolm of the Fifth Air Base Group. I can still see the joy on Driscoll's face as he saw his wife on the pier. I also recall the sadness in his voice as he said, "Oh, no, there's Grace" (Balcolm's wife). Balcolm had died in prison camp a few months earlier, but she had not yet learned of it. I was beginning to hope that bad news ended after those three occasions. First there had been the last night in Yokkaichi when a man by the name of Job had died in our camp only hours before we were liberated, then there was the man who died aboard ship only hours before we docked at Victoria, and now there was the sadness that had to greet Grace Balcolm.

The Wings of Madigan General Hospital just outside Fort Lewis, Washington, where we Project J servicemen were assigned was a series of low temporary buildings. We were allowed one telephone call. It was so good to hear my parents' voices, but I had not yet heard Fay's voice. I found out later that my parents had just received the letter I had written in Japan in October of 1944, one year earlier. So until they heard my voice, they were not sure whether I was alive. Letters from that time on seemed to take on a new tone.

There were the usual interviews and examinations awaiting us. Also it was here that we were issued our full complement of uniforms and other clothing, shoes, blankets, etc. We also received our stripes, ribbons, and medals. After that was taken care of, I contacted the air force liaison officer regarding my promotion. He advised me to wait until I arrived at my next stop, which would be in the military core area of my residence. (I was beginning to wish I had stayed a day or two longer in Manila.)

One of our first observations was how tall American women were and how long and skinny their legs appeared. And of course their white skin gave them the appearance of being anemic. It had been a long time.

In addition to this staff of nurses, there were quite a number of women employed at Madigan General Hospital—clerks, secretaries, stenographers. After having been out of circulation for so long, none of this escaped our attention, naturally. One woman in particular seemed to attract more attention and was the subject of conversation among us patients more than the rest. Perhaps it was because her desk occupied a more prominent location, where four main aisles intersected, or it may have been the fact that she was a very attractive person with a ready smile for everyone who passed her desk marked

"Personnel." I suspect it was a combination of both the location of her desk and the natural beauty and charm she exuded. At any rate, everyone hoped to get to know her better, but no one expected to.

On this particular day, I had been busy going to different clinics and interrogation rooms, so about 3:00 P.M., I decided to get a little sack time. As I approached my bunk, Hicks announced, "There's a note on your bunk." Sure enough, there was a note lying there with this message: "Sgt. Nordin— please report to the Personnel Desk at your convenience." It was convenient right then.

After greeting me with that very pleasant smile, she asked me if I was the Carl Nordin from Siren, Wisconsin. When I assured her that I was, she said: "Good. Ever since you men started coming home, I've been hoping you would come through Seattle and Madigan General." Then she drew from her desk drawer a copy of the *Inter-County Leader*, the local weekly newspaper of my area of Wisconsin, and she showed me an article about my probable liberation. She identified herself as Evelyn Peterson, whose father owned and operated a rural general store in the West Sweden community about ten miles from Siren. Furthermore, she had gone to high school with my sister Luella in Frederic, twelve miles from Siren. As it turned out, she and I had been confirmed by the same man—Reverend Carl E. Rydell—when he was pastor at Frederic and Siren. Not only that, she was presently attending the church he was serving near Tacoma, Washington. In fact, when he learned that I had been liberated, he and his wife took Evelyn and me out for dinner that next Saturday night, and later he showed me his church. That was especially meaningful to me because as a very young person, I had learned a lot from the midweek family Bible studies he used to conduct in homes. In the confirmation studies, he was an even greater source of inspiration to me. In fact, few people have left a greater mark on my life than Pastor Rydell. What a joy it was to see him and his lovely wife, and what an appropriate spiritual touch it gave my experience as it was culminating.

That meeting with Evelyn opened up a whole new social whirl because through our acquaintance, several of Evelyn's friends met several of my buddies, which in turn resulted in group picnics and visits to parks and other places of interest. In fact, it even spawned a romance that developed into the marriage of Odell Hicks and Dorothy Nelson from Milltown, Wisconsin (about twenty miles from Siren). Odell honored me by selecting me to be his best man.

Nothing is constant in the military service, however. Sooner or later comes the time to leave familiar faces and surroundings and move on to a new place. One afternoon I was informed that I was being shipped by hospital train to Gardiner General Hospital in Chicago early the next day.

That notice rather signaled the end of many things for me, almost like the end of an era. Some of us had been together for more than five years by now. Our detachment itself was over four years old, and we had been through a lot together. Sometimes we were separated for various periods of time, but always this group of men seemed to end up together. We had shared joys and sorrows, heartaches and laughter, suffering and survival, pleasures and agony. The breakups had begun when Valdez had to remain in Hawaii with a broken leg, and Bowden and East remained at Fort McKinley for medical reasons. The breakups continued at Camp Casising in 1942, when McKay and Didio went to Japan early. Later the Lasang detail had left Dapecol, taking sixteen who later perished. At Bilibid, Lt. Ricks, Mike Minotti, and Tom Earl were separated from our group. On the way home, some were separated in Japan, others in Manila. But this group had survived these many separations.

My good-byes that evening brought a lot of memories to the forefront. There was Bill Lowe, who had served as my barber in a time of great need. Although he was not in our outfit, he had been with us a lot. We considered him to be one of us. There was Ben LeBeau, who with Charlie Goodliffe and I had established a supply line in the Moro country, and there was Tony McCabe and Bob Dennis, the two Irishmen who had bandied back and forth for four years about who was clay pipe and who was shanty Irish. Most unusual of all perhaps were the circumstances concerning K. B. Larson, Odell Hicks, and myself. Like the rest, we had gone overseas and down to Mindanao together, but the three of us had been in the group of ten who had been caught between the lines for over twelve hours in Maluko before the surrender, had been in prison together in the Philippines, and had been on the same three hell ships going to Japan, where we spent a year in the same camp. We were liberated together, came out of Japan on the same planes en route to the Philippines, where we were billeted in the same tent, and had even returned to America on the same transport and were now in the same ward at Madigan Hospital. But it was more than saying good-bye, because we knew that for each of us, the way of life that had fashioned us into what we had become was about to end. Every one of us was about to enter a new, somewhat unknown phase of our lives at that point. The force of a good-bye between two special friends occurred at 4:00 A.M. the next morning, when Bob Dennis came into the bathroom where I was shaving to reminisce and say his good-bye. At that moment, we finally realized how deep and profound our friendship really was.

It seemed that no matter where we went, Project J personnel received special treatment. The hospital train was no exception. The clean white beds, twenty-four-hours-a-day nursing supervision, and meals brought right to us made us feel almost pampered as our train rolled eastward out of the mountains and toward Chicago. It did seem a bit strange, though, to board the train in pajamas and robe.

When the train left the station early that morning, leaving my buddies, who had become such an integral part of my life, I put that phase of my life behind me. To be sure, they would always occupy a special place in my heart, but now my sights were truly set on home. Now it really seemed as if I was going home, and I wondered how much longer it was going to be before I got there.

Hearing my parents' voices over the telephone at Madigan General Hospital had made me more eager than ever to see them. It seemed that after that call, their letters had more of a sense of urgency than ever before. My mother wrote the most precious letter that a son could ever receive. My father told me that when he picked up my duffle bag at the train station, which I had sent ahead, it was almost as if a part of me had already arrived. It was something tangible. Although I had not had the opportunity to talk with Fay, she was sharing in my family's joy, and her letters were becoming sweeter than ever. She was leaving no doubt as to what would be the next big event in our lives.

The family of my best boyhood friend from school days in Siren was currently residing in Omaha. They were practically all railroad people with the Union Pacific Railroad, some working right at the Union Pacific depot in Omaha. Kenneth Carpenter and I had been to their place for morning coffee during a stop as we changed trains en route to Salt Lake City in 1940. A number of them had come down to the depot on my way back to Salt Lake City from that one-day furlough in 1941. They were almost like family to me, so I knew that they must have been concerned about my fate these last four years, and I wanted to see them also. But how could I get word to them? I struck up a conversation with the head nurse, who turned out to be from Iowa. Since I was from Wisconsin, we were almost neighbors. When I thought that the time was right, I explained what I had in mind and asked if she would send a telegram for me at the next fifteen-minute stop. When she told me that she was not allowed to leave the train, I asked if I might have permission to do so. "It's against regulations," she said, "and besides, I can't let you have your clothes." "I don't need clothes," I told her. "I'll just slip in quickly wearing my bathrobe and come right back. I'll have the wording all ready." That did it. She relented, and at the next station stop, I quickly left the train, sent the telegram, and reboarded the train just as quickly to the accompaniment of quite a few stares. Now all I had to do was relax on my hospital bed, enjoy the ride, and hope that my plan had worked.

As is the case with any type of hospital situation or facility, there were all manner of cases on board that train. Men who had ridden troop trains, airplanes, warships, and troop ships off to war were now returning or being transferred from one hospital to the next on a hospital train. All had been strong and healthy once—the cream of the crop. Now far too many would never be whole again. The fortunate few would recover and take their places in society where they left off, a war and half-a-lifetime ago.

When the train pulled into the station at Omaha, sure enough there on the platform were Mrs. Campbell and three of her daughters. What a joyous reunion with old friends it was! They told me how they had kept in contact with my family, watching for any news there might be of me, and how they had kept me and my family in their prayers. I learned that my buddy was in the coast guard and his youngest brother was in the navy, both somewhere in the Pacific. Another brother was in the army. All in all, it was a reunion that seemed to bring me closer to home. And again I had left the train and stood around on the platform in my bathrobe to the accompaniment of stares.

Gardiner General Hospital was in the southeast part of Chicago. Before being converted to a wartime hospital, it had been the Chicago Beach Hotel. For that reason, it didn't seem so much like a hospital. There were wards to be sure, but I was fortunate to be assigned to a very pleasant private room that was light and airy. It seemed that the entire hospital was exceptionally clean and pleasant. As soon as was practicable, I contacted the air force liaison officer relative to my 1942 promotion. He tried to help, but was informed that once I had left the field, the promotion could no longer be validated except by the comptroller general in Washington, D.C., and that I would have to attend to that by myself. I spent two years in a an attempt to obtain that promotion, but to no avail. The irony of it all is that the others did succeed in getting their promotions. In one case, the military brought the stripes and the back pay right to the person's bed in Fitzsimmons Hospital. To my knowledge, I am the only person on that list of eight names who never did receive that promotion. The promotion General MacArthur gave us was the only advance in grade I received in three-and-one-half years, as it turned out.

Up to this time our world pretty much focused around people we had been associated with for the last four years. That whole scene changed for me when I left Madigan General Hospital at Fort Lewis, Washington, and came to Gardiner General Hospital in Chicago. Only one other man whom I had known in Dapecol and Yokkaichi was there—Motts Tonelli, who had played professional football with the Chicago Bears before going into the service. We would see each other at mealtimes and visit then, but that was about the size of it because we were quartered in different parts of the facility. But once it became known that he was still alive and back in Chicago, he was often in conference with agents for the Bears and members of the press so I was pretty much alone getting acquainted with the new world in which I found myself. Everything was new. It seemed that each day I would hear or read about various things of which I had no knowledge, but which were common knowledge to everyone else.

Then one day a volunteer brought the library cart into my room and asked if I wanted to pick out something to read. My immediate reply was, "I've been out of circulation for so long that I haven't the slightest idea what's current anymore." As I scanned the titles, I saw *American Guerrilla in the Philippines* by Ira Wolfert. "Hey," I said, "I was in the Philippines." Then to my surprise, as I glanced at the inside of the dust jacket, I saw that it was the story of Iliff Richardson. "Iliff Richardson," I said. "I know him. I spent ten weeks with him on the beach."

The book was a whole new revelation to me. Richardson had served with Motor Torpedo Boat Squadron Three, and after they had brought General MacArthur to Mindanao on his way to Australia, the squadron had remained at Bugo and operated out of that location. Rod McKay was in charge of the pier at that time, and I was running convoys out of Bugo. In fact, McKay and I lived in the same house in Bugo along with eight or ten of these men, and over the weeks we became acquainted with all of them. After the invasion, separated, and I never did know what happened to some of them. As it turned out, some eventually ended up in prison camp, some got to Australia, and others went to the hills. Reading that book was the first I had known of what had happened to Richardson. It was also the first account I had read about guerrilla activity during the war. It was quite a coincidence, I thought.

Letters from home began informing me that Siren's homecoming game was set for November 2, 1945; it would be the last football game of the season. Since my youngest brother Glenn was a senior, it would be his last football game with Siren High School. He was still in grade school when I left home to enlist in the service, so I had missed all of his high school years. I desperately wanted to see him play at least one game. Besides that, November 3 would be my mother's fifty-seventh birthday. The more I thought about it, the more I realized that I didn't want to miss any of those occasions. Besides, I had more than five months of furlough time coming. At that time, servicemen were granted thirty days of furlough a year, and I had already been in over five years. The fifteen-day furlough I had applied for four years earlier had been canceled before it ever began.

So I began working on the possibility of a furlough. The authorities were reluctant to consider it because my beriberi was still bothering me, and they wanted to do further observation and studies of my case. My history of dysentery was another factor which they were studying. According to their schedule, they were contemplating giving me a hospital furlough in a couple of weeks. When I reminded them that by then I would have missed my only chance of seeing my brother play high school football and that my mother's birthday would also have been passed, they finally relented, and I began making plans to go home at long last.

Home at Last

What a joy it was to be reunited with my parents at the Union Depot in St. Paul, Minnesota, the same station where I had sadly said good-bye to Fay and my sister Hazel more than four years earlier. With my parents were my sister An (Anna) and her husband Francis Smith. I began to realize how long I had been gone when I greeted another sister. When I said, "Hi, Lu," she replied, "I'm not Lu, I'm Betty!" She is eight years younger than my sister Luella, but in those five years she had changed from a girl in high school to a grown young lady, who looked just like Luella did when I left. After a reunion and lunch at the Smith's home in St. Paul, we took off for Siren because Dad had been informed by Fritz Puls, a World War I veteran and American Legionnaire, that the American Legion would be heading up the homecoming parade along with the American flag and Legion colors, and they wanted to include me in the parade.

We arrived in Siren shortly before the parade was about to start. My good friend from Siren, Harold (Mac) McBroom, and I were selected to lead the parade. He had just recently returned from the South Pacific, where he had served with the Seabees in New Guinea and the Philippines. It was a typical small-town homecoming parade, with the colors and color guard leading off, followed by the high school band. Mac, in his blue navy uniform, carried the blue Legion colors, and I, in my olive drab army uniform, carried the American colors. There was one difference in this parade, however. Marie Dahle, the first grade teacher, and her students had made a huge sign that read, "Welcome home, Carl Nordin," which was borne by some of her students at the head of the student group of the parade. Unfortunately, the wind damaged it as the parade wound through town, but it was a beautiful gesture. When the parade ended at the school grounds, I had another experience that reminded me of how long I had been away. As students and former friends gathered around to greet me and welcome me back, one high school lad grabbed my hand, patted me on the back and, as he welcomed me, he told me how glad he was to have me back. Wracking my brain trying to recall who he was, I finally had to ask him who he was. "Why, I'm your cousin," he said. "I'm Clifford Nyren."

I got a brief glimpse of Fay in the crowd at the schoolyard after the parade. It was enough to make me realize that already life was about to resume again where it had abruptly broken off four years earlier. We had an opportunity to be together for a while after the football game later on that evening, and from that time on, we saw each other practically every night. One of the popular songs at that time was entitled "It's Been a Long, Long Time," and we adopted it as our theme song. We were so happy and thankful to be reunited again. Countless prayers had been answered indeed.

There is no doubt that my mother's fifty-seventh birthday was the happiest one of her life. She had borne and reared eight children, of which I was the eldest, and now, after this difficult ordeal for the entire family, we were all together again in our farm home at rural Siren. What a memorable day it was!

The furlough time went quickly, but what a joy it was to partake of Mother's good home cooking each day, to become reacquainted with the family, and to go to town quite often and meet the guys who were returning almost daily from points the world over—China, India, Arabia, Europe, Alaska, the Pacific. I was rapidly beginning to realize more fully what a gigantic war it had been and how many of my relatives and friends had answered the call. It was all still so new to me.

In the midst of this joy and reverie, there was one unpleasant task that I felt obligated to perform, however. That task was to call on the parents of Kenneth Carpenter, the man with whom I had enlisted and left in Siren in 1940. He had died in Cabantuan Prison Camp in June of 1942, and there had been a memorial service for him some months before I had arrived home. There really wasn't a lot I could tell them about their son—only fragments of information that I had picked up from men who had seen him in his last days. There were some things I thought were better left unsaid, at least for the time being. I was happy that I was able to tell them that I had seen him in Manila, even though it was only while we rode in the back of a truck, as we were being taken to the pier in Manila to embark for Mindanao. I kept in contact with the Carpenters, even after they left Siren, and continued to send Mrs. Carpenter an appropriate Mother's Day card each year as long as she lived. I thought it might aid in providing some sort of link with their son.

When I arrived at the Union Depot in St. Paul for my trip back to Chicago, I happened to spy Vernon Johnson from Grantsburg, Wisconsin, a town about sixteen miles from Siren. He was returning to the hospital after furlough also, only he was returning to Vaughn General Hospital at Niles, Illinois, so we decided to sit together and compare notes. Vernon was returning to have some more work done on a finger which he had nearly lost when he grabbed the bayonet of a Japanese guard who had attempted to bayonet his buddy who was faltering on the Bataan Death March. I also found out that we had lived about the same distance from each other in Japan as we did in Wisconsin because he too was interned in a camp in the Nagoya area. The difference was that his prison group had spent most of their time excavating a huge cave out of the mountain into which prisoners of war were to be placed for execution in the event of an Allied invasion of mainland Japan.

There was one small incident on that train ride that gave us a clue to what we learned was a minority opinion back home, but which nonetheless did not set too well with us. We overheard a couple of defense workers in the seat behind us discussing the change in their lives caused by the ending of the war. Neither of them sounded as if they were happy that it had ended. Finally one of them told of recently buying a new home and how his job in a defense plant had made it possible to reduce his indebtedness quite rapidly. He concluded by saying, "If the war would have just lasted another couple of years, I could have had it all paid off." We could hardly believe our ears. Vernon jumped up to his feet with clenched fists and was about to take a swing at the man, but I restrained him, saying it would only start a brawl.

There is no doubt that from the standpoint of purely selfish personal economics, the man had a valid point, but to us, it was not only an insensitive statement, it was an insult. It was as if our homecoming had altered the status quo and spoiled things for him. It seemed ill-advised also because over half of the passengers in that train were military personnel in full uniform. We had already been hearing reports of neighbors back home who had bought and milked cows and resorted to other ventures in an effort to avoid serving in the armed services. That type of activity did not strike a pleasant chord with returning veterans.

In early December, I was advised that I would soon be placed on ninety-day T.D.Y. (temporary duty) at home. When that tour expired, I could either reenlist if my health permitted or take a discharge. There was one major item of business for me to take care of before returning home this time—the purchase of engagement and wedding rings.

Since there was going to be a change in my duty status, I had to go to Camp McCoy, Wisconsin, for a day or two of processing. This was to be my last association with active-duty servicemen, and it was interesting to note the general feeling of the men and the tenor of their conversation. Men were returning from practically the four corners of the earth daily, and throughout the United States, they were being discharged by the thousands daily. At the peak, there had been approximately fifteen million people in the United States Armed Forces. Now the talk was of reducing that number to about five million. Nobody denied that furloughs should be granted to the men with the required number of points or that there should be a reduction in the size of our armed forces. But there was concern about the rapid wholesale reduction that was taking place, and for a variety of reasons. For one thing, there was the matter of Russia. Although the Russians had been our allies, most people did not trust them a great deal. It gave many people pause that they were not demobilizing as rapidly as we were. Another cause of concern was China. Although the Nationalist government was friendly to freedom-loving and democratic-minded nations, the country was in turmoil. There was no threat from Japan or Germany in the foreseeable future, but their past actions had left us with the feeling that caution should be exercised. And to those of us who had been caught off-guard and had been forced to fight with not even enough of the bare essentials, the danger of unpreparedness had raised a specter that was difficult to erase. The attitude caused by the slogan "We don't want our sons to die on foreign soil" had been a costly one indeed. The men engaged in these discussions were not militarists—they were realists who had learned the hard way. They were men who had not fought for the purpose of making war or for any type of aggrandizement. They had fought to make peace, and they wanted to preserve it.

As I listened and learned more about the experiences of others, I became more keenly aware than ever of how different the fortunes of war can be. By the time most of these men became involved, it was already a big war, with plenty of planes, ships, ammunition, food, and men, and the overall prognosis was one of victory. Whereas for us, we were already in place when the war started as a rather small thing in an out-of-the-way place. We never had enough of anything. We were with the Americans when they were losing, and with the Japanese when they were losing. Always we had seen defeat.

I caught a train out of Camp McCoy for Eau Claire and went from there by bus to Rice Lake, where Fay met me late on a bright December afternoon. I had been guarding those rings with my life while at Camp McCoy and sneaking off to look at them and admire them in secret whenever I had the opportunity. Now I could wait no longer, so after pulling off the highway into the parking lot of a small nightclub, I slipped the ring on her finger. It was December 8, 1945—four years and two months after my aborted attempt to become engaged and four years and one day after the attack on Pearl Harbor that changed the world and sealed us into a fate of waiting, waiting, waiting.

December and January went by quickly. Fay was busy teaching school and also making plans and shopping for our wedding. I busied myself working in the woods of my father's farm, cutting bolts, pulp, and a few logs with my brother Kenneth. It gave us a chance to get reacquainted as we earned some money together, and it provided me with an excellent opportunity to get back in good physical condition, although my feet and legs still swelled from beriberi.

Fay resigned her teaching position at the end of the first semester, and on February 16, 1946, we were married in a lovely wedding ceremony in my home church in Siren. A few days later, with Fay wearing a nylon blouse made out of material from parachutes that the British used for dropping our first food after the war as part of her going-away outfit, we left for Miami Beach, Florida, where we spent our honeymoon. The entire trip was courtesy of the U.S. Air Force for all Project J personnel who wished to avail themselves of it. Each man was allowed two weeks at the hotel, all expenses paid, plus free travel for up to two weeks. For those of us who traveled by car, it amounted to about a month honeymoon. Each veteran was allowed up to two dependents. Some of the men brought their parents, but many of us spent our honeymoons there. For me, it was just like old home week. I got to see, and Fay got to meet, many of my former POW buddies, whom I never expected to see again.

It was a fabulous two weeks. Everything was free—entertainment, excursions, moonlight boat cruises, and after-dinner dancing. The weather was lovely and the water was warm, so we spent a number of afternoons at the beach with other newly married couples and went swimming in the ocean before going in and dressing for dinner. Nobody could have been happier than we were. We didn't know life could be so good. On our return, we traveled through central Florida to Pensacola and then followed along the Gulf of Mexico to New Orleans before heading north toward Wisconsin. By the time we arrived at Camp McCoy, the weather was really springlike. It seemed as if life was starting anew as I received my discharge on March 23, 1946, and entered civilian life again after a little over five-and-one-half years in the service. The big difference was that now Fay and I were embarking on a new life together.

By May of 1946, I was able to go back to my old job as clerk in the Siren Post Office. Clothes, cars, homes, and furniture were hard to find in those days right after the war. Practically all types of production had been geared to the war effort, so civilian consumer goods were in short supply. I tried to find civilian clothes in the Twin Cities, but demand in metropolitan areas was so great that there was very little from which to choose. I had the best success in the Twin Ports (Duluth-Superior). The same was true in finding furniture. We were not able to get a new car until 1948. We had received an unusually good price for Fay's 1941 Chevrolet, so we had sold it, thinking we could get a new one soon. Consequently, our only mode of transportation was my father's old Model A Ford pickup. We were unable to find a place to live in Siren, so I commuted the seventeen miles to work from the home of Fay's mother. Finally in July, a small apartment became available. It was only three rooms and a path, but Fay fixed it up really cute and what with some new furniture, a rug, and wallpaper, it was transformed into a pretty neat honeymoon cottage. We thought we had the world by the tail. After all, we had each other, a home, a job, and by now, our home had been blessed by the addition of our first daughter, Carleen.

"For better or for worse, in sickness and in health." We had heard those words in the marriage ceremony, had taken them seriously, and had pledged ourselves to them. But at that time, it seemed as though there was only a vague possibility that such things could enter our lives in the foreseeable future. In the spring and summer of 1948, however, I began having bouts of terrible headaches. It seemed that nothing would phase them when they came on. I had been taking flying lessons at the local air field and had progressed quite well, learning to use both ski and wheel-equipped planes. I had also checked out in float-equipped and multiengine planes, and after obtaining my private license, I began working toward my commercial license. By the fall of 1948, I had logged the required 200 hours of flying time, passed the written test for a commercial license, and had taken and passed part of the flight test. Since there was a rather large class of flight students, the FAA officials administering the test had to suspend further flight tests because of darkness. They were to resume the next Saturday. It was while I was out practicing different maneuvers one day that next week that I suddenly experienced a very strange feeling in my head. I turned the plane directly toward the field some twenty miles away, just hoping nothing further would happen before I landed. To save time, I entered the field air space without flying the pattern, landed, and left immediately for home. That night I was unconscious for fourteen hours with convulsions. I never flew again.

During the next six months, I was plagued with various manifestations of some rare disease that had doctors and specialists puzzled. I had bouts of partial paralysis, blindness, delayed sensory reaction, facial twitches, and a near-total lack of coordination at times. I tried to work in between times, but it was difficult to keep going. The money we had saved to build a house had to be used for doctor and hospital bills. Then I suffered another great loss. On February 21, 1949, my father died suddenly. It was our daughter Carleen's second birthday. It just seemed as if everything was going wrong again.

Suddenly one afternoon in early April, I began having violent seizures. I was conscious, but was unable to speak or use my left hand. At the doctor's office, I motioned for a pen and wrote down that I was conscious, and I explained on paper briefly what was happening. When the seizures subsided for a while, the doctor told me that he was sending me to the Mayo Clinic in Rochester, Minnesota. But I told him, "No, I can't go there because we didn't have any more money. Could I please go to the Veteran's Administration Hospital?" (In those days it was almost impossible to get into a VA hospital unless your local doctor sent you.) The doctor I had was a good doctor, but he was opposed to the Veterans' administration hospital because he thought it was a form of socialized medicine, so he had been sending me to specialists in the Twin Cities and this had liquidated all of our finances. When I explained that we had no money left and had even mortgaged our car, he finally relented. I continued having seizures as I was being driven to the Twin Cities that evening. I felt so sorry for Fay as we traveled to the Twin Cities. She went with me, so we had had to leave Carleen with my mother. And there we were, riding in the backseat as she tried to hold me in the seat and comfort me each time I had a seizure, neither knowing what the future held for us nor what to do about it. It was truly "for worse" for both of us.

I was admitted to the veterans hospital on April 5, 1949, and for the next ten days I underwent tests of every nature and description. Finally Dr. Pfefferman, a surgeon, came to my room and said: "Carl, we know where it is, but we don't know what it is. Our only hope is to go into your brain and see what's causing your problem. But there is a catch to it. We'd like to have you conscious during surgery because we are going to try and reproduce a seizure after we get your head opened up, and we want you to tell us how it compares with your other seizures. In other words, we want to see what's happening. But first, we need your consent to do this." That came as quite a shock. My first concern was about what my chances were if I didn't have the surgery done. Obviously, that was a difficult question for the doctors, but they feared that at the rate the problem was progressing throughout my left side, six months might be the maximum length of time they would guarantee me. Of course, if they found cancer, they couldn't guarantee anything. Finally the surgeon said, "I'll guarantee you one thing for sure—you will come through surgery." He seemed really certain of that. It was a positive statement, so I signed.

It was almost noon on April 20, 1948, when they wheeled me into the operating room. I raised up and waved to Fay and my mother as the gurney passed by where they were sitting in the corridor. I noticed that Fay was knitting for our expected second child. I had to make it.

I had been given a mild sedative, presumably to quiet my nerves, so I was a little drowsy. But I was aware of everything that was going on. They injected Novocain in my scalp before skinning that off the skull where the incision was to be made, so I didn't feel that at all. When they began drilling holes through my skull with a hand drill, I could feel that, however, and since it was so close to my ear, I could hear that awful grinding sound. The same was true when they sawed from hole to hole with a flexible saw. It didn't saw really cleanly, so I could hear and feel them tapping a chisel with a hammer before prying the plug loose and lifting it out. They now had a clear shot into my brain through a hole between three to four inches in diameter.

The induced seizure was not violent enough to provide adequate visual observation of the problem area to make any determination of how best to proceed. So they tried again, this time extending the electrodes of an electro-encephalograph machine right in next to the brain rather than attaching them to the exterior of the skull, which is the normal procedure. Then, just as the seizure was induced and the brain wave began acting wildly on the machine, they took pictures of my brain and had them produced on a glass slide. Then, and only then, were they able to identify the problem area—several yellow nodules on the brain that indicated some type of inflammation. When they placed the specimen under a microscope, they found it was just crawling with schistosomiasis bugs. In the words of the surgeon, "We found a regular love-nest of schisto bugs in your brain." Once the problem was determined, they put the plug back in my skull, rolled the skin back over it, and sutured that up. One of the most painful things had been when the surgeon called for a syringe to flush the blood away. When the water hit my brain, it sent sharp pain waves all through my body to the tips of my fingers and toes. The other was when they were sewing me up, as there was insufficient Novocain. Each stitch hurt. It was a long, difficult ordeal, but when they wheeled me out five-and-one-half hours after I had gone in, I was able to wave at Fay and my mother who were sitting exactly where they were when I went into surgery.

Following surgery, occupational therapy was necessary to develop strength and agility in my left hand, so I chose the project of making a leather hand-bag with both hand and shoulder straps for Fay. The project also involved a considerable amount of leather tooling which helped develop dexterity. Probably the biggest hurdle I had to overcome was the fact that I had to practically learn to read and write all over again. The doctor's recommended that I begin with books at the second-grade level because there are thousands of unused cells to be developed in the brain. I made the mistake of trying to carry on from where I left off. Because of that error on my part, it took me longer, and the task was more difficult than it ought to have been. In fact, that mistake caused me to have to work harder to do my job properly in the Post Office later on. Also, there was some damage to the optic nerve in surgery that affected the tracking ability of my left eye. That small handicap made the task of sorting mail more difficult because of the constant change in focus required.

Fay was seven months pregnant when I entered the hospital on April 5, but she continued to drive the eighty miles to spend an afternoon a week visiting me, always bringing our two-year-old daughter along to visit her daddy. Those visits were highlights to me and continued to make me cognizant of how much I had to live for. Then on June 8, 1949, our second daughter, Susan, was born. Fortunately, I was able to get an extended pass from the hospital, so I was home several days for that wonderful occasion.

Since there is still no known cure for the Japonica strain of schistosomiasis, the only method of treatment is intravenous injection of antimony. The idea is to try to kill the bug without quite killing the patient. Each treatment lasts two to four hours, and treatments are administered every other day for thirty-six days. At the end of the course, the patient is a wheelchair patient because the procedure is so hard on the heart. Also there is considerable weight loss and weakness because about halfway into the course, the patient becomes nauseated and unable to eat much in the way of solid foods. Even after the treatment was completed, it required several weeks of recuperation before I was strong enough to leave the hospital.

Finally on August 18, 1949, I was discharged from the hospital and was able to rejoin my family. It had been a long and arduous four-and-a-half months. But I had survived a rare disease and a difficult surgery and follow-up treatment. In addition, medical science had learned some things also. On one occasion they had called in doctors and scientists from all over the United States to study my case and to spend several hours interviewing me. Although there were a number of cases of schistosomiasis among the men who had been in the Philippines, especially Mindanao, practically all of these men sustained it in the intestines, liver, or spleen. I was only the third case at that time to have had it in the brain. Vincent Imme had brain surgery in Letterman General Hospital for schistosomiasis, and John Obell from Omaha had the same surgery at Fort Snelling about three months before I did. Surgery left him unable to talk, and it left Vincent Imme so depressed that less than two years later, he took his life.

I tried to work in December, but was unable to. Then on February 1, 1950, I began working half days, and on May 1, I was able to go back to work full time. I continued to go in for one-day check-ups once a month. Also in 1950, my government life insurance term was about to expire, and the recommendation was to convert to a modified-life policy. It was a better long-term policy, but the cost was greater, so on one of these visits, I asked the doctor just what my prognosis was regarding life expectancy. He hesitated, but had been with my case since before I had surgery, so he knew me well enough that he could say it like it was. His answer was, "With good luck, you could live ten years." Since term policies were for seven years, I gambled on the ten-year prognosis. That was 1950. This is 1994.

I had no further problems until 1953. We were just beginning to build a new house, and my brother and I had been working very hard to make the basement waterproof. The excessive fatigue triggered another seizure, so I ended up back in the hospital again, leaving Fay with the responsibilities and decisions that go with having a house built. She did a good job, but I felt terrible about it. I really had wanted to see it go up, but it was all in place by the time I got out of the hospital that fall and resumed work at the post office.

The next ten years were good years for us. Our two daughters had done well in school and were rapidly becoming nice young ladies. About the time they became high school age, Fay went back to work as secretary to the school administrator, so she was back in her former element, yet free of the cares and hassles often associated with teaching. She never lost her love and concern for the students, however.

On February 14, 1964, I became acting postmaster (the preliminary action before being commissioned by an act of Congress). It had been a little over thirty years since I had started as a clerk, so I was eager to begin my new responsibilities. When fall came, I began making plans for the annual Christmas rush. It is the one time of the year that the postal system is put to the ultimate test. I had everything in readiness—an adequate supply of the proper denominations of stamps, clerks' hours and schedules all formulated, so as to handle the heavy onslaught of mail both incoming and outgoing—and I was prepared for whatever exigencies might occur.

Then about the middle of December I suddenly became ill. The worst part of it was that none of the symptoms I was experiencing had ever occurred before. I was rushed to the veterans hospital in Minneapolis, where they began running all sorts of tests. A biopsy of my liver finally indicated that this time my problem was schistosomiasis of the liver. So on January 18, 1965, I began another thirty-six day treatment of antimony. It seemed to be harder on me than ever, so this time I was hospitalized until March 3, 1965, and was unable to return to work until May of that year.

Naturally, I hoped by this time that the doctors had been able to kill all the schisto bugs in my system. Early in 1966, however, they found more live bugs in my liver, so I was hospitalized again from February 22 until April 5, 1966, for my third course of antimony. Surprisingly, the bugs had lived at least seventeen years since my first treatment in 1949. It seemed that the scourge of schistosomiasis that I had first contracted in the rice fields at Mactan in Dapecol back in 1943 would never leave me. At this writing in 1994, however, I am happy to say that apparently I have finally conquered the problem.

Reunion for Peace

In a very real sense, the culmination of some of the most significant events which have been related earlier in this account occurred in 1977, the thirty-fifth anniversary of the fall of the Philippines. President Ferdinand Marcos issued a proclamation declaring 1977 to be a year of forgiveness—a Reunion for Peace. And in order to lend proper significance to the auspicious occasion, he invited not only the American veterans who had fought there, but the erstwhile enemies, the Japanese, to join in the observance. This gesture was made all the more significant by a special inducement provided by the Philippine government. This government and certain civic and veterans' organizations made our trips financially feasible because they picked up more than half of the tab on both airfare and lodging at some of the very best hotels in Manila. As an additional gesture of hospitality, there were a number of perks in the way of receptions, parties, side trips, and sightseeing tours.

So much for the obvious good intention of the government and the people of the Philippines to demonstrate to the Japanese and all the world, for that matter, that this was indeed a Reunion for Peace. We were to learn that their actions spoke even more loudly than their words.

Our first clue about the treatment and hospitality we would be shown occurred as soon as the plane landed and we disembarked onto the tarmac at Manila International Airport. There we were greeted by a band beneath a huge sign that said, "Welcome—Mabuhay," which is similar in meaning to the Hawaiian *Aloha*. As the band played, we were greeted by thousands of Filipinos on the field, in the galleries, throughout the airport and into the streets, as we boarded buses to go to our hotels. The cheering greeted us along the entire route to our hotel. What a thrill! What a difference, as compared to the mute stares that were our greeting as we marched from the hell ship through the streets of that same city en route to Bilibid Prison thirty-three years earlier.

Our view of Manila Bay and the city of Manila from the twentieth floor of the Manila Hilton Hotel, plus a tour of the city, presented us with a much different picture of the Manila I had last seen thirty-two years before. The harbor had been cleaned up, the city and streets rebuilt into what was now a gleaming city, bustling with commerce and interspersed with countless parks and gardens. What a magnificent job of reconstruction it was.

On April 5, we were guests at an impressive memorial service at Fort Bonifacio (formerly Fort McKinley) featuring the presentation of a huge floral wreath by the American Gold Star Mother of the Year. Fort Bonifacio is the largest American overseas military cemetery in the world. On a high point near its center is a huge concrete and marble ellipse, and on the face of the various huge slabs forming the ellipse are inscribed the names and identifications of all the men buried there. It is a most impressive, yet humbling sight. It was also nostalgic for me because as I stood there I could look off toward the Pasig River in the distance and see the exact spot where my tent had been when we were billeted in Fort McKinley before going to Mindanao in 1941.

There was more nostalgia in store for me when four of us visited old Bilibid Prison later that same day. To my astonishment, it was much the same as it had been in 1944 when we stayed there a few days en route to Japan. The gate was still the same, and the high curb along the left side when we entered was unchanged from what it had been when the men had stood there and watched us as we half-walked and half-dragged ourselves in on that day so long ago. And even the numbers on the outside walls of the building marking the cells were unchanged. I noticed as I glanced over to where I had been billeted that there was the same big "17" where I had stayed in 1944. But there was one big difference this time. After mail call on that fateful day in 1944, I had lain on that concrete floor, pondering why I had not heard from Fay or from my folks, but this time I had Fay with me. I finally began to realize that on this trip, I had come full-circle from those terrible times, and the experience was just beginning.

It was just a few days before we had left Siren that I had received word from my brother, Col. Glenn Nordin, that he had finally located Ikuta-San, my former honcho in Japan. At that time, Glenn was vice-commander of the Fifth Air Force stationed at Yakota Air Base near Tokyo. His secretary, Maggie Surles, was from near Yokkaichi, and while home one weekend, she had made the contact. I had no opportunity to make further plans, except to notify Glenn that we would try to extend our trip to Japan and that I would make further contact from Manila. After trying to find Ikuta-San, mostly through the efforts of Glenn while he had been on various assignments in the Orient (for sixteen years), I did not want this opportunity to slip through my hands. Consequently, I spent most of April 6, a free day, at the American Embassy contacting Glenn and making the necessary arrangements. From there I went to the travel agency to make those arrangements as well.

There had been another unexpected twist just before we left, as well. Shortly after midnight of our last night at home, I received a long-distance telephone call from New York. It was United Press International (UPI). Somehow, and to this day I have no idea how, they had heard that I was going to the Philippines to participate in the Reunion for Peace program, along with other Americans, the Filipinos, and the Japanese. They explained that their reason for calling me at that late hour was to request an interview. So for about fifteen minutes in the middle of the night, I was interviewed via long-distance telephone by UPI.

There was a third out-of-the-ordinary element involved in the whole scenario also. Sig Schreiner, owner of the tour company selected to handle this particular tour and a former POW of the Japanese, had asked us to bring our state flags along. He also contacted me and asked me to request a letter from the governor of Wisconsin to the president of the Philippines, which I did. (I did not know Sig Schreiner before this trip.) So I dutifully carried the Wisconsin state flag and the official letter from Governor Lucey to President Marcos with me to Manila. I had no idea what to do with them or what was going to happen next.

Each evening a group of us fellows would gather in the lobby after dinner while our wives wrote letters, put up their hair, fixed their nails, or whatever women do before they retire for the night. Since about one-fourth of the veterans in the group had fought there in the early part of the war when we lost the Philippines and three-fourths were men who were in on the recapture of the Philippines, there were a lot of previously unanswered questions among the groups. As we shared war stories night after night, each of us learned a lot about those parts of the war with which we were unfamiliar.

It was at one of these sessions that a young Filipino sought me out and identified himself as the UPI representative for that part of the world. He also requested an interview, wherein among other things, the topic of the state flag and the letter from Governor Lucey to President Marcos surfaced. In the course of the interview, we went to our hotel room, where he met Fay and included her in the interview as well. He took a number of pictures but appeared to be especially interested in photographing the letter in the nine-by-twelve manila envelope, whereupon was written, "To His Excellency, Ferdinand E. Marcos, President of the Republic of the Philippines—from Patrick J. Lucey, Governor of the Sovereign State of Wisconsin, U.S.A." Inscribed off to the side and down a little were the words, "To be hand-delivered by Carl S. Nordin."

The last words of the UPI representative before he left that night were, "I have orders from my boss in New York to get a picture of you delivering that letter to the President of the Philippines." Dumbfounded, I said, "How do I do that?" To which he said, "Just engage him in conversation." Then, as an afterthought, he called out, "Bring it with you to Mt. Samat."

In the forenoon of April 6, we were guests of Carlos Romulo at the Department of Defense. He was a most gracious host and was an interesting man to listen to, having been educated both in the Philippines and at Columbia University. He was a literary man, but he served as an advisor to Manuel Quizon, president of the Philippines, was on General MacArthur's staff in Malinta Tunnel on Corregidor, and later was his aide-de-camp in Australia. After the war, he served his country in a number of capacities, including delegate to the United Nations, president of the U.N. General Assembly, and ambassador to the United States.

Later that afternoon and evening, we were guests of Col. and Mrs. Santos at a lovely garden party in their spacious home, that was almost like a villa. He had been a senator and, I believe, a Supreme Court justice of the Philippines.

Our tour of Corregidor the next day was marked by two poignant coincidences. As we were standing at a certain point, a man from La Crosse, Wisconsin, named Buster Brown, who had parachuted into Corregidor on the retake of the Philippines, said to his wife, "Right here is where I was hit." Immediately, Dr. Harris Braun, a dentist from Walworth, Wisconsin, asked, "What day was that?" As they compared notes, Doc Braun all but verified right then and there that Buster was one of the casualties he and his crew of medics removed from the carnage of Corregidor to a field hospital at Subic Bay on one of their many rescue trips.

Later on, as we toured Battery Way, which was a battery of four eight-inch guns, a man from New Mexico explained that he had been an ammunition handler for one of the guns, but as the gun crew began to get killed off, he found himself almost worked to death, handing eight-inch shells to all four guns. That continued until an enemy shell hit an ammunition depot, killing most of the men left. Having nothing to do, he went topside to Battery Geery, a sixteen-inch gun, whose crew had been partially decimated. Recognizing the authority with which this man spoke, our tour guide wisely asked him to tell us all just what happened. He explained that they had fired Battery Geery so fast that they had to stop to let it cool so that they could rebore it. Then his eyes became transfixed, and his voice seemed to hit a dead calm as he explained what happened next. Being dead-tired, he spread his denim jacket on the ground, lay down, and went to sleep. When he awoke, a Japanese soldier stood over him with his bayonet inches away. "I became a guest of the Emperor," he said simply but eloquently. Surely those two seemingly insignificant episodes spoke volumes regarding the cost of freedom— first the fight to the last to retain a piece of real estate that represented freedom and then the humiliation of losing it. Then there was the high cost of retaking it, as illustrated by Buster Brown, and thousands like him.

April 9, Bataan Day, is always a special day in the Philippines, with the patriotic connotation much like we used to enjoy in America on the Fourth of July a century or so ago. There are patriotic celebrations throughout the nation, but on Luzon, there is always a commemorative service on Mt. Samat, where one of the fiercest battles of the Bataan campaign was fought. Now it is marked by a 97-foot monument and a 295-foot steel-and-concrete cross with fluorescent lighting, making it visible for miles around. At night it can be clearly seen on Corregidor and way out into Manila Bay. This cross was dedicated on 1967 on the twenty-fifth anniversary of the fall of the Philippines.

The thirty-fifth anniversary, featuring the Reunion for Peace theme, was more special than ever. It began with prayers for peace by an American, a Japanese Christian pastor, and a Filipino priest. Featured in remarks were His Excellency Kiyokisa Mikanagi, ambassador extraordinary and plenipotentiary of Japan, and His Excellency William H. Sullivan, ambassador extraordinary and plenipotentiary of the United States. The main address was by His Excellency, President Marcos of the Philippines. Summing up the Reunion for Peace, he said of the former combatants, "Why did they come back to socialize for a week with their former enemies? Let it be said that they have come back here to give personal testimony to the final end of the war." The ceremony ended with a twenty-one gun salute.

As the president and the first lady were departing through a corridor in the crowd, I felt a tap on my shoulder and heard someone say, "Now." I turned, and there stood the Filipino UPI representative, pointing to the president. I ducked down, working my way through the crush of people to the open corridor. It's a wonder I wasn't shot as I walked up to the president. I began by saying, "Your Excellency, I'm Carl Nordin from Siren, Wisconsin," and, displaying the letter as I walked alongside him, I continued, "I have a letter from the Governor of the State of Wisconsin, and it says, 'To be hand-delivered by Carl Nordin.' It is my pleasure to do so." His eyes lit up, and he said, "Ah, Wisconsin, Wisconsin," and we talked of Wisconsin for several strides before I returned to the crowd. (I learned later that, all this time, the UPI representative had been taking pictures of us which he used for a news release that showed up in the *Hong Kong Standard, Washington Post, Pacific Stars and Stripes, St. Paul Dispatch,* plus other papers in Wisconsin, Illinois, and Florida.)

Following the ceremony, there was a huge barrio fiesta at Arani honoring the American, Filipino, and Japanese veterans and spouses. As we sat in our respective groups, I said to a man next to me, "If this is a reunion for peace, we should do more about it than just remain in our separate groups." So he and I went over to some Japanese and began talking to them in their own language. That both surprised and pleased them. It also broke many barriers, as we began introducing our wives and friends. They gladly responded in kind. To my surprise, the first man I talked to was a post office employee in Japan, just as I had been before my retirement. Not only that, he had been a prisoner of the Americans on Luzon. Another man had fought at Davao. Selected excerpts from newspaper accounts bear further evidence that it was truly a Reunion for Peace:

> Beneath a 295-foot-tall steel-and-concrete cross erected to the memory of 12,000 Filipino-and-American war dead, an old Japanese held hands with a Filipino wearing a World War I flat steel helmet.

Carl Nordin delivering a letter to President Marcos from Governor Lucey of Wisconsin at Bataan Day ceremony on Mt. Samat. (Reunion for Peace, April 9, 1977.)

An American shouted to his wife, "I found him," and approached a former Filipino comrade. The woman hugged the Filipino.

Sig Schreiner said, "You can't write off a whole race because of some of its people."

"I don't see what we can gain by keeping an open sore," said Donald Blackburn of McLean, Virginia.

Japanese smiled and talked in halting English with Americans. Cameras clicked as former enemies stood side by side.

"This reunion is confirmation that nothing of that war lingers on," said President Marcos.

It seemed entirely fitting that Bataan Day should be followed by Easter, a day commemorating reconciliation and victory. An impressive outdoor Easter Mass was celebrated in the shadow of a large veterans' statue and memorial in Ayala Triangle, attended by hundreds of Filipinos, Americans, and Japanese. Father Ortiz delivered an eloquent sermon which was followed by open Communion in which he made it very clear that all were invited to participate regardless of religious affiliation. As I partook of the sacrament, I could not help but think about how magnanimous this was of Father Ortiz and the Catholic Church, and how fitting it was in the spirit of this entire event in which we were participating.

Following the service, we were guests at a five-course luncheon in the officer's club at Camp Aguinaldo. A program of excellent entertainment and speeches by several dignitaries followed the luncheon. Concluding the afternoon was the presentation of the various state flags to General Espino, chief of staff of the Philippine Armed Forces, accompanied by a brief presentation statement. Since the Wisconsin state flag has figures denoting progress and industry with the word *Forward* emblazoned on it, I called the general's attention to the word *Forward* and said, "Just as servicemen from Wisconsin went forward with the Fil-American forces in the heroic battle for the Philippines, so do we now pledge to go forward with your country in its quest for lasting peace." Then I saluted him and returned to my seat, pleased to know that the Wisconsin state flag, along with about twenty other state flags, will hang in the Philippine Hall of Flags from that day forward.

The weekend of Bataan Day festivities concluded that evening with a moonlight military parade in Rizal Park, which was excellently done and a most fitting way to bring that special observance to a close. Interestingly, a number of Japanese whom we had met at the barrio fiesta were already seated in the stands as we approached that evening. On seeing us, several rose from their seats, smiled, and motioned for us to come up there for a few moments. After a brief greeting, we returned to our seats and discovered that we were sitting between a Japanese veteran who had fought at Davao and the Japanese lieutenant general who headed up the Japanese delegation to the Reunion for Peace. Considering everything that had transpired in the last few days, there was ample evidence of the success of the event.

Fay and I took advantage of the next several free days for a nostalgic trip to Mindanao. My good friend Salvador Albarece met us at the airport outside Cagayan. On our way to Tankulan (now named Manolo Fortich), we toured Bugo and drove over to Tagoloan so I could point out the mouth of the canyon where the 30th Bomber Squadron had been bivouacked in the early days of the war. Rod McKay and I had been attached to them for rations when we had been stationed on the beach at Bugo. We had made that trip on foot twice a day for our meals, so it had some meaning to me.

Del Monte had a big pineapple plantation and cannery in 1941, but I was amazed to learn how much larger the operation had become by 1977. Now known as the Philippine Packing Company, it had expanded into bananas and a huge cattle ranch, where thousands of head of beef were being raised. In fact, the first honest-to-goodness working cowboys I had ever seen in my life were at that ranch in Mindanao; they were mounting up to ride herd. From there we went to what had been Camp Twelve in 1941. It was now a large processing center. One of its specialties was fresh pineapple. These were prepared and stored under refrigerated conditions to be shipped out in refrigerated ships and planes. When I asked where the best markets were, I was surprised to learn that their leading market was Japan. I noticed also that their heavy trucks were Japanese models by a ratio of about five to one, whereas in 1941, the only trucks I saw were American-made. Curious about this, I broached the subject to Salvador. Not wanting to offend me, he said, "Well, how shall I say this, Carl, but as you know the roads are not very good over here, and these trucks must carry very heavy loads. It has been their experience that the Japanese trucks stand up much better." I registered surprise at the extent to which Japan had become a major trading partner. But my faith in humanity was bolstered when Salvador said, "I know what you are thinking, Carl, but the war is over, and they are our neighbors. Now we must forgive them and be friends." This was coming from a man whose land had been invaded, overrun, and ravaged, a man who had fought against the Japanese in the guerrilla army while his family barely subsisted in the hills. I learned one more thing of some significance: the name of Camp Twelve had been changed to Camp Phillips in honor of an American officer named Captain Phillips who had been spirited into the area to do surveillance work behind the Japanese lines prior to the reinvasion of Mindanao. Unfortunately, the Japanese captured and executed him near Camp Twelve.

Arriving in the former Tankulan was almost like coming home for me. About the only change in over thirty years was that they now had a municipal water system. Salvador was especially proud of the water system because he had played a significant role in obtaining it. He was almost as proud of the shower and toilet in his home, although it was exceedingly crude (there was no hot water). About the only other changes were that the little Catholic chapel had been replaced, and the Albareces had moved across town to a lot next to where the 89th Quartermaster had been headquartered during the war.

That evening all but one of their eight children plus a lot of grandchildren gathered at their house for a banquet of roast pig and lots of other food in honor of our visit. Sharing in the honor of the festivities was of a grandson, who was baptized with Fay as one of his sponsors. It was a joyous occasion, and it was good to meet their family. They have seven sons and one daughter, all college-educated and all with good jobs. Salvador was principal of the school in Tankulan, and his wife Marcelina was a teacher before and after the war. Later he became superintendent of schools of Bukidnon Province, and after he retired, Marcelina succeeded him in the position.

As we traveled in a southerly direction out of Tankulan on a sightseeing trip the next day, there were memories galore—the curves, the canyons, the places we had been ambushed by planes at one time or another, the spot where I had last seen the Albareces from the truck in the convoy taking us out of Camp Casising as I heard them yell, "There he is, there's Carl." We stopped at Maluko, and I was able to show Fay one of our schoolhouse storage depots. I was also able to pinpoint exactly where I had lain in the hollow of an abandoned outhouse and watched the bombs come down as the Japanese tried to rout ten of us caught between the lines. She had heard me tell about Impa-su-go-ung, the spot of our last stand. Now she saw it with her own eyes, as well as what remains of Camp Casising just outside of Malaybalay. To my surprise, even the old pump, our only source of water at that first camp, was still there. We continued on as far as Valencia, where there is now a fair-sized junior college. We wanted to go to Maramag, but were unable to because our driver wanted to get back to Cagayan before dark. How different from 1942 it was when we would beat up and down those same roads in cumbersome trucks at all hours of the day and night, completing the trip even if it took till morning.

As I used to make the trip between Cagayan and Iligan back in 1942, I would often wish that somehow Fay and I could share the beautiful scenery along that route. Naturally, I thought that this would be our opportunity to do just that, but it was not to be. A state of unrest had been in existence for several years involving Communist Hukbalahops (Huks), the Nationalists, government forces, and the Moros. As a result, most of western and south-western Mindanao was pretty much off-limits to tourists and outsiders. A permit was required in most cases, and even if we could have obtained one, our driver was not very keen about going, so we decided against it.

We flew to Davao the next morning, where we were met by the Albare-ces' youngest son Valentine. He was a sales representative for a seed com-pany, and had most of eastern Mindanao as his territory. Our first visit in the Davao area was a trip up the slopes of Mt. Apo to the former agricultural experiment station. I was reminded again of how I would gaze toward the east from that high vantage point, allowing my dreams to extend across Davao Gulf, past Samal Island, and across the vast Pacific to America, home, my family, and Fay. It almost seemed too much to hope then that those dreams would come true. Looking around the area, I was disappointed at what had happened. Evidently, the war had interrupted the program and the original concept of the project to the point that it was never revived. Most of the nice trees were gone. There were only a few pieces of lumber where our camp had been. The rami fields had been taken over by weeds, there were few reminders of the abaca industry, and most of the field roads we labored on were grown over. The state of decline was disappointing.

For years, I had been telling people about the dense jungle in which the Davao Penal Colony was situated. In fact, it was reputed to be the densest, most malaria-infested jungle in the Philippines. That's why they had built a prison there. The only access in those days had been a small road that narrowed down to two wheel tracks for miles before approaching the gate. Imagine my surprise as we sped through open country on a concrete highway twelve inches thick at the rate of 85 kilometers per hour (55 mph). But that surprise was practically nothing compared to the surprise that greeted me on arriving at Dapecol. Instead of a rather large compound, there was one barracks—nothing else.

Instead of a jungle for miles around, there was one tree. Instead of being inhabited by hardened criminals, and later prisoners of war, now the site was a juvenile detention camp. There were no longer gardens, orchards, and rice paddies; the jungle had been cleared and developed into huge farms owned by wealthy landowners who raised a variety of crops on a big scale. In fact, they were some of Valentine's best customers. It was also down in this area where Philippine Packing owned and operated banana groves comprising thousands of acres. Of all the changes that had occurred in the previous thirty years, this was the most extensive. Davao was a dichotomy, however. We had seen the large, expansive farms, and yet just outside the city, poor farmers were trying to eke out an existence on small plots of land with one carabao and a few crude tools, living in small houses on stilts, with possibly a pig and a few chickens occupying the ground below the house. The Insular Hotel where we spent the night is as nice a hotel as one can find anywhere. In fact, of all the hotels we have stayed at anywhere, few, if any, have more beautiful or better-kept grounds. In the city itself, there are many fine stores and interesting bazaars. Yet, just outside of town on the road up Mt. Apo was a little so-called refreshment stand dispensing tuba with a tin can or a stick from a large open kettle with flies hovering around and floating on the surface. Coming up the hill was a man driving a carabao that was pulling a scoot, reminiscent of the era before the wheel was invented.

Back at Cagayan again the next day, we took Salvador and Marcelina's daughter Susan and her husband Ray Tan to lunch. Both have good jobs there. I was struck again by what a fine family the Albareces are. We spent our last night in Mindanao at the VIP Hotel in Cagayan. Salvador came in from Manolo Fortich to bid farewell as our plane left for Manila.

As our plane headed north from Cagayan and I left Mindanao, perhaps for the last time, I reflected on what we had seen and experienced. I loved the scenery, the climate up on the plateau, and the people, especially in the central part of the island. I was pleased that they had recovered from the effects of the war to a remarkable extent. It was somewhat troubling, however, to see that although certain segments of the economy were forging ahead, there still seemed to be a peasant class. It also appeared that those who were reaping the most profits were not putting a proper proportion back into the infrastructure. There was a new highway down the east coast from Surigao, but the Sayer Highway which runs through the central part of the island, connecting Cagayan with Davao, was not yet finished, and the section between Valencia and the north coast was actually in poorer condition than it had been in 1942, as a result of heavy usage by big trucks. I was troubled also by the state of tension that seemed to pervade. While the entire country was under a state of martial law at the time, it was much more noticeable on Mindanao. This was especially true in the Davao area. The armed guards at the Davao Airport were much more numerous, and it seemed that they were at the ready with their rifles. Perhaps Fay's assessment says it all best: "Mindanao is a beautiful island, but it is very primitive."

The day following our return to Manila, we participated in a tour of the Cultural Center, Folklore Theater, and the International Convention Center, with a luncheon atop the Cultural Center with a beautiful view of Manila Bay. The next day, our last full day in Manila, we were guests at a fancy luncheon in the Army-Navy Officers' Club. That evening, we all participated in a lovely mabuhay (farewell) banquet on the top floor of the Manila Hilton Hotel, at which we were entertained by some wonderful folk dancers and a soloist from Hong Kong. It was a class act and a beautiful way to conclude our memorable return to the Philippines.

My mind was filled with many thoughts the next day as our plane carried us toward Japan. So far, the last two weeks had seemed almost like a dream. Just the mere fact of returning at all was almost more than I had dared hope for. There had been so much more than we had ever envisioned. Of course, the trip to Mindanao and seeing the Albareces had been special to us, but all of the festivities commemorating the Reunion for Peace program and the spirit in which they were carried out had been beyond what a person would imagine. Now, I wondered about this next reunion. Would Ikuta-San remember me? Would it be a letdown? And yet, something deep inside me seemed to impel me to go in order to complete the mission, to finish the dream.

I need not have worried. When our party of five—my brother, Glenn, his wife, Mary, Glenn's secretary, Maggie Surles, Fay, and I—arrived at the Ishihara Sangyo Factory in Yokkaichi, Japan, the first thing that caught my eye was the American flag flying at the same level as the Japanese flag. Then, as we were ushered into a reception room, the thing that struck me first was the large number of people in attendance, the cameras, and the strobe lights. The press was represented by two daily papers out of Tokyo, an English-language paper, a radio station, and two national television networks. I later learned that when a Japanese captive would come all that way to look up his former captor, it really made news. In addition, there were a number of factory officials and the man who had acted as Glenn's interpreter on a visit several years earlier when Glenn and Mary had gone from Okinawa in an attempt to locate Ikuta-San. A rather large rectangular table with flowers and Japanese and American table flags occupied the center of the room. I was at once humbled. Sitting in a wheelchair at the near end was Ikuta-San with one of the largest smiles I have ever seen. It almost seemed as if my heart would melt as I faced the man who, through tears, had said, "Sayonara, Nordin," as he waved farewell to me when our ferry left the pier thirty-two years and another world earlier.

Putting on my old Japanese cap with prison number on it, I turned to him, saluted, and said, "San Yaku san ju yan, waukaru?" (334, remember me?)

Then I stepped up to his wheelchair, and putting my arm around his shoulder, I said, "Ema tomadatchi" (Now we are friends, meaning no longer enemies). It was really quite moving. Inwardly, I felt so good, as if I were completely fulfilled. The ache I had felt at not being able to effect the reconciliation I thought we both desired when I marched away was now completely obliterated. It appeared that the feelings were mutual.

Once this first meeting was over, we talked of each other's health and well-being. I learned that he suffered from arthritis, hence the wheelchair. Our conversation drifted to old times, such as the earthquake and the tall chimney falling, the eruption of acid mains. He inquired about Shorty Batson and Goat Yaeger. He knew that when we called E. J. Batson "Shorty," we were referring to his size, and he indicated that that was not very nice of us because no one wants to be short or have that fact referred to in a name. He was amused again about Goat Yaeger and thought that he was aptly nicknamed. He felt bad about Tim Hardy, Corson, and others who had died so young. He told me that Sato-San had died, but he was unsure of what had happened to Shinogi-San.

There were a lot of questions from the various segments of the press. Not wanting to appear disrespectful to my hosts, I was quite polite and cautious in the answers I gave to questions about the life of a prisoner of the Japanese and various other questions about our treatment. After a while though, Glenn told me to tell it as it was because they would probably understand, and he believed that they ought to hear it from someone who was there. In telling my story, I was determined to give Ikuta-San credit for the decent acts of kindness he had shown, however.

The factory had been enlarged a lot in the years since the war, to the point that I hardly recognized it. When I mentioned that I would need to see the Shinto shrine we used to bow to in order to orient myself, they included that in a grand tour of the factory. Before leaving on the factory tour, the press wanted pictures of the four of us outside with Ikuta-San. Following the photo session, Ikuta-San had to leave, as he was tired, so we said our farewells. As his son was about to wheel him away, he paused and told me in quite good English, "You will never know how happy you have made my father today." Mission accomplished.

The tour ended at a beautiful marble memorial shrine that the factory had erected to honor those who had died. Glenn and Mary had seen it when they were there in 1964, but then it was quite plain, and the inscription was in Japanese. Now however, it was enhanced by plantings of beautiful shrubbery and flowers, and there was an English translation of the inscription as well, which read: "Nothing is more sublime than to give one's own life for the sake of others." This monument is dedicated to those who fought and were killed for peace and freedom in World War II.

I stood transfixed for a moment. Then, to my surprise, I was handed a beautiful floral wreath to lay on a marble slab in front of the shrine. I felt honored at the request, yet humbled by the significance of what the shrine and this wreath symbolized. After placing the wreath before the shrine, I saluted, then bowed my head and breathed a silent prayer. I am pleased that the wording on the shrine is so inclusive, but flooding my mind right then were thoughts of Hardy and Corson, Ernie Meyers and Sgt. Driver, Corporals Brown and Job, the Englishman who was beaten to death, the Dutchman whose mess kit I had borrowed before he got both kidneys blown out of his body by our own planes, the men who had just plain expired because of their bodies' inability to live another instant.

Among the countless thousands memorialized by that shrine were Mac Davis, Corporal Bowden, Clucas, Christensen, and the rest who accounted for exactly fifty percent of my outfit who never came back. Of singular importance to me in this respect are memories of Kenneth Carpenter from Siren, Wisconsin, with whom I enlisted; John LaVoie from St. Paul, with whom Kenneth and I both trained at Fort Snelling, Minnesota, and with whom I served prison time in Dapecol; Al Saranian, with whom I soldiered in Fort Douglas and on Mindanao and later suffered in two prison camps; and Lt. Col. Rogers, camp commander at Lasang, who for some inexplicable reason sent me back to Dapecol when I had dysentery, thereby eliminating me from the fate of those who went down when their hell ship was torpedoed. I am sure that act of his saved my life, and I am so sorry that he had to lose his. Included in that same group is Jug Imlay, my very good friend, who risked his life to get me back to camp in the first place when I became ill with dysentery. Sadly, he also perished.

The men named above represent only a portion of my loss during World War II, but the great cost of war becomes much clearer when we begin to speak in terms of individual buddies rather than in terms of abstract numbers. The real horror of war comes when we realize that these men were fathers, sons, husbands, brothers, sweethearts. They surely ought to be memorialized, and a memorial built by a former enemy is particularly significant.

That evening all of Japan had an opportunity to witness what had transpired earlier that day in the reception room of Ishihara Sangyo Factory in Yokkaichi because the two major television networks broadcast it on the evening news. The same was true the following day, when the newspapers came out. I was happy that they had given Ikuta-San good press also. In my case, I even heard from a woman whose mother had done menial work at the factory at the time we were there. She also sent a gift of exquisitely hand crafted dolls.

The fact that the timing of our trip coincided with cherry blossom time opened up one more unique opportunity for us. Each year, when the cherry trees are in full bloom, the Shinyuko Gardens are closed to the public for one morning. The Japanese government issues passes to 400 people in the

Carl Nordin after laying wreath to fallen comrades at former prison camp, Yokkaichi, Japan (April 1977). The inscription on the monument reads: "Nothing is more sublime than to give one's own life for the sake of others. This monument is dedicated to those who fought and were killed for peace and freedom in World War II."

international community, including top people in the military, for the purpose of viewing the gardens at their leisure. At about 10:30 A.M., the prime minister and his wife arrive to officially greet those present. As it turned out, one of Glenn's friends and his wife were on vacation back in the States, and before they had left, they had given Glenn their tickets for us to use. Consequently, for a period of four hours, Fay and I were Col. and Mrs. Lancaster. Although this particular honor was not in any way associated with our mission or a reason for coming to Japan, nevertheless, just shaking hands with the prime minister and his wife did sort of serve as frosting on the cake.

Before leaving Japan, I was interviewed further by the large daily newspaper *Mainichi* and also by *Pacific Stars and Stripes*. Following the interviews, I received one last big surprise. Mr. Futoshi, Glenn's protocol officer, came to see me as we were spending our last afternoon in Glenn's home. He was visibly moved by the very favorable publicity the press and other media had given our visit and the positive reaction by the public. He flattered me by telling me what a positive symbol of forgiveness and peace our visit had displayed to the nation. As his way of thanking us and showing his appreciation, he wanted to take us to a luxury resort on the other side of the island. Since our schedule did not permit that, he presented me with a beautiful muglike vessel made of Arita pottery with a base of fine wood. It is a mug that had been in his family for many years and had been used for partaking of ceremonial tea on special occasions. Now he was giving it to me out of gratitude for our visit. What an honor that act signified! Obviously, I prize it very highly. (Earlier, Fay and Mary had each received a coffee or luncheon set for four from Maggie's brother and his wife at a dinner party in Nagoya following our visit with Ikuta-San. We, in turn, had presented Maggie with a gift for all she had done in helping to arrange the meeting, and for being my translator whenever my Japanese faltered at the meeting. The gift which I presented to Ikuta-San had been purchased in such haste that I had not noticed that on the back it said, "Made in Japan.")

There had been an element of sadness associated with leaving the Philippines a few days earlier, and yet the Reunion for Peace effort had turned that sadness into a feeling of satisfaction. A corner had been turned. Leaving Japan was accompanied by similar feelings—sadness at leaving which was accompanied by a feeling of reconciliation, a feeling of satisfaction. Beyond that, words fail me.

Perhaps one or two excerpts from newspapers covering the events sum up the trip best. From the *Chunichi Shimbun*:

> At approximately 1:30 P.M., Mr. Nordin arrived at the factory, where he was met by Mr. Mankichi Ikuta. Mr. Nordin ran up to Mr. Ikuta, put his arm around Ikuta's shoulder, and said in Japanese that he learned during his prison camp days, "Tomadachi, tomadachi" (Friend, friend). Mr. Nordin put his cap on, which showed his prisoner number 334, and asked Mr. Ikuta, "Do you remember me?" He shook Mr. Ikuta's hands; his face showing his excitement, Mr. Ikuta managed to say, "You gained some weight and look so fine and healthy," but no other words could follow, as he was overcome by emotion.

From the *Pacific Stars and Stripes*:

> My first thought was, "Mission accomplished," Nordin said. "I finally get to see him." He identified himself to the wheelchair-ridden Ikuta through his prison camp number 334, and was amazed to find the old man not only recalled him but asked about other Americans who had been in the camp.
>
> Nordin wouldn't talk much about what the two discussed. The most terrible memories are often the most private. But when he left Japan late Friday, Nordin had something else to remember the rest of his life.

A Promise Kept

Except for the two bouts with schistosomiasis of the liver in the 1960s, our lives had taken on a normal and pleasant aspect once I regained my strength. Our daughters were active and popular in school. Fay and I both enjoyed our jobs and our lives together. Our family managed to take camping and other trips together every summer. In later years, Fay and I were able to do a considerable amount of traveling, visiting all fifty states, every province in Canada except for two, plus a number of countries in both Europe and the Orient. We were definitely experiencing the "for better" part of the marriage equation.

But we were not only getting a lot out of life, we were also attempting to put something of value back into life. Each of us took an active role in community, civic, and church work, with a major emphasis on the latter. On the local level, we both taught Sunday school for many years, and in addition, Fay was Vacation Bible School superintendent for a number of years, and I was Sunday school superintendent for fifteen years. Fay was also very active in the women's church organization for many years, and I served a number of terms on the church council over a thirty-year period. Then in 1966, I was elected to a three-year term on the Synod Evangelism Committee of the Lutheran Church in America. Since the synod level in church government is somewhat akin to the state level in our federal government, this new assignment afforded me a larger view of the church at work. That was the beginning of a new career of service, so to speak.

At first glance, this new dimension of service might appear to be primarily happenstance because I did not know for several years that I had been nominated by a person from another town. But as time went on, and more opportunities for service and ministry began dropping into place, completely unplanned, I came to realize that it might be part of Someone Else's plan.

The realization that some other Force was at work in directing my life did not come as a result of any great burning voice or any other miraculous manifestation. The more I wondered about it and thought about it, the more assured I became it was the result of my own prayers a number of years prior to these new developments. And it had all come about in a gradual sequence. It began in my late middle-age years, when I had begun to contemplate retirement and how I could or would deal with it in a constructive manner. I had no plan, no agenda, no specifics. I merely began to pray that if I could be used in any way or in any type of service, that a way would be shown to me and that I would recognize and act favorably on the opportunity. There was another consideration that entered into the equation also, and that had its origin on the sand bank of a small stream in east-central Mindanao when a war-torn soldier made a desperate plea for divine guidance. I have never forgotten the promise I made to do His bidding at that time and the commitment I made to serve Him from that time forward. I recognize that this can be construed as dangerous theology, but there was no deal-making on that strip of land. It was just an earnest plea for guidance and a sincere commitment to service.

As time went on, new areas of service opportunities opened up as I moved from the Evangelism Committee to American Missions to the Executive Committee, World Concerns, World Hunger, and presently the Synod Stewardship Committee. When my second three-year term on this committee expires in 1996, I will have served on the synod level in one form or another for thirty consecutive years. Included also are three years as chairman of the Subcommittee on Ministry to the Native Americans, plus developing and directing a summer ministry for tourists for eleven years.

During these same years, my home congregation elected me to serve as their delegate to close to twenty annual synod conventions, and the synod elected me as one of its delegates to ten of the biennial conventions of the national church body. As a result of this added exposure to the workings of the church at large, I became more cognizant of the church and its ministry in the world.

Looking back on my life, especially these last fifty years, I realize that I have so much for which to be thankful. First and foremost, I have a loving God who watches over me. I am thankful for Fay and our family and my parents and family who waited and prayed for my return. I am truly thankful for one of the most precious things in life: *freedom*. Life without freedom is not life as God intended it to be.

Time and again over the years, I have gone back to that strip of sand beside a stream in that faraway land, figuratively speaking, seeking guidance, comfort, and counsel. Not only has there been a Listener, but answers have been given, perhaps best expressed in this scripture verse: "And I was with you in weakness, and in fear, and in much trembling, and my speech and my preaching was not with enticing words of man's wisdom, but in demonstration of the spirit and of power" (1 Corinthians 2:3-4).

Military History of
Carl S. Nordin

Carl S. Nordin enlisted in the United States Army at Fort Snelling, Minnesota, on September 18, 1940. Shortly after enlistment he was sent to Fort Douglas, Utah, where he completed his basic training. During the next year, he worked as a clerk in the Property Office, as secretary and manager of the Post Carpenter Shop, and later as manager of the Post Utilities Warehouse.

In October of 1941, Nordin was shipped overseas as a member of the newly formed Det. 2nd Q.M. Supply (Avn), which was attached to Fifth Air Base Group and landed in Manila, P.I., November 20, 1941. On December 1, 1941, the Fifth Air Base Group and attached units were sent to the southern Philippine Island of Mindanao to establish an air base on the southern periphery of the Philippine Islands. Exactly one week later, following the attack in Pearl Harbor, the United States declared war against Japan. One of Nordin's first assignments was to accompany two other men into the Moro country of central Mindanao, where the three negotiated contracts with local farmers and their representatives to supply foodstuffs for the troops, an effort that served well for the duration of the fighting. He later was in charge of convoys hauling supplies and foodstuffs to the various depots and fronts of the island. After invasions at five different points of the island, practically every serviceman ended up in combat duty.

Nordin was taken prisoner May 10, 1942 (Mother's Day), and was held prisoner in two different camps on Mindanao. On June 6, 1944, the entire camp was evacuated via hell ships. They arrived in Moji, Japan, September 2, 1944. Nordin spent the remainder of the war working on the railroad at Yokkaichi, Japan, until he was liberated on September 4, 1945.

Carl Nordin was "posted" for his second promotion during wartime in April, 1942 but since the only telegraph line to Washington was taken up with the Bataan surrender details, the message never did get through. Consequently, he only achieved the rank of sergeant.

Nordin was awarded the Bronze Star for Meritorious Service, a field citation for "Outstanding Performance of Duty in Action," the American Defense Medal, the Asiatic-Pacific Medal and Philippine Defense Medal with four battle stars, three presidential unit citations, the Good Conduct Medal, the Victory Medal, and the Prisoner-of-War Medal.

Index